THAT SON OF A GUN HAD SENSE

*Mule Stories from the Bootheel Area
During the 1930's–1940's Era*

Lonny Thiele

Front cover photo: *Walter McGhee at age 14 in 1941 cultivating corn with Pete and Peewee, a pair of brown mules. See McGhee's story on page 165.*

Second Printing, 2011

Printed by Stinson Press, Poplar Bluff, Missouri

Dedication

This book is dedicated to Melvin Bradley (1922–2003) who spent years crisscrossing Missouri researching for his 540-page, two-volume book set entitled The Missouri Mule: His Origins and Times. Bradley's work helped lead in 1995 to the mule being named Missouri's official state animal.

Acknowledgments

This book could not have been written without help from many people and without cooperation from the people interviewed for their mule stories.

I would not have had the idea of putting a mule book together without the writing and reporting background I experienced after changing my career in 1989 from finance to journalism. I am also indebted to personnel with the Daily American Republic newspaper in Poplar Bluff for letting me cover agricultural stories, some of which included mule stories.

There were several who assisted me in editing and reviewing stories. Their work was very appreciative and improved the book considerably. These people included: Teresa Oyler, journalist, who was a co-worker of mine while I worked at the Daily American Republic; Andy Valentine, friend and book enthusiast from Nashville, Tennessee; Myra Dye, journalist; and Tammi Bryant, English teacher and a niece of mine.

Others who assisted me were: Thomas Sallee, agricultural statistician, USSA-NASS in Columbia, Missouri; Brea Black, special collections librarian, Topeka and Shawnee County Public Library in Topeka, Kansas; Kathy Dickson, artist; and Dr. Frank Nickell, director, Center for Regional History at Southeast Missouri State University at Cape Girardeau, Missouri. I received library assistance from personnel with the Poplar Bluff City Library and the Kansas City Public Library.

I received some assistance with changes and corrections from the first printing. A couple of those who assisted me with this were: Fred Coulter of Moxee, Washington, and Bruce Beck of Poplar Bluff, both long-term acquaintances.

And finally, for working full time during the more than three years I collected stories and for all of her help with computer work, I am grateful to my lovely wife, Pauline.

Map of the
Missouri
Bootheel
Area

Cape
Girardeau

Wayne

Bollinger

• Marble
Hill

• Leopold

• Zalma

Cape Girardeau •

• Delta

Scott

Carter

• Greenville

• Williamsville

• Ellsinore

Wappapello •

Stoddard

• Puxico

Butler

• Grand n

• Poplar Bluff

Ripley

• Dexter

• Bernie

Sikeston •

• Charleston

Missis-
sippi

New
Madrid

East Prairie →

Fairdealing •

• Doniphan

Harviell •

• Naylor

• Broseley

• Quln

• Powe

Glennonville

Neelyville

Parma

Catron

Lilbourn

Supply •

Malden
Campbell •

Arkansas

Holcomb

White Oak

Rector •

Hooker •

Kennett

• Senath

• Hornersville

Dunklin

• Gideon

Portageville

• Peach Orchard

Pemiscot

• Hayti

Caruthersville •

• Cooter

• Blytheville

New Madrid

Mississippi River

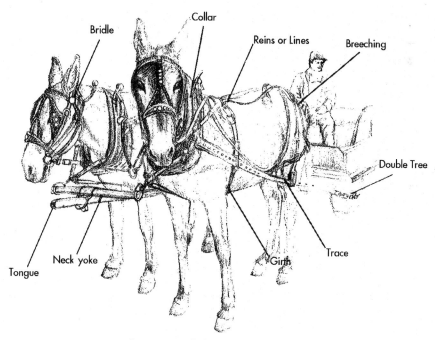

Bridle

Collar

Reins or Lines

Breeching

Double Tree

Tongue

Neck yoke

Girth

Trace

Mule team with harness parts labeled.

Table of Contents

II. Mules

III. Farming With Mules

IV. Robert "Uncle Bob" Boyers Family of Butler County

V. Mules That Worked by Voice Commands/Without Lines

"A Mule Kicked Him" "He Was Called, 'Doc'" "Pete" "Mule Races" "Missed the Footrest" "Turn Around Jude" "I Didn't Like It. I Had to do It" "You'll Pull That Mule's Tail Off" "He Would Roll Over on His Back and Start Kicking at You" "That Scatter-brain Got Loose and Jumped Plumb Over It" "If the Other Mule Wouldn't Come Around. He'd Take His Head and Hit Him and Make Him Come Around" "He'd Find That Row and Then He Was Gone" "All He Wanted to do Was Jump That Fence" "He Just Took a Two-By-Four and Hit Him Right Between the Eyes" "He Cut Himself Up Real Bad and Died That Night."

Definitions

Bit–metal mouthpiece on a bridle, acting as a control

Breaking plow---a farm implement used to cut, turn up, and break up the soil

Bridle–a head harness for guiding a mule or horse; it consists of headstall, bit, and reins

Britchen—Mule harness that fits over the mule's rump. This gives the mule something to push against when holding a wagon back or backing.

Burro—small members of the ass family, native to the southwestern U.S.

Buster–large wedge used to break open furrows

Collar—a part of the harness of draft animals fitted over the shoulders and taking strain when a load is drawn

Cultivator—an implement for loosening the soil and destroying weeds around existing plants

Disk—a heavy frame with sharp, thin, circular metal pieces that revolve, used to break up soil for sowing

Donkey---worldwide nickname for the ass family

Doubletree—a crossbar to a wagon, plow, etc. to each end of which the singletrees are attached when two mules are harnessed abreast

Gee—a command word to a mule meaning turn to the right

Halter–a headstall usually with noseband and throatlatch to which a lead can be attached

Hame–one of two curved supports attached to the collar of a mule team to which the traces are fastened

Harness–the leather straps and metal pieces by which a horse, mule, etc. is fastened to a wagon, plow, etc.

Hand–One hand equals 4 inches used to measure height of mules and horses.

Harrow–a heavy frame with spikes drawn by mules and used for leveling and breaking up plowed ground, covering seeds, rooting up weeds, etc.

Haw–a command word to a mule meaning turn to the left

Hinny–a cross between a stallion and a jenny

Horse Mule–a male mule over one year old

Jack–male of the ass family

Jenny–female of the ass family

Lay-by–final cultivating of crop, usually corn

Lines–long narrow strips of leather attached to the mules bits that run back to the driver and are used for driving and whipping mules to go faster and for stopping them

Mare Mule–a female mule over one year old

Mule–a cross between a jack and a mare (female horse)

Plantation–an agricultural estate, usually worked by resident labor

Rein–a narrow strap of leather attached to each end of a bit in the mouth of a mule, and held by the rider or driver to control the mule, also called lines when referring to harness rein

Sharecropper–a tenant farmer esp. in the southern U.S. who is provided with credit for seed, tools, living quarters, and food, who works the land, and who receives an agreed share of the value of the crop minus charges

Shoot Craps–when a team of mules don't pull together, instead one pulls, then the other

Sickle Mower–an agriculture implement with a cutting mechanism that consists of a bar with a series of cutting elements

Singletree–a wooden bar swung at the center from a hitch on a plow, wagon, etc. and hooked at either end to the traces of a mule's harness

Sulky Rake–A 2-wheeled vehicle having a seat for the driver only with a rake consisting of teeth or prongs for gathering loose grass, hay, etc.

Trace—either of two straps, chains, or lines of a harness for attaching a draft animal to farm equipment to be drawn

Double shovel without handles

John Van Gennip (right) and brothers by sickle mower

Team with sulky rake
Photo courtesy of Ralph Freer family of Butler County.

Forward

Older people have vivid memories of their younger days. This book utilizes that.

From January 2007 to April 2011, I interviewed 78 elderly people for 90 mule stories. Two people, Buck Farmer and Lloyd Massey, each contributed four stories; six others contributed two stories, Robert Boyers, Mike Cooper, Chalk Givens, Bud Henry, Ralph Higgerson, and John VanGennip.

Some of the people were difficult to interview. Two of them I talked with two hours in order to get maybe 10 minutes of story material that I could use. One of them I left thinking I didn't have a story, only to find after typing up the notes there was a story in there. Some were difficult for me to understand, and I would ask them over and over to repeat certain words. Some were easy to interview. Several were good storytellers, two of whom were Farmer and Massey. There were several people interviewed whose stories are not included for some reason or other. Some of the reasons are; unwilling to sign release forms required by the publisher to use their story, not enough information for a story, and noticeable exaggerations. Two men decided they didn't want their mule stories published.

The breakdown of stories per county are: Butler 24 (10 of them for the Boyers family chapter), New Madrid 14, Pemiscot 12, Dunklin 9, Stoddard 5, Mississippi 5, Ripley 3, Bollinger 4, Wayne 3, Cape Girardeau 3 and Scott 1. Five stories came out of northeast Arkansas and two came from northwest Mississippi.

Mules were irreplaceable for hundreds of farmers in Missouri's Bootheel during the 1930s and 1940s. Many of the people interviewed said they couldn't have made it without mules. Mules could pull a cultivator for 10 or more hours a day as many days as the farmer wanted to work, and they did it on minimal feed and minimal injuries. Many people interviewed said they fed their mules about four ears of corn for lunch, perhaps 12 ears a day. Flora Currie, who grew up on a sharecropper's farm in north central Mississippi, said at times they never had grain or hay to feed their mules, just grass.

The 1930s and 1940s was an era where chemicals weren't used to eradicate weeds, which is why it was necessary to plow (cultivate) a crop several times.

Of the 78 people I interviewed for mule stories, I can only recall one of them talking about having a veterinarian out to treat a mule, and only two mentioned a mule breaking down while doing farm work.

One thing the book doesn't express well is the hours, and hours, and adverse weather conditions boys, girls, men and women spent and experienced walking behind mules. If they just worked mules 60 days a year, a conservative figure, that would be about 500 hours a year following mules. They could easily have worked 1,000 or more hours a year. Only two of the people interviewed said they were bored working mules. Most were happy to be working mules, because if they weren't doing that, they would probably be chopping cotton, which was much harder and more tedious work. Another thing the book doesn't express well is the sounds associated with working mules, such as the sound of farm equipment digging into the soil and the groaning and braying of the mules. Smells associated with mules and other farm animals are mostly pleasant but cleaning out stalls as mentioned by Tim Whitney, Sr. and Lloyd Massey, could be pungent.

The biggest surprise to me from the interviews was the number of people who started working mules as early as 7 or, 8 years old. I questioned this the first one or two people who mentioned this until I saw a photo of a young boy working a team of mules to a plow.

Mules are still popular today, especially for pulling wagons, plowing demonstrations, riding (some are gaited), and hunting due to their ability to jump over fences.

Lastly, I had a feeling and a few of those interviewed expressed it without my asking, they missed the times they spent with mules. Some even said they wished they had a mule. One thing for sure, they liked, and didn't hesitate, talking about their farm mules.

Special Introduction to Mules

as told by Wyman Hampton

Let me tell you about mules. God didn't create mules. Mules are a hybrid. They do not reproduce themselves. In the Bible, a man discovers mules in the wilderness.* King David, I believe he had 40 sons, and they rode mules.** But George Washington introduced them to the United States.***

A mule is a cross between a jackass and a mare. A cross between a stallion and a jenny is called a hinny. They're not worth anything. They don't get big.

Mules have sense horses don't have. They get their size from their mother, and have the sense of a jackass. Horses will prance around on a mountain. They could fall over. But a mule won't do that. If a team of horses runs away, they might go through a fence. Mules won't do that. Horses will drink water until they get sick (when hot). A mule will drink a little water, then stop.

Horses need 10 ears of corn to work on, a mule will take five or six. A little mule down to four ears will still do as much as a horse. A little mule will work as much as a bigger horse on half the feed. They will work horses to death. They are a very tough animal.

Cotton fields are associated with mules in people's minds and sayings. They did use them an awful lot in cotton fields. Mules were used for everything, breaking the ground, pulling the harrow, drilling the seed, cultivating, cutting hay, raking hay, everything you could use a horse for. But a mule is better. Mules are tougher, have smaller feet, and won't chop down the ground like horses will.

People in the North run mules down saying they're ornery and will kick you. Oh no, I suspect a horse will hurt you first. I like horses though. They are better for riding.

My Uncle Grant Hampton, who raised horses and mules, told me this. He would tell his boys never to put a jack with a stallion, that the jack will ruin the stallion. Stallions fight mainly with their hooves and will kick at a jack and make a dive at them. And when they dive at them, the jack will grab it by its ear or nose and ruin him. The favorite place for a jack to grab a stallion is its nose or under its jaw. They will hang on like a bulldog and bawl all the time. The stallion will rear up to paw him; and when it does, it's lifting the weight of the jack, because the jack won't turn loose. It will wear the stallion down to the ground and then stomp it to death.

One day my cousins had company, and my uncle was gone. They put ropes on the jack and the stallion to see what they would do. The jack made a dive for the stallion, and the stallion kicked him and sent him rolling. The jack got up and came after him. That's when the boys pulled them apart. You castrate mules when they're young, so they won't get big and get the jack in them.

*Genesis 36:24, "This was that Anah that found mules in the wilderness, as he fed the asses of Zibeon his father."
**II Samuel 13:29, "Then all the king's sons arose, and every man got upon his mule, and fled."
***Melvin Bradley in his book, *Jack Stock and Mules in Missouri*, page five, writes, "In 1785 the King of Spain sent a fine jack and two jennets to George Washington, and the following year, in 1786, Lafayette sent him a jack and two jennets from the island of Malta. These importations may be considered the beginning of mule breeding in this country, as the animals were selected for that purpose and were representative specimens of European jack stock."

Wyman Hampton died before he had a chance to proofread this introduction, which was compiled from notes taken when he was interviewed in June 2007.----Lonny Thiele

Introduction

I wrote this book as a voice for Missouri farm mules from the 1930s and 1940s—a voice for more than 245,000 incredibly hard working, resilient, versatile equine survivors who possessed a keen intelligence, that in many incidents seemed to be a sense of humor.

For more than 165 years roughly 1785 to 1950, this country relied on mule and horsepower for farm power. Horses were bred for pleasure and farm work. Mules were bred for farm work.

The sheer numbers of mules in the United States and in Missouri in the 1930s and 1940s, is phenomenal. According to Thomas Sallee, agricultural statistician with the United States Department of Agriculture's National Agriculture Statistics Service in Columbia, Missouri, there were 245,554 mules in Missouri in 1935 and 193,565 in 1940. Mule numbers in the U.S. for these years were 2.4 million and 1.9 million respectively.

Stories in this book are firsthand accounts by people who farmed with mules in the Bootheel and surrounding area, mainly in the 1930s and 1940s. They farmed with mules as adults, teenagers, many as preteens, some as young as 6 or 7 years old. Most of the people when interviewed for their mule stories were in their upper 70s and 80s.

According to several men interviewed for mule stories, mules are usually smaller, eat less, withstand heat better, and pound for pound, work harder than horses. These traits made them the farm animal of choice in the South,* and in the Missouri Bootheel area where cotton was the main money crop in the 1930s and 1940s. Mules worked 10 or more hours a day, six days a week.

Mules' intelligence enables them to have good survival skills. A mule will usually not go somewhere it senses is dangerous. Many people featured in this book refer to this trait. There are no studies I am aware of that compare the intelligence of mules to horses. However, it has been common knowledge for centuries that mules will not overeat and founder themselves as horses will, that mules will not work themselves to death as horses, on occasion will, and that mules are more surefooted than horses. Mules are usually more independent and tend to have more personality than horses.

Mules have amazing skills, one of which is their ability to tell time down to minutes on a daily basis. Another is their ability to work strictly on voice commands without the use of driving lines. Another is their ability to learn to open doors and gates. Dozens of people featured in this book refer to these skills.

In the 1930s and 1940s most rural Bootheel people did not have electricity or running water. According to Robert H. Forister in his book, *Complete History of Butler County, Missouri*, in 1935 only 11 out of 100 farms had electricity and in 1950 there were still many farms in Butler County without electricity. Betty Boyers Webb, in her story about Pat and Jet, stated they didn't have electricity until 1949.

I spent more than three years working on this book. About six months into the research, I became surprisingly aware of how many preteens farmed with mules in the 1930s and 1940s. One reason for this was most farm implements in that era were walk-behind equipment, and most men, weighing 180 pounds or more, simply could not walk the 20 or more miles a day, five or six days a week, that was required for making a living farming. However their young sons, who weighed 40 to 80 pounds less, could. Some of the stories refer to teens working mules by walking behind equipment, while their dads worked other teams with planters, which had seats.

According to a USDA Bulletin, one horse could plow .84 acres per day, and harrow 7.08 acres per day. I am using these statistics because I couldn't find one for mules. Therefore, a typical mule team could plow 1.68 acres a day, or harrow 14.16 acres per day. According to Charlie Jennings (see story), there are 11 quarter-mile rows per acre. Which means while plowing, mule drivers walked on average four and a half miles per day. Several men told me they harrowed 10 acres a day, which computes to walking 27 miles. One person mentioned going 30 miles a day.

As a reporter for the Daily American Republic (DAR) newspaper in Poplar Bluff (1995-2004) I wrote a four-part series about farming with mules. The stories were well received and helped me win an annual Missouri Press award. The Associated Press picked up one of the mule stories for regional coverage. While I was interviewing people for these stories, I became aware there were many more mule stories out there; these stories were not being recorded, and people who had farmed with mules were elderly and were passing on.

About six months into the research, I decided to set two parameters; to only interview people who actually farmed with mules, and to talk to people who farmed in or within 30 miles of the Bootheel counties of Pemiscot, New Madrid and Dunklin.

The intro story provided by Mitzi Chase is an exception to both parameters. I ran an ad for mule stories in Rural Missouri, an electric cooperative monthly magazine, and Chase emailed me her story. I kept reading it over and over, and I couldn't resist using it. I only found one person (Alfonse Webb) who farmed with mules on a plantation in the Bootheel area. There are probably some out there who I missed, but I did find one who farmed with mules on a Mississippi plantation, so I decided to include the Tim Whitney, Sr. story. And I decided to use the Flora Currie story because she was the only black lady I found who had farmed with mules.

In addition to Chase, three others wrote their own stories. Dallas McElroy, Lloyd Massey and Alvin Hager. McElroy had written two mule stories as part of a book he had planned to write. With his approval, I edited the two stories into one. I interviewed Massey using a tape recorder, from which I obtained two stories, then he handwrote two more stories and mailed them to me. One of these is in the Runaways chapter, and the other is "Dad's First Tractor." And Alvin Hager, from Paducah, Kentucky sent me a story he had handwritten for the Boyers' family chapter.

I chose the Missouri Bootheel area for several reasons; it is relatively close to where I reside, this is the top cotton-producing area for the state and mules were preferred over horses working in cotton fields; Missouri was one of the top mule states in America, and the Bootheel counties were three of the top mule-raising counties in Missouri.**

This book is in no way intended to be a complete collection of existing mule stories in the Bootheel area. I collected enough stories that I felt represented most of the area, and represented people of various social, cultural, and educational backgrounds. There are eight stories told by black men, six stories told by white women, one story from a black woman, and the rest are from white men.

Several of the contributors quit school to help their dad farm and never went beyond grade school. Others were college graduates, some obtained doctorate degrees. Many were retired farmers; several were retired school superintendents, one is a retired circuit judge, one is a retired entomologist, and one is a medical doctor who was still practicing medicine, when interviewed in 2008.

•   **Melvin Bradley on pages 146 and 147 in his 540-page, two-volume set titled *The Missouri Mule: His Origin and Times* writes, "The mule was the preferred animal for field work in the South. The southern farmer firmly believed that mules required less rations than horses when working, and could subsist on roughage when not in draft: that mules were much hardier under careless treatment." And, "It is unrealistic to compare horses with mules as a power source under the conditions of cotton production in the South. When horses begin to overheat, they tend to panic and will often increase their pace. If not stopped for cooling, they are likely to drop and die where they fall. Most mules will slow down when dangerously hot and many will stop and refuse to budge before they reach a killing temperature." Bradley is quoting Robert Lamb from his book, *The Mule in Southern Agriculture.***

** Melvin Bradley, Table 8-1 on page 164. The three Bootheel counties were in the Top 12 of total mules in Missouri in 1920. New Madrid was 3rd with 7,563 mules, Pemiscot was 8th with 6,211 mules, and Dunklin was 10th with 6,147 mules. Calloway was the leading county with 8,454 mules. Missouri has 114 counties. Ten of the contributors died before the first printing of the book in November 2010. They were: William Cato, Ping Davis, Chalk Givens, Wyman Hampton, Troy Hartle, Artie Hillis, Joe Hillis, Lindell Hoggard, Arnold J ones and Bob Lincoln.

We Were Soon Buried Up to the Running Boards
by Mitzi Chase

I am 75 now. I was 10 years old when my family decided to visit an aunt and uncle in the Forest City, Missouri area near Mound City. We were a little on the poor side, but World War II was starting and my father was working at Cushman's (Cushman Motor Scooters) in Lincoln, Nebraska improving our income considerably, enough to purchase a Packard automobile. I don't remember the year but I do remember it was like a boxcar, very big and heavy.

When we left Lincoln it was a beautiful spring day, and when we arrived at our relatives the spring rains were in full force. After a nice visit, my father loaded us into the old Packard to start our return trip to Lincoln.

Well, as the saying goes, the bottom had gone out of the country road. But this was not an obstacle to my father, since he had this big-heavy automobile.

We were soon buried up to the running boards.

Our relative hitched up a team of his working horses. They could not budge the car. After a few calls to nearby neighbors, one soon showed up with a team of Missouri mules. They were hooked to the Packard and they started pulling. They got down on their bellies and they brought that mired down Packard right up out of the mud.

As I said, I was a 10-year-old girl, and I have never forgotten that day, or what wonderful magnificent animals that team of mules were. I try to go to the state fair only to see the Missouri mules as often as I can. To me a beautiful picture is a picture of a team of matched Missouri mules, but sadly most people seeing that picture, do not know what wonderful stories they could tell. And more sadly, they become less and less.

Mitzi Chase was born April 25, 1932, in Rockport, Missouri, to George and Clara Knapp. She has an older sister, Evelyn, and a brother, Bob. She attended school at Rockport until the family moved to Lincoln, Nebraska in 1940. "We had a family tragedy, and my mother died in 1942; and we moved back to Missouri to be close to relatives," she said. She was graduated from Forest City High School in 1950. "I was an administrative assistant to the nursing director of a small hospital and sang in a championship Sweet Adeline chorus for 25 years," she said. She raised two sons. Her husband, David Chase, was a TWA captain (now retired), and in 2008 the couple resided in the Lake of the Ozarks area.

He Was There for Me When I Needed Him
Harry
As told by Marie Fikuart

Harry was the first and last mule I remember working with. Daddy bought him from a mule farmer from Sikeston. I just loved him. I would hug him around the neck every time I was close to him, like you would pet a dog or a cat. He was there for me when I needed him. I was so young. I was just nine years old when I started working him full time.

Harry was a very gentle, medium-size gray mule. He was an independent mule. He was a smart mule. When he wanted out of the barn lot, he'd jump the fence or open the gate. We had a big wide gate, 10-foot long, and it had a slide handle to release it. Harry learned how to move that handle and he'd open the gate to get outside for some new grass or clover. He always stayed close to the lot. He just wanted something different to eat. When he opened the gate there would be two or three other mules get out with him. But we knew Harry was the only one that opened the gate because he was always one of them.

Poppa farmed 500 acres north of McMullin (Grant City) and had 30 mules. We raised wheat, corn, soybeans, cotton and watermelons. I harrowed, raked hay, cultivated and broke ground with Harry. All of it was riding equipment. I was so small they would put a sack of sand on the plow to help hold it down. The point on the plow was so shinny, it was just like a mirror. Some of the mules we worked with him were Maud, Rodie and Ida. We made a lot of money in the summer off the watermelons. They'd send them to Chicago by rail. I would drive a wagon load of corn to Grant City to load on the railroad.

I'd ride Harry to the mailbox bareback. We didn't have any saddles. I'd climb upon a feed trough to get on him. He'd poke along going the mile to the mailbox and after you picked up the mail, he'd just fly. We lived right beside a railroad track. A lot of times I would holler and wave to the conductor while getting the mail. That's the only time I got to ride him. Poppa wouldn't let us ride him for pleasure.

Poppa saw that Harry and I got along together, and he just kept letting me work with him. It was less trouble to farm if you had a mule you liked. He was a smart mule (to work with). All I had to do was say, "gee, haw, whoa, gettyup." That's all you needed to know to communicate with him. I would climb on the feed trough to put his bridle, collar and harness on. As soon as I came in from the field, I'd take the bridle off of Harry and turn him loose in the barnyard and I'd go help Momma put dinner on the table while the men stood around outside. There was a lot of stuff I missed since I was a girl.

I saw a tornado once that was about three miles away. It tore up Daddy's wheat thrasher that he had stored in a barn. We would have wheat-thrashing dinners where the farmers would come from all around to help with the harvest. Poppa would haul that machine to their farm. One year I got to be water boy and ate at the first table. We didn't work together very often.

I would work from sunrise to sunset. Sometimes when we came in there would be a sore on their neck. We'd take a knife and cut holes through the collar to relieve the pressure. We took good care of them. We piled a lot of corn in the feed trough and the mules would come and eat what they wanted. We had windmills in the pastures.

I wore hand-me-down blue jeans and a cotton shirt of some kind. I didn't wear shoes because I didn't have shoes most of the year. I'd get one pair of shoes in the fall. One year we lay by corn on a Saturday in June and we had five cultivators in the field side by side, all pulled by mules.

There was one thing I didn't like to do on the farm, that was plow the corn. You had six shovels on each side and you had to adjust them just right or they'd pull to the side. You had to use your knees to keep them pulled together. That was hard to do. I'd accidentally plow up some corn, and I never wanted Poppa to find out.

One year Daddy rode around on a horse with a saddle overseeing everyone. We had tenant farmers. He thought he was King of the Hill. But he didn't fool us very much.

I worked with Harry until I was 16. After I graduated from high school I was expected to get a job in the city, which I did, but I missed the mules. He was the only mule Poppa ever put out to pasture. Harry died about 10 years later and he was buried in the pasture near where they found him. Poppa liked him. The whole family liked Harry.

The special friendship Harry and Marie enjoyed stayed with her throughout her life. Linda Culbertson of Sikeston, one of her daughters, described it this way, "My mother is 90 and all my life I've heard about Harry, her mule. She worked in the fields as just a young girl and Harry was her partner. He made a lasting impression." Culbertson estimated her mother was 4-foot tall and weighed 60-lbs. at age 9. On the day she was interviewed for this story, Marie took me into her living room and showed me a stationary bike she exercises on she calls "Harry" where when exercising she recalls the times she would be on Harry racing at a full gallop back to the barn after picking up the mail. - the author

 **Marie Vaughan Fikuart was born Sept. 27, 1920 to Green and Ethel Joyce Vaughan at Gray Ridge in Stoddard County. She had two brothers and four sisters. In 1923 the family moved to Scott County, seven miles north of Sikeston, east of McMullin or Grant City. Marie attended Sand Prairie, a one-room school, for seven years. She graduated from Blodgett High School in 1937. After graduating from high school she worked at F.W.**

Woolsworth in Sikeston in the stockroom for 12 years. She married Windle Fikuart in 1941 and raised three children. Windle died in 1995. "I had two older brothers but they didn't like farm work," she said. "The oldest was a mechanic. He worked with his Uncle Jim. The younger brother liked to hobo. He and a neighbor boy would hop trains in the summer and go as far as Colorado."

I. Mule Teams

She Walked Out in the Dark and Said, "Where's Your Daddy?"
Shorty and George
as told by Bud Henry

My uncle said they run off with him all the time and he couldn't do nothin with them, so he sold them to my dad. This was in 1942. They were four or five years old, weighed 900 to 1,000 pounds. One of them was shorter, stood about 14-hands, that's the one we called "Shorty." They were dark brown. George was almost black and had a white nose. My sisters and I rode them. We'd ride them up and down the turn rows, over to our neighbor's house. Most of the time we'd ride Shorty. My sisters were scared of George. Dad bought me a little saddle in 1943. I used it on Shorty and used two girths to go around his belly.

I was riding him one time in a neighbor's yard and he ran under a clothesline with me and it caught the saddle horn. Shorty pulled with all his might and the clothesline was strong enough it popped that girth and I went off his back. That saddle horn still has the marks on it.

When I was four or five Dad and I went up the levee in the wagon with Shorty and George looking for cattle that ran on open range. We got about 10 miles from home and ran into a guy who told Daddy that he had seen some of his cows. He said he would take us where they were at. Instead of following him in our wagon, Dad said I had to get back home because he might be gone all night.

He turned those mules around. I was holding them lines up. I thought I was driving them. They never trotted. They walked the whole way. I got nervous when it started getting dark. We lived on the riverbank and I rode that wagon all the way back home. We got over near the river, they came to a crossing, they went over that levee, down through the bar (borrow) pit, across the field and came out at the barn where we kept them. It was dark and we didn't have electricity. Momma had been waiting on the porch and heard us drive up. She walked out in the dark and said, "Where's your daddy?" I said he went with a man looking for cows. She said, "You're so little. He shouldn't have sent you back home alone with those mules." She unhooked them from the wagon and left them in the lot with their harness on.

Next day my dad came in walking and she unloaded on him. Dad said, "Ah Mildred, I wasn't worried about him. Them mules would find their way back home."

The first job I did with Shorty and George was plant corn, when I was seven. The planter had two big levers on it you had to trip to let it down and you'd raise it up at the end of the row. I was so small I'd have to take both hands to work those levers. It made blisters on my hands. I got the big idea when I got to the end, my hands were hurting so bad, I'd just turn those mules and leave the planter in the ground. And it did, but it bent it all to one side. I walked over to the barn where my dad was and told him the mules had run away and tore up the planter. I suspicioned he knew those mules didn't run away. But he went along with it, took the planter apart, straightened it back up, and put it back together. Later on in life, I felt so bad about that. One day I said, "Daddy, those mules didn't run away." He said, "I know they didn't. But you got away with a lie to try to keep from getting a whippin."

Shorty was the gentlest and was probably the strongest. He was a pulling little rascal. They were really stout. My uncle had a big thrashing machine that they throwed sunflowers in. They grew a lot of sunflowers then. My uncle got it down in a slough. He had a 35 John Deere tractor. They tied a team of mules to the tractor and together they couldn't pull it out. So my uncle came to my dad's house to get another mule team. We lived about four miles from him. When we got there, Dad had him unhook all that stuff and said, "Let me hook Shorty and George in there."

My uncle had five sons. They were there and they went to laughing and going on saying you think them mules are going to pull that out. Daddy said, "Let me hook them to it." They were still laughing when he hooked it up. He put their check lines on their collars and backed away and started talking to them. Man, they went to pulling and got their bellies plumb on the ground. Dad kept talking to them, "Come on now, get down there and let's get it." He didn't lay a hand on them. He didn't have a line on them, nothing. They pulled that thrasher out of the slough. Those boys shut up. They said, "Whitson, them's the pullingest little mules." That's the way those mules were. If you hooked them to something, they were going to move it if they could.

We didn't have a car. We used the mules to go to town. We'd get up at 3 o'clock to get ready. It was an all day affair. Dad and Mom would sit on the buckboard. My sisters and I would sit in the wagon. We'd pull in behind one of the grocery stores and unhook the mules, bring them around to the side of the wagon, take their bridles off and hook them from their collars to the side of the wagon, put a flake of hay in there for them. There'd be several wagons back there. Time we got done getting groceries and shopping and get back home, it would be dark.

Dad and I farmed with those mules until 1953. We also had an H Farmall tractor. I was in high school one day and Dad took them off to a man he knew at East Prairie and sold them to him. After that I can remember him saying, "I made one of the biggest mistakes of my life" and there were tears in his eyes because he had sold them, and they were part of the family and should have died there on the farm.

Whitson E. "Bud" Henry was born Feb. 15, 1938 to Whitson Edward Henry

and Mildred M. Joiner Henry at their home at Higgerson Landing, located 11 mites east of New Madrid along the Mississippi
River. He had an older sister and three younger sisters and one
younger brother. Bud attended Higgerson School, a one-room
school built by his grandfather, through the eighth grade. He
walked the four miles to the school throughout the eight years.

He graduated from New Madrid High School in 1957, attended
Murray State University in Murray, Kentucky for two years and was drafted
into the U.S. Army in 1960, and served one year active duty and six years in
the National Guard. He married Beth Hunter in 1966 and farmed with his dad
until 1966 He started farming on his own in 1967 and farmed up to 4,000
acres. Bud continued to farm until 2003 and retired shortly after his wife
passed away in June, 2003. Bud is first cousin to Ralph Higgerson who has a
stories in the Farming With Mules and Mules That Worked by Voice Com-
mands/Without Lines chapters. The Spring floods of 2011 covered the farm
Henry grew up on.

Bud in 1945 with his dad and George   *George and Shorty (1948).*
and Shorty.

*Martha Henry Hunter (Bud's oldest sister) on
Shorty (1946). "He was so gentle. We could
just climb on his back and ride him. I was riding him down to my grandparents one time and
one of my cousins jumped out and spooked
him," Hunter recalled. "Shorty stopped so sud-
denly, I went over his head. I don't know what
kept me from breaking my neck. He ran to the
barn, I had to walk the rest of the way."*

Directly the Water Started Coming in the Wagon Bed
Shorty and George, Part II
as told by Bud Henry

We were always shearing the mules and messing with them. Inside the back leg of a mule under the tail is soft and tender. Shorty and George liked to be rubbed there. So they got where when you'd go to the barn, they'd go backing up on you. We knew what they wanted and we'd rub them. If we were at the barn and if strangers came up talking to us, those mules would start backing up to them. They thought they were backing up to kick them. It would scare them. Daddy would say, "They aren't going to hurt you. They just want to be rubbed."

Back in the 1940s they had a 4-H fat barrow show here in town in April. And it was a big deal here in New Madrid. They had a parade, bands, and all those tents. We got in it ourselves in 4-H. We didn't have any cars. The mules were our transportation.
I think it was in 1947, we hooked Shorty and George up one day before daylight, got in the wagon and started to town. It was around 11 miles from where we lived.

Backwater from the Mississippi River comes up every spring and it covered all that country around where we lived. We came out those muddy roads, wasn't no gravel roads, come through the woods and got over there across the levee and we ran into water over the road.

Dad started driving those mules in that water. He could see where it came out on the other side and thought it was low. My mother was sitting in there. Me and my three sisters were sitting in the wagon. Directly the water spurted through the cracks and started coming in the wagon bed. My sisters and I got our butts wet and jumped up, and I looked out at the mules and water was up to their sides.

When the mules started to jump and swim Daddy knew then the water was too deep. The wagon bed started floating up from the frame and he jumped out on the tongue to the wagon. Mother was screaming and carrying on, thinking we would drown as Daddy was the only one of us who could swim. Dad reached in the wagon bed and got some baling wire and used it to tie the wagon bed down to the stakes that were on the sides of the frame.

This road wasn't very wide, but he turned Shorty and George around and they pulled that wagon out. Once we got in shallow water, Dad got back in the wagon with all that water running out. That scared us all and we went back home. I never will forget that. When we got home floodwater was up across the farm so we took all our livestock to the levee and turned them loose.

There Wasn't Anyway of Stopping Them
Kit and Beck
as told by Dr. Gene Leroux, MD

Mules were the main stay you might say. Back in the 1930s and 1940s, that's what we made a living with. They were real necessary. My memories of mules couldn't be better. They were dependable. I knew what to expect out of them, and they understood you.
We had a horse or two, but most always Dad had four to six mules.

Dad's cousin, Henry Richmond, had Kit and Beck. Dad bought them from him as 2 year olds. I think Richmond had an extra pair. They came out of the same mare but different jacks. They were both black mules. Kit had a black nose, and Beck a light brown nose. Kit, a horse mule, was shorter and heavier than Beck, a mare mule.

Kit was the spirited one. He on occasion would take the bit between his teeth and run off. When we would put the hay frame on the wagon used at haying time it would make a racket, and Kit would start to prance and dance. If no one was there to hold him, he would take off.

One time they took off with the wagon and jumped over a 4-foot barn lot fence without tearing the fence down. I guess they had enough jerk and bounce to jerk the wagon over the fence. There wasn't any way of stopping them. It would be like trying to stop a freight train. We found them in the woods a straddle a tree.

Beck was good to ride. A lot of times I rode her bareback. If I was working them in the field, at lunch time I would unhook them, jump on Beck, and lead Kit to the house.

Gene Leroux 1942, when weighing 140 lbs.

Garold, one of my older brothers, was a little high-spirited. Ole Beck sometimes would take a notion she didn't want to get bridled. Garold would get one of her ear's in his mouth to hold her head down to get the bridle on her.

They were excellent workers. I started working them at age 11 (1939). I wore overalls and most of the time I wore shoes. A lot of times I didn't wear a shirt. There were times when the ground was soft that I went barefoot. But during hay season I wore shoes. I always tell people I got one pair of shoes a year whether I needed them or not. I never did get tired of walking behind them. One time when it was hot, my older brother and my dad said I needed to stop and let them rest a while. I guess I was pushing them too much.

Dad had bought an F-14 Farmall in 1938 that he used for plowing and disking. He used the mules for cultivating and planting. In 1941, I started driving the tractor some. It was nice to sit down and ride while plowing and disking. I used Kit and Beck through the 1940s for cultivating, mowing and raking hay, and pulling a wagon in corn-fields while gathering corn.

We had 160 acres of our own we farmed and sometimes we rented more land to farm. We had the tractor and two mule teams. My dad usually drove the tractor, and me and one of my brothers would work the mules. We primarily raised cotton and corn, some soybeans, wheat, oats, and rye. We raised 25 to 30 acres of cotton. Cotton was our cash crop. During the depression, from 1929 to 1934, we were able to pay our place off in five years.

We always had lots of chores to do in the morning, and it would be 9 o'clock before I would get the mules out to the field. I would quit at noon. I got accurate at judging time by the way my shadow cast. I would go back at 1 p.m. and work until 7 or 8 in the evening, when we'd quit. I would feed them two or three ears of corn at lunchtime, and their main meal was at night. I would feed them heavy at night and pump water by hand.

Leroux's brother with Kit (front) and Beck 1941.

Back then you could drive a pipe 20 to 25 feet in the ground and have water.

In 1942, my older brother joined the Army, and my oldest brother drove a stock truck, and my youngest brother was five years younger, so I was using the mules pretty well all the time. During the first cultivating when the plants were small and the ground more firm, I probably cultivated a half acre an hour. As the plants got bigger, I could go faster. There are 11 quarter-mile rows to an acre. So I was walking 13 or more miles a day behind the one-row cultivator. When the weather got hot, they'd have to rest. We'd go pretty good for two or three days, and a week or so later, we'd go again. Most of the crops would be laid-by (final cultivation) by the Fourth of July.

I can remember gathering corn late in the fall and the wagon

Kit and Beck (1937) with James Leroux.

would get mired down in the mud with a full load. They'd (Kit and Beck) get down and pull to get that wagon out. One time a neighbor got his old Chevy pickup (1930s model) stuck in the ditch about a quarter of a mile from where we lived. Dad hooked Kit and Beck to the front end and got them to pulling, while the man drove the pickup. They pulled it right out of the ditch. One time in the spring of 1944, which was a wet year, I got the Farmall stuck in a ditch in a field and hooked Kit and Beck to it to pull it out.

During the winter months we kept the mules in a 100-acre fenced area, mostly woods, that was a half-mile to the back. We would get them up in February. We would walk out to get them, and they would run from one end of the woods to the other three or four times. When they got ready they would run into the barn.

Beck learned to open the crib door and gates with her nose. We've had two or three of them get in the corncrib with her. They ate a lot of corn and made a mess but never hurt themselves. She'd open a pasture gate with either a hoop over it or a sliding latch. She learned how to open both.

They (Kit and Beck) were heavy pullers. Back in the '30s, before combines, we used binders to cut wheat. It took three or four mules to pull them. We used Kit and Beck and Kate, a reddish mule. That was a heavy load. Some mules will balk with a heavy load. But these three never did. I guess they would have kept on pulling until they fell.

 Gene H. Leroux was born Aug. 16, 1928, to William A. and Mary Ann (Crook) Leroux. He was raised on a 160-acre farm south of Naylor in Ripley County. He had three brothers and three sisters and was next to the youngest boy. He attended Taylor School, a two-room school, through the eighth grade. He was graduated from Naylor High School and was 1947 valedictorian. In 1950 he was drafted into the Army . He served 13 months in Korea, and was discharged Aug. 28, 1952. He married Louise McGonigal on March 29, 1951. After being discharged, he went back home and farmed for two years and realized there was a shortage of doctors in the area. He obtained his pre-med degree from Arkansas State University at Jonesboro in 1956 and was graduated from Missouri University's School of Medicine at Columbia in 1960. After practicing medicine at Ellington, Missouri for a while he moved his practice to Doniphan in 1962, where he was still practicing medicine part-time in 2009. "I still make two or three house calls a week," Dr. Leroux said at his office in Dec. 2007. "Back in the 60s I worked 12 to 18 hours every day, seven days a week; and I'd drive 200 miles at night after working in the office. Many nights I never even got to bed. I would get up twice, or occasionally three times to treat someone at the emergency room, or deliver a baby, or make a house call. I averaged working 18 hours a day, seven days a week from 1961 to 1973. I've never had to sit around waiting for patients." When Dr. Leroux was asked if he got tired walking 12 or 13 miles a day barefoot while cultivating, he said, "We didn't have rocks down there. That helped a lot. We were raised up in that (environment). We didn't know any better."

If Those Galluses Hadn't Of Broke. She Probably Would Have Killed Him
Rock and Rodie
as told by Buck Farmer

We had a mare mule out of a bronco mare. She was feisty. Rock was a black-horse mule. Rodie was a brown-mare mule. Rock and Rodie, they were a good team.

Rock, was raised by a fellow whose farm we rented. He was 2 years old when we got him. Rodie came from a fellow who lived south of town, and he had a good pair of mules named Dave and Rodie.

Rock was broke on the new farm we moved to northwest of Charleston when I was 8. I put Rock beside Spider (see Spider and Ella story in this chapter) and in the middle pulling a sulky plow. He wasn't any trouble to break. Rodie was already broke.

We had a 240-acre farm. Dad had eight mules and a horse named Trixie. We had three sulky plows. It took three mules to pull each one. I was so small when I started plowing, Dad would tie a piece of railroad iron under the seat, so that when I hit a hard spot it wouldn't come out of the ground.

Our farm was laid out in 40-acre tracts. My dad bought me a new International walking cultivator that was used for cultivating watermelons. They're such a tiny little plant. When they came up you had to be very careful not to cover it or damage them. One of my sisters would sit on the tongue and drive the mules, so I could keep my eyes on the cultivator. When we came in for lunch, Dad would ask how many rows we had plowed, and we generally plowed 50 rows in half a day. You figure that up at a quarter a mile a row, and I walked 25 miles a day in plowed ground.

I'd get up at 4:30 in the morning, and my mom would give me a cup of coffee so I wouldn't fall asleep while cultivating, working the mowing machine, or whatever. Rock and Rodie were so trained, I'd leave the cultivator in the alleyway. I'd bring them out harnessed, and they'd line up on that tongue unassisted.

I had to have them home by a quarter till 12 and quarter till sundown, that's when Dad wanted his mules in. I could look at the sun and tell exactly what time it was. Dad never would let me go barefooted. One year I went through the whole year without wearing a shirt. I just wore trousers. I would get sunburnt and a good suntan.

Rodie would bite you. When she'd bite at me, I'd slap her on the nose. When we sheared her, we used a twister. I had a cousin who worked for my dad. He was about 4 years older than I. He was pretty good at shearing a mule. So it come a rain and Dad said, "Shear the mules." So I caught ole Rodie and put a twister on her. I had a hitch line and I tied it in the galluses of my cousin's overalls. I turned the twister loose and it was by the grace of God; if those galluses hadn't of broke, she probably would have killed him. When she took off it swung him around and that scared her and she really took off. We had to catch her and finish the shearing.

As a young man I started strawing watermelon cars. The straw was used to pack watermelons on and to put between watermelons, to keep melons from being damaged in shipment. I'd get a dollar a railroad boxcar. After wheat harvest I'd go to a farmer who had a straw stack. I'd either buy it or he'd say I'll give it to you if you clean it up. Rock and Rodie pulled a big wagon that held enough straw that I could do three boxcars.

I had a black man helping me. He'd throw it up (into the boxcar) and I'd stomp it down. I was strawing a car one day and flies were bad. And ole Rodie was throwing her head up and down. I was in the car. And she came up with her bridle off. It hung under the neck yoke. I hollered and jumped in the wagon, and when I pulled the reins, the bridle slapped her in the chest, and then they took off.

There was a narrow road next to the track. There was a melon grower there and he'd bought a new Chevrolet automobile. And they were headed for that new car. He was out there trying to flag them down. They turned right, down through a cotton patch. The way I stopped them was to jump off and run and cut them off and grab a hold of their bridles. I was just a kid, probably 14. I caught them in about 100 yards, but it was an experience I'll never forget.

I did a lot of work with Rock and Rodie. A friend built a filling station and a restaurant across from the shoe factory at Charleston, and he needed some dirt to fill in some low places. I used a two-by-four dump wagon that had two-by-twelve sides, and two-by-fours in the bottom. I would go to the ditch banks outside of the city, and using a shovel, fill the wagon to the extent the mules could pull it. I'd pull in on the lot and start turning the two-by-fours over, and that would spill the dirt. That made it very simple.

This Rodie mule had never been ridden. One day I had taken a wagon over to a sawmill. He had a corduroy road, where they lay wood planks side by side for a road. I would see the owner coming out with six or eight mules pulling a loaded wagon, hauling logs to Charleston. I had unhooked the mules and I just decided I was going to ride Rodie (and lead Rock). It spooked her when I jumped up on her. She was more scared than I was and that's pretty scared. Her ears stayed up all the way home. When Dad saw me riding her, I thought he was going to faint. She was a tough mule. She and ole Rock could stand the heat when a lot of them would pull out.

When I went in the service in 1942, my dad sold them (Rock and Rodie) to a fellow for $500. That was almost unheard of during the Depression. At that time you could buy about any mule for $100.

This is the first of four stories by Buck Farmer. (See "Old Timer and Alfred" and "Spider and Ella" in this chapter and "My Gosh a Mighty! The Dirt Was Flying," Dave in the Mules chapter.

Charles F. "Buck" Farmer was born Dec. 19, 1919, to Charles F. "Charlie" and Cordilla Farmer. He had four sisters, one younger and three older. His father farmed in Mississippi County, 18 miles west of Charleston. When Buck was eight they moved to a farm three miles northwest of Charleston. Buck attended Dihlstadt School northeast of Charleston through the third grade and Charleston schools into his sophomore year, when he quit to help his dad farm. Buck enlisted in the Army in 1942 and was trained as a military policeman. He was selected for officer training and later was trained for the Secret Service. He spent time overseas in China, Burma and India. He lost Juel, his wife of 65 years, in August 2005. Buck was a Ford tractor dealer, then worked for Implement Sales Company in Memphis, Tennessee, retiring in 2005. He was board chairman at Implement Sales. Recalling mule farming he said, "In those days if you saw a team of mules hooked to a hitching rail in town, you knew who their owner was. If a mule got loose and came to our house, we knew whose mule it was."

I Can't Believe I'm Not Dead
Dink and Kit
as told by Armon Keaster

Dink and Kit were a pair of black mules. Dink was a horse mule, and Kit was a mare mule. They were large, good-looking mules, and were the envy of the neighborhood.

Dad purchased them as 2 or 3 year olds in 1939 from Dwight Clodfelter, a farmer who lived around Kinder or Puxico. He had bought a tractor, which is why he sold the mules.

They were a hard-working team of mules. They responded to commands, gee, haw and whoa. Their only problem was sometimes they tended to run a little bit. Kit could be lazy and Dink was a worker. She always put him in a difficult situation. She was the flighty one. She was also slightly larger.

My older brother, Densil, did most of the farming with Dink and Kit, until 1942 when he went into the military. After he left my dad and Uncle Harold took over the farming. We owned 20 acres and farmed between 30 and 40 acres, mostly cotton, and we always grew 5 to 10 acres of corn to have to feed the farm animals.

I sometimes worked the mules, but my main job was chopping cotton and picking cotton. From ages 14 to 19, I consistently picked 300 pounds a day. I also picked for other cotton farmers and earned $2.50 per 100 pounds.

In May 1945, we had a flood and had to move our livestock to a neighbor's a mile and a half away. We stayed at the house and had to put our furniture on blocks. Our neighbor, Albert Fox, came to eat with us one day, and when we opened the door water came running through the house. He kidded us that for the first time we had running water. (The house didn't have running water).

Keaster's dad with Dink and Kit.

The ground was wet that year until the 29th day of June. That's when Dad started planting corn with Dink and Kit. There wasn't enough time to plow the ground. He used a lister planter, which used a double mold-board plow to make a furrow in which to drop seed. It probably took him about two weeks to get it planted. In two or three days the corn came up.

We had that team of mules cultivating corn every day. We were up at daylight and came in at dusk. Dad used a riding cultivator, which is why they were worked so hard. He always took a 30-minute break at noon. The mules were given water, grain and hay, which was mostly clover.

Mother milked the cows. My chores were to feed all of the livestock. We usually had a dozen or so hogs. I cleaned out the stalls and raked out the corncobs from inside the barn every day and cleaned out the chicken house two or three times a year. I even swept the yard. People couldn't believe that I actually swept the yard with a broom.

We kept our house and fences painted. People thought we were well off, but we were fortunate to have enough to eat. We kept a large garden and fruit trees.

When I would walk out to the barn early in the morning to feed the mules, they would be pawing at the gate that led to the barn lot wanting to be fed. The gate was 75 feet from the house, but I could hear them pawing when I opened the door. They would follow me to the barn and I would feed them first.

Mom also worked in the field. One morning she had finished milking and was walking down the hallway of the barn, and she startled one of the mules, probably Kit. They were probably asleep or grazing on some hay. Kit instinctively reared up. Mom said when Kit recognized who it was, she made every effort possible to keep from hitting her, but when Kit came down she grazed her front. Mom came to the house and opened the door and said, "I can't believe I'm not dead!"

When working in the field, Dink and Kit had a propensity to run. Densil kept trying to find ways to keep them from bolting. He finally put leather bands around their front legs and tied the bands to a rope, which ran up through the harness, and he kept the end of the rope around his back. When they would run, he would lean back and their front feet would come back under them, throwing them on their noses. He only had to do that two or three times. We all laughed about it.

Densil was a smart cookie. He could shuck 100 bushel of corn a day by hand, which was almost unheard of in the Bootheel. He would shuck the ears of corn from the husks and throw them in the wagon. They always said he had an ear of corn in the air at all times. He had to take the wagon to the barn and scoop out the corn. He took a lot of pride in his ability to pick so much corn.

He taught Dink and Kit to keep the wagon moving slowly along rows going away from the house. He would pick two rows at a time. The rows were a quarter of a mile long. When he got to the end of the row, he would jump in the wagon, turn the mules toward the house, and run them to the other end; then he would start up on two more rows. There was no way to keep those mules walking slowly going towards the house.

In 1947, Dad bought a B Farmall tractor for $700 and sold Dink and Kit to Albert Fox for $500. Even though Fox had tractors, he wanted that pair of mules. They were still the envy of the neighborhood. Their only problem was they still had a tendency to run.

That next spring, in 1948, Fox was hooking them to a cultivator, and they got away from him and started to run down the road to our house. They had run a half- mile or so; I saw them coming. When I attempted to herd them around, they ran off the road and towards a tractor disk. They tried to jump it and Kit cut her knee. The wound healed, but she was never the same after that.

Dad never worked horses. He said mules were calm compared to a horse. Dad didn't want to be a sharecropper. He paid cash for everything, and saved his money. He didn't want to go into debt.

 **Armon Keaster was born March 12, 1933, to John P. and Nora Keaster. He was raised about 10 miles southwest of Lilbourn in New Madrid County. He had five siblings, two brothers and three sisters, and was the youngest boy. Armon was graduated from Risco High School in 1951 and attended Southeast Missouri State University a while before obtaining his B.S. degree in entomology from the University of Missouri (MU) in 1959. He earned his master's there in 1961 and his doctorate in entomology in 1965 at MU. He researched corn insects at MU for several years and taught entomology courses there from 1970 until he retired in 1997. In December 2007 at the time of the interview he and his wife, Mona, had been married 51 years and resided in Columbia.**

We Used Them a Lot of Times When the Corn Got Tall
Old Timer and Alfred
as told by Buck Farmer

They were both big tall mules. One was a red mule Dad called Old Timer. We had a black mule we worked with him we called Alfred. Alfred was a stringhalted mule. He had strained his leg. I can still see him going through the field, and he'd stretch this leg out even going through the field. It was sprung by over loading him. I was 12 when we had them, so it would have been 1931.

They worked good together, and we used them a lot of times when the corn got tall. During a drought my cousin came over to help us. Dad had heard they were using mower wheels, cast wheels off of a mower; they were heavy, we'd take those wheels and drag them through the middles to try to bring moisture to the top of the ground. We used those two mules.

They were 17 hands tall. We rode them to be above the corn. In those days open-pollinated corn would get 8 foot high. When the first hybrid corn came out it would only get 6 feet high and there would be two nubbins to each stalk. Then the hybrid corn came in, and that's what you see out there now.

If you didn't get above the corn to get air, you'd smother to death. We hooked a singletree with a chain on it to the mower wheel. We had a lot of fun riding those mules down those rows.

It was a pretty good job to get up on those ole tall mules. We'd grab the hames and swing up on them. We didn't get off unless we had to.

One of the funniest things happened. My cousin and I were coming out the end of a row and I saw my mom and dad coming. They had a small can (baking powder). I thought, "Boy, they're bringing us something to eat."

Mom handed me the can. Somehow or other they had gotten hold of some bedsprings out of a mattress. They stuffed them down in this can. I grabbed it because I was closest to them. I jerked the lid off and those things flew everywhere. It scared those old mules to death. But they weren't the type of mules to run off. I'll always remember that. They did bring us a little something to eat.

My uncle borrowed one of them and got him mired down in seep water. We thought we were going to lose that mule. He took a log chain and a big ole mule that he had, tied it around his neck, and pulled him out backwards. It's a wonder it didn't kill him.

This is Buck Farmer's second of four stories. See "Rock and Rodie" and "Spider and Ella" in this chapter and "Dave" in the Mules chapter.

They All Thought I Was Dead When They Picked Me Up
Matt and Andy
as told by Max Ray Moore

I'd go to the field after school. All I ever wanted to do was farm. I think I was 6 years old and I remember when I was with my dad that I'd want to drive (the mules). When you turned the dirt over with a mowboard plow, there were men that followed with a harrow. I'd hang around him (Dad) and sometimes I'd walk along beside him. I remember one afternoon I got down there and he was really tired from walking that ole loose ground all day. And I said, "Why don't you let me drive them?" He said, "Well, do you think you can?" "Yep." "Now, don't let them turn around too close at the end now or they will get away from you."

They were worked down and everything. And I went out and made it just fine and made two turns (with the harrow.) He sat down up there and waited on me, because he was give out. But I would have done anything to get to work them. I thought I'd hung the moon.

I remember their names, Matt and Andy. Andy was a gray that had turned white, and Matt was a bay. They were 10 years old.

I was always walking around out there, cause I was just interested in farming. I went by and my uncle was planting. He had two mules. He had one to a single plow that he'd run on top of the bed and make a furrow. He'd go around and then he'd stop him. Then he'd take the one hooked to a one-row planter and he'd plant up and back, and he'd do the same thing over again. When I went by, he said, "Reckon you could hold this. Reckon you could plant this." I said, "I don't know now. I could hold it (planter) up till I get to the end, but I can't turn it around. I'm not strong enough to turn it around." He said, "Well, I can turn it around."

Each one of us had one mule. He went out front with the plow. He'd turn around and he'd say, "whoa" and they'd stop. I couldn't even hold the handles. I had to hold below. We'd get it in a furrow and I just kept it in that furrow. But I could hold it up, and he gave me a quarter. That was the first quarter I ever made in my life. I was 6 years old.

Andy was very gentle and everything. When I'd go to the field, I'd hang around till quittin time and I'd ride him to the house. One time it was just before dark and (we) went through a lot and kind of a little gust of wind blew the crib door, and it popped! He jumped sideways just a little bit.

I fell off and my leg got hung up in a chain and he run around. He was in a lot and kept running in a circle. It's a wonder it hadn't killed me. They said when he'd go around my weight would swing out. Finally when he came back my head hit a box, turned me over, and I come out. My head hit the ground first and it knocked me out. They all thought I was dead when they picked me up. They took me to the hospital in Jackson, Tennessee. I just had a little cut over my eye. They said if I had anything, it would be a slight concussion. Both of my eyes were black and swelled too (closed). They took me home and in a few days I was up running around. My eyes sure were black for a while. I was 7 when that happened.

 Max Ray Moore was born April 15, 1928, to Harvey and Beulah Moore in McNairy County, Tennessee. His dad farmed 50 acres three miles northeast of Leapwood. He had two older sisters, both of whom had died, at ages two and three, before he was born. In February 1937, when he was 8, the family moved to Dunklin County, Missouri near Hornersville. Moore attended Cotton Plant School, a two-room school north of Hornersville, from the third through the fifth grades. He then attended schools in Hornersville, graduating from Hornersville High School in 1946.

He spent four years in the U.S. Air Force, 1951 to 1955, mostly as a jet fighter instructor at Amarillo, Texas. He farmed with mules through 1941. His dad sold their 65-acre farm near Hornersville and bought a 400-acre farm nearby in November 1941, and left the mules and horses to the man who bought their farm. On the new farm, they farmed with two M Farmall tractors. They sharecropped two years, and during this time they made enough money to buy the farm. Moore was 14 when he first farmed with a tractor. He and his wife, Margaret, had been married 59 years in 2009; and Moore, at age 81, was farming 3,250 acres with his son, Marty. Moore said when they unhooked mules from farm equipment they put the O ring of the trace chains over the hames. This loop is what he caught his foot in.

Moore also has a story in the Runaways chapter.

Author's note: There are two other stories in this chapter that recall incidents of falling off a mule and having a leg hung up in a trace chain. See Wilburn's story on Blue and Red, and Shipman's story on John and Slim.

Learned to Cuss Farming With Those Mules
Judge and Beck
as told by Judge Bill Batson

I was born and raised around Campbell and for a while my parents, Clifton and Lucy, farmed in Arkansas. My dad always farmed with mules. In 1934, he sold his two mule teams, a large pair and a smaller pair, that he farmed with in Arkansas and bought a tractor. He used it one year. He couldn't afford it and went back to mules.

When I was 12 (1937), they left the farm they had rented in Arkansas and bought a 40-acre farm near Qulin. It was practically all in timber. We would clear ground and burn the logs. Back then we used mules to build piles of logs 15 foot high to burn. We would hook a log chain to the mules, and pull the logs up on logs used as runners. When it was wet we used what we called a mud sled that Dad had made to haul logs on. It was much easier than using a wagon.

Dad had heart trouble, which kept him from doing labor, so I did most of the farming from the time I was 15 to age 17. My two older brothers were in the service, my younger brother was five years younger. I quit school after the eighth grade. I had started ninth grade, and during the six-week, cotton picking vacation, I decided I had all the school I wanted and didn't go back to school. It wasn't hard to talk my folks into it. They needed someone to work the farm.

The mule team I worked were named Judge and Beck. Dad bought them from a friend who lived near Riddle Hill, located about four miles west of Malden, and east of Crowley's Ridge. They were a reddish color and medium to large in size. Judge was a male mule, and Beck was a female. They were matched in size and color.

They were older mules, but still young enough to put out a good day's work. We farmed 25 to 30 acres, mostly cotton, corn, wheat, and hay. We hauled in loose hay, enough to feed the mules and three or four milk cows.

Batson (center) with his mom and dad. Photo taken in summer 1940 at front yard of Qulin farm. Highway 53 is in background, along with cotton and corn. Along the woods is where Batson learned to cuss and where his dad stepped out and surprised him.

I used those mules for everything. I would start working them in early February with a breaking plow. We would sometimes have to plow ground covered with water. They would plow right through it where you couldn't go with a tractor. It would take a month or so to get all the ground broken. We would do a little over an acre a day using a 10-inch or 12-inch plow.

We had a lot of new ground to plow at Qulin. I used a new ground plow which had a flat piece of steel called a coulter that ran in front of the plow. The coulter would tell you when you hit a root. I could tell by how the root felt whether or not the mules could pull through it. I've sliced roots half in to. If I felt the root was too big, I would lift the plow over the root and go on plowing. I walked behind the plow and kept the reins around my waist. I've been jerked over plow handles many times. Sometimes I would misjudge the stump and get hung up. It would take several minutes to get the plow loose.

After plowing I would pull a drag type disk over it. Where we had plowed in wet ground the clods would get real hard when they dried out and there were spots we had to disk over and over again. Then we would harrow. I used a new ground harrow, which was an "A" frame shape that was made out of four-by-fours with a cross member for support. It had two rows of iron spikes that did the harrowing.

I could only plow a little over an acre a day in new ground, but in old ground I could plow two acres a day.

I figured it out one time that I averaged walking 20 to 25 miles a day plowing. The mules probably averaged 2 and a half mph, and I was working them 10 hours a day. I was proud of my plowing. I would start by going down the center of the field and flip dirt one way; then I would come back and flip dirt the other way, and would plow in 30-foot strips.

Mules are a lot more adapted to working new ground than horses. If horses hit a root and are jerked to a stop, they will prance around for a minute or two. If mules hit a stump, they just stop and wait until you get the plow out.

After the ground was prepared, my dad had a two-row riding drill. It had different plates for planting cotton or corn. You just changed the plates. He would do the planting. That's all he did. He'd take a long stick and goose them mules a little bit and they would walk fast. I guess the reason he wanted to do it was he didn't have to walk like I did.

I would get up at 4 a.m. and the first thing I would do was feed the mules, while Mom started cooking breakfast. Sometimes I would milk a cow. Most of the time, the milking was done by my younger siblings.

Usually by sunup I was out with the mules starting to work them to a double shovel. I learned to look at my shadow and tell what time it was. When my shadow pointed north, I knew it was noontime. I would unhook Judge and Beck and drive them in the barn lot and I would take their bridles off and feed them two or three ears of corn apiece.

After lunch I would lay down for a nap. With the front and back doors of the house open there would be a cool breeze. I would get up around 1 p.m. and go back to work until sundown. One of my younger siblings or my mother would bring me some cold water to

drink at midmorning and midafternoon. Sometimes I would be working close to the barn and would stop and go get a drink from the pump. The mules drank at noontime.

It's hard to tell how many miles I walked behind those mules. Mom would tell me that at nights I would be moaning in my sleep and that she'd come in and rub my legs. I never would wake up.

I worked those mules six days a week, 10 to 12 hours a day. In the three years I worked them they never did go lame. I worked mostly by myself. We never did work on Sunday.

One day I was working when the temperature was around 100 degrees. The mules would get hot and flies were thick. Judge had his underbelly covered with flies. I felt sorry for him and reached under him to scrape the flies off. He instinctively raised his leg up, and when he put it down; it got both of my thighs and knocked me to the ground. I told him I wouldn't give him any relief after that. I learned to cuss working with those mules.

One day I was cultivating corn and we approached a big stump. I wanted the mules to go to the right of the stump. Instead, they went to the left. I gave those mules some choice words. I didn't know it, but Dad was behind some trees and heard me cuss. He stepped out and said, "What did you say?" He knew exactly what I had said. I didn't even bother to stop. I cracked the butt of those mules with a whip and took off for the other end of the field.

When the corn would get 6 or 7 feet tall, I would take one mule to a middle buster and do what we called "laying it by." We would split the middle that would cover the weeds up where they would have to grow real fast to catch up with the corn. You wouldn't know anybody was doing it until you saw them come out at the end of the row. My clothing would be ringing wet with perspiration. There would be sweat all over the mules' shiny coats. I had to let them rest every once in a while, so they could cool off a little. It would usually be June before we lay the crops by.

There was only one time they ran away with me. I was working another person's farm and was going home in a wagon, and some way or other the reins got loose. They took off and they got in a fast trot, and then went pretty fast. I never let that happen again.

The mules were used for heavy work in the spring and early summer. After that they had it pretty easy. In the fall we used them to pull a wagon in gathering corn and for pulling loads of cotton to the gin.

William C. "Bill" Batson, Jr., was born March 21, 1925, to Clifton and Lucy Batson. He had two sisters and three brothers, two of them older. He enlisted in the U.S. Navy at age 17 and served in the South Pacific during World War II. He started high school in January 1946, after being discharged from the Navy, and started college in the fall of 1946 under the GI Bill. He graduated with the Qulin High School Class of 1947 and did undergraduate work at Southeast Missouri State for two years before being accepted into law school in the fall of 1948. He graduated from University of Missouri Law School in February 1951, and went to work as an insurance ad-

juster at Macon, Missouri, then moved to New Madrid before settling down in Poplar Bluff in 1954. He opened his own law practice in 1957 and from 1957 to 1970, worked either as an assistant prosecuting attorney or prosecuting attorney. He was appointed associate circuit judge in 1976 and retired in 1988. He spent several years in the 1970s and 1980s developing Batson Mini Farms, a 385-acre subdivision complex, located four miles west of Poplar Bluff. This is where he resides with his wife, Ruby Jane. The couple celebrated their 62nd wedding anniversary in November 2009.

Batson said when he returned from the Navy, his father had sold Judge and Beck. "I loved farming. I had planned to teach agriculture before a friend talked me into going into law school," Batson said. "When I went back to high school I wrote an essay on how I loved turning the ground. I enjoyed it. A lot of people used horses, but mules were the mainstay for power and energy in farming. I read a lot of articles about Missouri being the mule state of the United States. Even in the history books we were taught how important mules were for farming."

Well, It Was Right Up One of Them's Butt
Mag and Jig
as told by Ed Beasley

In 1941, my dad and my brother-in-law, Cecil Kilgo, went to Mississippi, and they brought back 30 head of mules, all young mules. They hauled them back in a bob truck. They may have made more than one trip. I imagine he bought them from individuals. Back then a lot of people raised mules. Dad wouldn't have a horse, because they'd balk.

Dad sharecropped, and was straw boss for U.S. Holiman. Holiman gave Dad the money to buy the mules. He had a bunch of land south of Gideon, and probably had 15 sharecroppers. We lived in a four-room house on the farm.

Dad had a pick of choice of the 30. He picked the two he wanted, and that's the ones he kept. He called them Mag and Jig. They were good-sized black mare mules, probably weighed 1,200 pounds.

I was 10 and wasn't big enough to break them. But my brother and three or four guys broke them to work. To break them, they'd hook two of the unbroken mules to a wagon and get them in a plowed field. There would be two in a wagon. They'd each get a hold of one line to make them turn. They'd make them run until they wore themselves down.

My job was to pump water for the mules with a hand pump. When I got in from school of the evening, that's what I had to do. It was a 500-gallon tank, and when the mules would come in from the field, and when they took the harness off of them, they went straight to that water tank. Well, my job I had to keep water in it. I might pump for two hours. A couple of years later, my dad got a one-cylinder, gas-powered water pump. You had to hand crank it. That was the best thing that ever happened to me.

My dad had a way with mules; he'd keep them under control. He could talk to them and get more out of them, than beating (them). He would see that they had the best feed and hay. He said, "That's what made our living." Once a month on a Sunday he would shear them (manes and tails). He kept them looking good. That was our way to go to town, mules and a wagon. We used them to haul wood. That's all we had back then, were mules.

Me, and my brother-in-law, Hob Baker, were planting corn one time with Mag and Jig. They were young at the time. I had just filled up the planter with seed, and Hob was in the seat driving them. They took off running and he jumped off. They got astraddle a pasture fence and tore it up, probably for a 100 yards or so. When they stopped, they had the bottom of the planter upwards. And one of the mules was down. And one of the feeders, that's what I call them, they hit the ground for the seed to go in; well, it was right up one of them's butt.

They were just shaking; they were so scared. After they settled down, we got them up and he started working them again.

When I was 11, my older brother left for the service, and I started farming with my dad. That's the way it was back then. I started out with Hawk and Dink. Hawk was white and Dink was black. They were old mules, probably 20 years old and gentle. That's the reason my dad put me with them. I wasn't big enough to harness them, but I could take the harness off.

I would work with my dad. He would work Mag and Jig, and I would follow with the older team. They were slower and would lag behind. There wasn't nobody running no race. Most of the time, I'd go barefooted and I wore overalls without a shirt and a straw hat if I had any at all. Fresh plowed ground was easy to walk on.

When you'd take Jig's bridle off, she'd sling her head every time. If I'd hung on to that bridle, she would have slung me across the lot.

When I was 14 (1944), my dad got me a one-row riding cultivator. That was another best thing that ever happened to me. Always before I used a walking cultivator. I would hook Mag and Jig to the cultivator. They were no comparison (to Hawk and Dink). They'd step on out there and get it. They were just good mules, no letting up for them. They just kept going.

Back then it was hard to find a good pair of mules that would pull together, generally one of them would slack off. These two just got down together and pulled.

In 1944 we moved, from three miles south of Gideon, to north of Gideon, and me and my dad built a house, a shotgun house, what they called them back then. Dad bought a Ford tractor. After he got the tractor, he started renting land, and he got an old man and woman to plow with Mag and Jig. I was driving the tractor. They lived about a quarter of a mile from us. After they were done for the day, the old man would unhook the mules and turn them loose, and they'd come to our house. They'd come straight to the barn. Me, and my dad, one of us, would take their harness off and feed them.

My dad kept Mag and Jig until 1945. Back then $600 was a lot of money. He sold them to a guy north of Gideon, and that's what he got for them, $600.

Ed E. Beasley was born Dec. 1, 1930, to P.O. and Dolly Beasley. He had seven sisters and was the middle one of three brothers. His older brother, Leon, was 11 years older. Beasley went to Frazier School through the fifth grade near Laplanta, Arkansas. The family moved to New Madrid County in 1941. While sharecropping for U.S. Holiman, P.O. Beasley farmed 220 acres,

mostly cotton, using his two teams and hired hands, who had their own mules. Ed Beasley attended Gideon Elementary School through the eighth grade, then quit school to farm with his dad. In 1947, he was drafted into the Army Air Force, where he was trained in crash rescue. After being discharged in 1952, he worked in crash rescue at Anderson Air Activation in Malden for seven years. In 1960, he started driving a bulldozer, making drag lines. When he retired in 1982, he was running drag lines for a coal strip mine in Illinois owned by W. M. Crumpecker. In April 2004, his wife, Pauline (Polly), died. The couple had been married 56 years.

He Killed Dad's Favorite Mule.
Us Kids Buried That Mule
Rock and Sam
as told by Lloyd Massey

Now going to the big mules, ole Rock and Sam, my dad kept them to haul logs. Anytime he wasn't having to farm, he'd take those mules back in the woods where people were cutting trees for lumber. They were perfect. When loading logs he didn't have to use the lines or anything. He'd just holler at them, "get up, whoa. haw."

There were a lot of times out on the roads people would get stuck. We'd take Rock and Sam out and pull them out.

I've never seen any mules larger. They weighed close to 2,000 pounds and were at least 16 hands high. Sam was reddish. Rock was dark brown. They were older than the little team (See, Jim and Bill in Mules That Worked by Voice Commands chapter). Dad had them several years. He used them on the farm some, not as much as we did the little ones. But anytime he needed them, he used them on the farm.

When (after) he'd lay by crops in July, he'd leave home and go eight or 10 miles to the Wordell area, and use the big team to haul timber. He'd stay up there two or three weeks by himself, camping out.

One time my half brother, Paul, who was 12 years older than I was, had the two of them back in the wood lots on the farm. We were dragging logs out to the edge of the woods to saw up for wood, using a handsaw. And it started raining. We hooked them back to the wagon and Paul and I got on the wagon. He got up to drive them and hit them with the lines and hollered at them. We were getting wet. We run them all the way to the house that way. And Dad told Paul to drive them down in the ditch because he needed Sam to get wet for some reason. The ditch is by our house. It's still there. I don't remember what he was going to do with them, maybe to clean them off.

Anyway, ole Sam got stuck in the mud, plumb down, just his head sticking out of the water. It just happened we were able to get Rock out and we took a trace chain and hooked it to Sam's head, and Rock pulled him out by his head. We took them back and un-harnessed them and left them in the lot. By that time we were wet.

Later on, Paul, he was cutting the mane on Sam and I was holding the bridle. And he got up between his ears, and he had me pull the bridle off of his ears where he could cut between the ears. And the mule slung his head and slung the bridle plumb off, and took off running out of the barn.

Paul come back with the shearers with his arm all the way back and throwed hard as he could at that mule and hit him right behind the ear. It stuck into his brain and he fell like he had been shot with a rifle. It killed him instantly. He killed Dad's favorite mule. Us kids buried that mule.

Paul wouldn't have nothing to do with it. Us kids, my older brother, my sister and I, buried that mule. It took us a half a day to dig a hole out in the field to bury him. They'd drug the mule (carcass) down there with another mule. About the time we started to roll him in, Paul said, "Don't put him in there with them legs, they'll stick out on top." So we cut his legs off with a chopping axe and rolled him off in that hole and covered him up. This was in the spring of 1934, when I was 13.

Dad bought another mule to go with Rock and went ahead logging. Dad got a tractor in 1938, and I think he gave the little mules away and sold the big mules.

 This is Massey's first of four stories. He also has stories in Mules
That Worked Without Lines and Runaways chapters, plus "And
Guess What. That Tractor Didn't Stop."
Lloyd Massey was born July 25, 1921, to Harvey L. and Effie
Inez Massey. He had one older brother and two younger, and
one sister. His father farmed on Ingram's Ridge in Pemiscot
County, six miles northwest of Hayti. Massey attended Ingram
Ridge School through the eighth grade and was graduated from Hayti High
School in 1939. He has a perforated ear drum, which kept him out of the serv-
ice. He farmed with his dad until his dad passed away in 1955 and continued
farming until 1991, when he turned the farming over to his son, James Massey.
By then the Masseys had accumulated 960 acres and were farming 1,700 acres.
In May 2008, Lloyd and Gertrude, his wife of 67 years, were still residing on
the farm.

I Heard Him Start to Chuckle, "Hee, Hee,"
All of a Sudden It Got Quiet
Beck and Tobe
as told by Francis Hulshof

Dad bought Beck and Tobe in 1932. They were the gentler team.
They weighed around 1,000 to 1,100 pounds. He bought a younger
team, Mike and Rube, in the late 1930s. They weighed 1,200 pounds.

For lighter work we would use Beck and Tobe. For heavier work
we used the bigger ones. We used the younger mules to a tandem
disk, and we cultivated with Beck and Tobe. They were easier to
work.

Beck and Tobe were brownish red. I was 10 years old when I
started working them to a cultivator. At first Dad harnessed them. I
harnessed them by myself when I was 12. That harness was a little
heavy to sling over. Dad would tell us what field to go to, how to set
the cultivator and not lose moisture. He'd do a round or two so we
would know how to do it. Dad or one of my brothers would work the
other team.

We had to walk behind the one-row cultivator. I would work the sweeps to get close to a row, so it could cover up the weeds. I can remember resting at the end of a row and taking a drink of water. They at times would reach over and bite each other. Mules would get wore out too.

I used Beck and Tobe to haul cotton when I was in the eighth grade. I would get up at dark, catch and harness them, and hook them to a loaded cotton wagon. I would get to Highway 61 by daylight. I could get on the highway, get to the gin on the other side of town, and get home in time to go to school. I did that for about two weeks, and by that time I was wore out.

My brother, Joe, got kicked by Tobe one time. He (Joe) was always trying to do something funny. He slipped around the barn, caught Tobe when he wasn't looking, and slapped him with a one-by-four, 3 or 4 feet long. I heard it. I was across the road and he was in the lot. I heard him start to chuckle, "hee, hee, hee." All of a sudden it got quiet. The mule had kicked him. And it knocked him down. Then I heard the squalling and crying. Tobe kicked him right across the face, and that Sunday we couldn't go visit kinfolk because he still had that imprint of the mule hoof on his face. Luckily he didn't break anything.

I worked Beck and Tobe to a sweep rake. I would line the hay up to a windrow and dump it. Then it went into a baler. We would put up 1,500 to 2,000 square bales of clover hay each year. Usually we sold some of it. We would plant clover seed in February early enough for there to be a thaw and a freeze. That way the seed would melt in the ground and come up. We sowed eight pounds to an acre by hand. We wanted it to be muddy so the seed would sprout in the ground and come up. A lot of time we would plant clover in the wheat. We'd harvest the wheat, and later on cut the wheat straw with the clover, and bale it for hay. The next year we'd have a clear cutting of clover hay that was pretty-good hay.

One day I was working Beck and Tobe to a walking cultivator and ended about a half-mile from home. I got up on the tongue and was going to ride it home. They got about 100 feet down the road, and all of a sudden those two mules took off as fast as they could go. It knocked me off. I rolled over on the ground. I just got up and looked at them. There was a trail of dust behind them. They went to the barn where they usually go and waited for me to get there.

I think Dad paid $200 or $300 for Mike and Rube. They were not fully broke when he bought them. Dad said, "We're going to break them a little more so they won't be so dangerous." We had 10 acres of fresh-broke ground. Dad said, "You hook to that A-frame harrow and take them mules up and down that plowed field. Keep going back and forth. It don't matter if you harrow it two or three times. Just wear them out." That's what you had to do to break them, wear them out.

We did that all morning and all afternoon, and about quitting time, Dad said, "We'll see if we broke them." You wouldn't dare try to get on a mule before they were broke. I patted one of them on the back. He nodded his head and didn't do anything. So I got on him and rode him home.

Dad had 100 acres on the original farm and bought another 120, and we farmed 200 acres with the two teams of mules, and a F-20 Farmall tractor.

We could always tell if we kept our mules in good shape through the winter. As soon as we went to work, if they would keep on working and didn't act like they were wore out, then we knew we had fed them good enough to keep their strength and health up. We would get all the horsepower out of them we could.

We would try to plow in March. I can remember several wet years, '47 was real wet. One year we didn't get cotton planted until June. Sometimes we'd get a bale of cotton picked in August. Most of the time it was September. Some years were extra hot and dry.

We (sometimes) rode the mules on Sunday. It depended on how vigorous we felt. We'd ride the first ones we caught. We rode bareback. We'd get the mules running in the lot, and they may dart at something, and you'd fall off.

Just mules were all we ever had. I can't remember any of the neighbors having horses. All had mules.

I was drafted into the Army in 1951, and went to Korea and came back in 1952. We still had the mules when I left. But Dad used the F-20 for most of the disking and plowing. My brother Paul wrote me that anthrax came through the area in 1951. It wasn't contagious to humans, but it killed cattle, hogs, and the mules. He wrote that about ever other day they had to haul and pile carcasses up and build a fire. It got all of the mules.

 **Francis Hulshof was born July 23, 1928, to Henry and Emma Hulshof. His dad farmed three miles northeast of Portageville in New Madrid County. He had three sisters and was the oldest of four boys. He attended Saint Eustachius School in Portageville through the eighth grade. He served with a 105 howitzer artillery unit in Korea as a forward observer. He farmed with his dad for several years after being discharged from the service. His dad bought him an 80-acre farm near the home place in the 1950s, which Francis still owns. He mainly grows cotton, corn, and soybeans. He still helps out at the farm, which is now run by his son, Randy. Francis and his wife, Sally, celebrated their 54th anniversary in 2008. "When I was working the mules to a walking cultivator, we would do 30 rows in the morning and 30 rows in the afternoon, 60 rows a day. We would cover six acres; and with quarter- mile rows, that would be a total of 15 miles. We'd get our exercise," he said.**

Dad Got Out His Pocketknife and Picked the Pellets Out of
Tom and Kate
as told by James Dement

My parents, James Francis and Wilma Dement, were married in 1921. Eleven months later I was born. About this time my step-grandfather loaned my dad some money to buy a team of mules. He bought some young mules that hadn't been broke. Ole Tom and Kate were about the same age I was. They were brown, medium-size mules. Dad got them trained up real good.

A lot of jobs on the farm required two people. When I was 5, Dad put me in the wagon to drive the mules, while he picked corn. I got those lines and tried to whip the mules to make them move. That got them upset. They started running off and wouldn't stop. Dad caught up with the wagon, and got in and ran them in circles for a while.

When I was 6, I was leading them to pasture, and while I was trying to open the gate, one of them stepped on one of my bare feet. I was screaming, hollering, kicking. The mule took its time getting off.

We had some problems, ole Tom, Kate, and me. I was about 8 before Dad would leave me alone in the field with the mules. I started working Kate and Tom to a double A harrow and to a disk. Dad would do the plowing and planting. When we came to the end of the row, instead of making a wide circle around, I would try to make a square turn.

One time I cut the corner too short. It got ahead of me and turned on its side and flopped over towards those mules. I hollered "whoa" and they stopped with the harrow leaning on their rear ends. I took the traces loose and got them to move up, out of danger.

A similar experience happened one time when I was disking. I turned it too short and the disk flopped over. I hollered "whoa" and they stopped. One of them had 3 feet on the ground and one foot on a disk blade. I again disconnected the traces and got them free of danger. This time I had to get Dad to help turn the disk over. He couldn't get too mad at me because I was helping him out. Most times a team will panic and run away under these circumstances. I guess these incidents were proof that Tom and Kate were ready to work with me.

We would be working in the field and when Mom rang the dinner bell. If Tom and Kate were headed for the barn they would speed up; if they were headed away from the barn, they would try to turn around. They knew it was time for a rest. One time the pole the dinner bell was on was leaning over, and puffs of wind would sway the pole back and forth causing the bell to give a couple of dings. The mules would hear the dings and speed up, but when the bell did not continue to ring they would slow back down. The process kept repeating. This almost drove the mules crazy when the bell would not do a steady ring as they had learned it would do.

By the time I was 10, I was big enough to help with haying. Dad would pick up loose hay and pile it on a wagon that he had put a frame on to extend its width and length. I would stay on the wagon and move the hay around to stack it. When it got up high enough we would head to the barn. Dad forked the loose hay from the wagon into the barn loft. I would move it around and stack it in the loft. That was a job I hated, especially when there were two people throwing hay up. When that hay started filling up to the top of the barn, it would get hot and dusty and there were wasp nests. I made a solemn vow I would never do that when I got big.

Tom and Kate were good about opening gates, by lifting up the latch. One time they opened the gate and got out in the cornfield. Dad and Mom tried to get them in but when they came to the gate, they would throw their tails in the air and run by it every time. My dad had a lot of patience, but they pushed him too far. He got his 12-gauge shotgun and went back to the cornfield, and when they took off running he blasted them with the shotgun. They ran through the gate, through the lot, into the barn, into their stalls.

Dad got out his pocketknife and picked the pellets out of ole Tom and Kate. You could tell where each shot was located by the bump on their hide. It taught them a lesson.

We always fed the mules five ears of corn each twice a day, and loose hay when we were working them. We fed them corn in the stable, and hay in a rack outside. My dad was not a large man in size. He was about 5 feet and 7 inches tall, and weighed around 150 pounds. For his size he was very strong, and had large muscles in his arms and legs. When the mules got to be 17, ole Tom developed kidney problems, and Dad sold them. It almost broke Dad's heart to have to get rid of them.

Dad purchased a beautiful team of blue horses from Doniphan to replace them. They were only partially tame and were wild. They would kick the side of the barn out, and get in a corner and dare you to put bits in their mouths. Dad and I were both afraid of them. Horses are not as smart as mules. A mule will not run into a fence, but a horse will run through a fence.

Tom and Kate played a very important part in the life of our family and were almost considered a part of the family.

 Jim Dement was born Aug. 14, 1922, to James Francis and Wilma Dement. From ages eight to 18, he farmed with mules (1930 –1940). He had three younger sisters and was raised on a 40-acre farm about one mile south of Broseley in Butler County. Dement graduated from Broseley High School in 1941. He was in the U.S. Army (1942-1946) during World War II. He served with the 1st Combat Cargo Group in southern China as an army aerial engineer. He made several flights over the Hump (Himalayas), from Burma to China. "We dropped food for mules in Burma and flew them, five at a time, into China in C-47 cargo planes," Dement said. "They were backpack mules. The guys would kid me and say, 'Hey, Dement, those ole mules make you homesick.' One time a mule went wild in the C-47 and started kicking while we were flying and they had to shoot him. We would fly at 17,000-feet altitude, so the mules would get sleepy. They didn't have enough oxygen." After returning from the war Dement received his undergraduate degree from Southeast Missouri State University in Cape Girardeau and a master's degree in biology and education administration from George Peabody College in Nashville, Tennessee, and also a six-year special degree in education administration from Vanderbilt College in Nashville in 1953. He started teaching in 1953 and was superintendent at Holcomb Schools for 18 years before retiring in 1981. In 1974, he and his wife (Betty) divorced after 28 years of marriage.

Kate Shoved Mike Off the Bridge
Mike and Kate
as told by Joe Hillis

I was raised on a 160-acre farm one mile north, and one and a half mile east of Broseley. When we moved to the farm in 1930, Dad had a pair of young mules called Mike and Kate. They were with us all the time I was growing up. I got to know them pretty well. They were part of the family. Mules are just like people. They have their own personalities, and they're all different.

There were 30 acres of the 160 acres that was cleared. We cleared the rest of it with those mules using crosscut saws, chopping axes, and dynamite. We kept 12 acres in woods. We'd cut logs and the mules would skid the logs and haul them to the mill. We built a barn with the wood, and rough lumber was used in building our house.

Dad had mares and we would raise mules and break and sell them. We had Mike and Kate, and we also used the mares as a team. Horses are prettier, but mules are easier to handle. I'd rather farm with mules. We raised cotton and pasture on the sand hills, and on the low ground corn, milo, soybeans, and wheat. We also grew cantaloupe and watermelon.

Mike was laid back. You had to prod him along to keep up with her. If you smacked him, she'd jump. You had to stay on him all the time or she'd be pulling most of the load.

I started working with those mules when I was 11. I broke ground with them when I could barely reach the plow handles. I would head them down a row and they knew what to do. When we got to the end of the row, I would flip the plow over and them mules would circle around. I didn't have to lift the plow.

Dad would tell us this story. He was crossing a creek (1928, 1929) with Mike and Kate near Hilliard over a bridge without rails. They got to pushing against each other, and she shoved Mike off the bridge. And from that day on you could never get them to cross a bridge with her on the right and him on the left. When working them the custom was to work the mare mule on the right and male mule on the left.

It was always funny. Everybody in the country knew Dad's mules wouldn't cross a bridge unless he switched them. When we would take the mules and a wagon to go fishing in the St. Francis River where we had to cross a bridge, we would hook him to the right and put her on the left. When we came to a bridge, they were a little spooky but they would cross it. We would catch carp with dough balls and mom would pressure cook and can them and make fish patties. They tasted like salmon patties.

I farmed with Mike and Kate for four years, plowed, cultivated, planted, raked, mowed. If you got those mules headed down a row, you didn't have to worry about them. When it was lunchtime I would unhook them, hop on one of them and go to the house. You could ride either one of them. I would put them in a stall with their harness on and take their bridles off and let them rest, or they could eat hay.

I would keep the lines around my shoulder and waist, and hands on the handlebars. I worked a disk plow, which required three mules, and a riding cultivator that you guided with foot pedals. If they were pulling a hard pull like a harrow or planter, Mike and Kate would start breathing hard and I'd stop and let them rest.

Every morning I would clean, brush and curry them, comb their tails and try to get cockleburs out. Every night when you'd come in the first thing you'd do was un-harness them. The first thing they would do is get in the sand and roll. Then you would feed them generally hay and shelled corn. In the summer they grazed in a pasture. We would always give them corn twice a day when working them, in the morning and at night.

We also used them for picking cotton and gathering corn. We put a muzzle on them when gathering corn. After picking cotton all day, I would take a wagonload of cotton to the mill at Broseley. I might have to sit there until 10 or 11 p.m. When unloaded I would hook the lines to a wagon post, and sit down in a corner. I wouldn't have to guide them going home. When they got to the gate (at home), they would stop.

We hayed with Mike and Kate. Dad had 10 acres of alfalfa behind the barn. We cut it three times a year. We used Mike and Kate to cut hay, rake it, and we shocked it in piles, and we hooked the mules to a wagon to load it using a pitchfork. When we got to the front of the barn, we would unhook the mules and take them around back, where we hooked them to a rope that was tied to a hayfork on the other end. The mules would pull the hay up to the loft, and one of us boys would be in the loft to trip the rope (attached to the hayfork). We would swing it out before tripping to get hay in the corners.

If you wanted to ride Mike or Kate, all you had to do was go out and put a bridle on and ride them. When you approach mules you have to say something. One time my brother (Jim) forgot.

Jim Hillis describes what happened one day in 1943 when he was 13:

I went out to feed some hogs in the barn lot. I had a sack of corn over my shoulder and dumped the sack of corn on the ground behind Mike. He was standing in the lot. It scared him and he kicked at me.

His hoof missed me but the top part of his ankle hit me on the side of my head. It knocked me to my knees. I got up and got out of there. I didn't hit him. It was my fault for not letting him know I was behind him.

Joe Hillis continues: Dad kept Mike and Kate until they were up in their 20s. He sold them to a friend, Fred Brown, in the mid-1940s.

Mules were very important. That was your power. Today they farm with tractors. Our power was mules and horses. But we didn't have tractors; we had the mules.

Joe Hillis was born April 18, 1927, to Jess and Minnie Hillis. From ages 11 to 17, Hillis farmed with mules (1938-1944) in Butler County, one mile north and a half mile east of Broseley. He had a younger brother, Jim, and twin sisters. Jim was interviewed by telephone for part of this story. Joe was initially drafted by the army in 1945, but was turned down due to being color blind. He was drafted into the army in 1950 and served in the Korean Conflict for nine months and in Japan nine months before being discharged in 1952. He received a B.S. degree from Southeast Missouri State University in 1955 and his master's degree from Arkansas State University in 1961. He spent 14 years teaching in various school districts and then 17 years as superintendent at Neelyville and then Twin Rivers schools before retiring in 1981. In 2007 he and his wife, Billie, celebrated their 54th anniversary at their Poplar Bluff home. "Dad purchased his first tractor in 1944. I graduated from Broseley High School in 1945, so I didn't get to work with tractors very much," he said. Joe Hillis was interviewed in July 2008. He died on April 12, 2009 at age 81.

Mike (foreground) and Kate.

They Could Pull the Devil Off of a Cross
Spider and Ella
as told by Buck Farmer

When I was 5 years old we lived on the biggest sand hill in Mississippi County, about three miles northwest of Charleston. One day the sand was blowing to beat the devil, and my mother sent me to take some water down to people who were plowing watermelons. My dad was there and we had an old plow (cultivator) you worked with your feet. It was hot and Dad had an extra team so he could let one of them blow, rest under a tree.

They were a yellow team named Spider and Ella. So I got up on the cultivator and was pretending I was plowing watermelons. And I seen him motion to me. He had been plowing the row, and the cultivator he had resting had been plowing out the middle, and I said, "Dad, let me go plow?" I got on it and did that, and from then on Dad always had me working the cultivator.

Dad had Spider and Ella from as early as I can remember. They were broke processing cypress timber by a black man, who wore a patch over his eye, Sam Phillips. He could take a whip and knock a fly off of a mule's hip. He wore this whip around his shoulder all the time, and used it only when he needed to. In logging cypress stumps, you've got to have a mule that will slow down when you would say, "steady, steady."

I started going with the threshing machine crew when I was 13, and I took Spider and Ella because they were gentle and had been around me some. I inherited the job of pulling the cook shack. They'd hang all the utilities on that shack and when you went over a railroad track, you don't want to go at a high speed. All I'd have to say was "steady" and they'd just creep over it.

Spider and Ella were buckskins with stripes down their back. I think that's how he got his name. They were brother and sister and were big mules, probably stood 16 hands. They probably weighed 1,250 to 1,300 pounds. They could pull the devil off of a cross. They would pull. Spider was bigger and stronger than Ella.

In those days the roads were in bad shape and Model Ts would get stuck, and people would walk to our house. We'd take ole Spider by himself, and hook him to whatever, and he'd just groan and pull, and pull it loose. We'd hook him to whatever we could get to, usually around the spring. The bumper would be too weak.

There was a borrow pit about a quarter of a mile from where we lived, where they'd borrow dirt to fill up the road. This man knocked on our door one night and said, "Charlie, I'm stuck up down here." We took ole Spider and went down there and the man said, "Please don't tell anybody." Cause he was with his secretary. We took ole Spider and pulled him out. He had parked where nobody could see him. My dad owed him a little at that time and later he threatened to sue Dad. He was something else.

It used to be when you had a Model T, you'd get up in the morning and they'd be cold. You'd drain them at night and in the morning, put hot water in them. But it was hard to get them started. So Dad would say, "Go get ole Spider." And we'd take ole Spider and he would pull it until we got it started. My dad would be in the T and I'd lead the mule. He'd push in the clutch and throw it into gear. We used the Model T to go to school.

We used Spider as a wheel mule to a (wheat) binder because he was big and stout and wasn't going to spook at anything. When pulling a binder there were three mules to the wheel and two in the lead. As the off mule, Spider was strong and would carry the load. I never saw him pant in his entire life.

In 1939, Dad traded Spider and Ella for a down payment on a Ford tractor.

This is the third of four mule stories told by Buck Farmer. See also "Dave" in Mules chapter and "Rock and Rodie" and "Old Timer and Alfred" in this chapter.

You'd Better Be Ready, Because
They Were Going to Go
Gray Jack and Black Jack
as told by Earl Willcut

Gray Jack and Black Jack were two horse mules. One was gray, the other black. They each weighed 1,300 to 1,400 pounds. Dad bought them along with harness for $72 at Kennett in 1947. He used them for skidding logs and farming. Gray Jack would try to bite you or kick you.

Gray Jack was the weakest. When you hooked the tongs (to a log), Gray Jack would stand firm. When you picked up the lines, you'd better be ready because they were going to go. Gray Jack would set up to the doubletree, and Black Jack would bring the load up.

When you called on Black Jack he'd thump those feet, trollin with them. I've heard that mule groan. He'd be pulling so hard I could see wrinkles in his hip. He knew he'd better pull it or he'd get a whippin.

One time we were loading logs and they wouldn't pull the logs up (on the truck) and I kicked Black Jack, and he kicked back with his two feet.

If you hooked them to a stump, they would pull this way and that way, go clear around it to pull it out. If we came to a branch (creek) when they were skidding a log, we'd stick a pole under the log and I would yell, "gee" and they would go right on through.

I started working Black Jack and Gray Jack when I was 12, when I wasn't big enough to break ground, but I could plow cotton with a riding cultivator. I would get on a nail keg to put their collars on. I would have to get up there to buckle the collars and shovel their hames over. I started breaking ground when I was 13. I would step off 20 feet from the woods and start plowing. I was small enough that if the plow came out of the ground I couldn't set it back in. I would have the mules make a circle to set it back in.

When I was 16, I started working them to a sulky plow. It was a 14-inch plow you'd walk behind. It had a dead wheel that flopped around behind it. After plowing we used a middle buster to bed the ground and then we would harrow off ridges, and planted on top of the ridges with the mules pulling a drill. It would drill two rows at a time.

When corn was in the roasting-ear stage, Black Jack would reach over the fence and ride it over and get out. Gray Jack would bray and Dad would tell me to go to the field (to get him out). He just did that when it was roasting ear time.

We fed each mule 10 ears of corn when working them. They had hay if they wanted. We didn't feed them little bitty nubbins; they were used for cows' feed. At noontime we would unhook them, drive them to the barn, pull their bridles off and hang them on the hames.

We also had a horse team, Spot and Prince. I liked the mules. Horses are cold-shouldered, they have to be warmed up, mules ain't. The horses walked like they were on rollers. Mules are more sure-footed.

You couldn't trust the mules too far, had to watch them. When you hooked them up, you hooked the gentlest mule first. You'd say, "Get over there." You snapped the breast collar first, then the double-trees. You'd say, "Back up, back up here" and they would back up. You'd say "gee" and they would go right "haw" and they would go left. They'd learn it. We were never allowed to ride the mules. We had saddle horses. That's all we had to farm with, those mules.

I worked those mules until I left home at 17. I started picking cotton in 1940 when I was 6, and picked until 1957 when I was 23. I was married in 1955. I would pick 300 pounds a day and my wife would pick 200 pounds. We were paid $15 a day.

 **Earl Willcut was born April 7, 1934, to Elmer and Myrtle Will-cut. He had seven brothers and four sisters and was the sixth boy born. His mother died when he was six. His father farmed in western Butler County along Beaver Dam Creek, about nine miles west of Poplar Bluff and four miles from the Lone Hill community, which had a store, church, and school. Eighty acres**

were tillable, and they raised 10 acres of cotton. They also raised cattle and hogs. Willcut attended Hemp Hill School, a two-room rural school, through the sixth grade. His wife, Aline, died in 1963. Willcut farmed until 2000, and in 2009 was residing on his farm near Poplar Bluff.

Never Tear Down the Bridge That Brought You Across
Queen and Kate
as told by Arnold Jones

I started working with mules when I was 7. My dad would do the harness. We had two mules, Queen and Kate. Queen was a big black mule with a white mouth. Kate was a smaller mule and was all black. She weighed around 1,100 pounds. You could ride Kate but not Queen. It was two miles from the house to the field. We'd ride Kate and lead Queen.

They worked fine together. We used them for plowing with a double shovel, harrowing. Dad always did the cultivating. You'd break a root and it would fly back and hit you in the shin. When plowing with them and it got close to noon, they would head for the house. They weren't stupid.

I would take turns working the mules with my brothers. One would work them one day, and the other the next. If you weren't plowing with the mules, you were choppin cotton. We farmed 22 acres of our own, and rented additional farm ground.

Kate would jump out of the lot and go down the road. She'd break into another pasture, and get in with some neighbor's horses. We would put a chain around one of her front legs, and tie a wooden block to it. She would still get out with the block on. When she walked down the road, she would walk with the wooden block off the road. I think she did that to keep us from tracking her. One time by the time we caught up with her, the chain was on her, but the block was gone.

My dad told me you couldn't ride Queen. He told me the story of my older brother, who one time wore her down working her all day, then tried to ride her.

Arnold's brother, Lee Jones, 12 years older than Arnold, describes what happened:

I tried several times to ride Queen. After we were done with a day's work of 10 hours or more, I would take her gear off, and lead her up to a stump. She was as gentle as she could be until you got on her back. That was it. She'd throw me off!

Arnold Jones continues:

We put corn in a barn. If Queen would get hungry, she'd go to the back of the barn where the corncrib was and paw at it until she got a plank off. Kate would join in, in eating the corn.

Ole Queen didn't like crossing bridges. If there was any hole in the bridge where she could see the water, she'd go to backing up on you. You'd have to whip her to show her who's boss, and she'd go across.

We used those mules in the fall to grind sorghum. And we used them in the winter for hauling wood. Once a month Dad would hook them to a metal-wheel wagon, and one of us would go with him to Gurley's store to get groceries at the junction of 158, which was about four miles away.

I worked those mules until I was 16. One time the mules got out, and ended up in a neighbor's barn. I walked in the stall to put a bridle on Kate, and she laid her ears back and bit me on the wrist bad enough to draw blood. I just put coal oil on it and went on.

We cut oats for hay. We'd put a post in the ground, and pile the hay around it in a teepee shape. It would be 12 foot high and would last the mules through most of the winter. We also fed them corn. We'd pump water in a number 3 metal tub that held 15 gallons. A mule can drink five to 10 gallons of water. If we didn't leave enough water; in the middle of the night, they'd start kicking that tank, and Dad would say, "Go out and pump water, Son."

Dad bought a used 8N Ford Tractor to farm with in 1962, and kept those mules another two years even though we didn't use them. I asked him one time why he kept those mules and he said, "Son, never tear down the bridge that brought you across."

Arnold W. Jones was born Dec. 26, 1948, to Frank J. and Evelina Jones. He had four brothers and three sisters; two of the brothers were older. He grew up in the Bacon Pasture area about five miles south of Poplar Bluff in Butler County. He attended Willow Oak, a two-room rural school, for eight years and Wheatley High School in Poplar Bluff one year, graduating from Poplar Bluff High School in 1967. He was drafted into the U.S. Army and served in Vietnam in 1970-1971. He worked at Dunlap Implement for 12 years before joining the City Water Department in Poplar Bluff, where he has worked for 20 years and in 2007 worked there as a water line foreman.

Jones standing next to team disk.

In 2007 he and his wife, Joanne, celebrated their 20th wedding anniversary. Jones was interviewed January 14, 2008. He died October 16, 2010.

I Decided I Would Ride That Sucker
John and Slim
as told by J.C. Shipman

I started out when I had to have a box to stand on, to get the harness on the mules. I worked a big ole pair of mules. They were close to 16 hands tall. They were black, John and Slim. I wasn't big enough to turn the plow. I'd have to let them turn it.

They could work, and plow (cultivate) you 10 acres a day. I farmed with mules from age 7 to when I married at age 22 (1942) and had to go into the service. I never farmed after that. When I got home from the Army, things were tough and I couldn't get a tractor.

My dad farmed in Dunklin County, one and a half miles east of White Oak. He rented 120 acres (sandy soil) from the same man (M.A. Hogue of Holcomb) for 20 years. They never had a written contract. If Dad wanted something he would go to him, and Hogue would say, "Mr. Shipman you know more about farming than I do. If it makes you money, it will make me money."

We raised mostly cotton, corn, hay, and soybeans. Dad had three teams of mules. He would work one pair, me another, and my younger brother (a nephew) one. We usually worked together. We would go out at daylight and come in at dark. Rows were a quarter of a mile long. There were no breaks except for lunch. We would come in at noon and feed and water the mules. It took a lot of work for one team to work 40 acres.

I wore overalls with patches on them. I can still hear my mother say, "It's no disgrace to wear patched clothes. But it's a disgrace to go dirty." I went barefoot. I've chopped cotton where the sun got the ground so hot I would have to dig a hole and get in it. I'm not ashamed of my farm life.

Slim was a little on the crazy side. John was gentle. One day we were working and it came up a rain and we all went to the house. We turned the mules loose in the barn. I decided to trim their manes. I caught the gentle one first and trimmed him. Ole Slim wouldn't let me catch him. They were in the hallway and he would run from one end of the barn to the other. He would run to the end, and turn around and look at me. Then go the other direction when I approached. I got so mad at him I threw the hand shearers at him, and they stuck in his hind end. Slim's hind end got sore and his back end like to have rotted off, but he healed up. Dad never found out what happened until I was a grown man, and he said, "Son, I ought to whip you yet."

One hot summer day my brother and I were working about a mile from home, and I decided I would ride that sucker (John). He never had been ridden. My brother was working Slim. We had been busting out corn middles. I told Glen, "I'm going to ride that sucker home." He said, "You'd better not."

I jumped on him and we had gone about a half-mile, when all of a sudden he jumped and lunged forward. I wasn't expecting it, and while falling off got my leg hung up in a trace chain, and it scared him and he started circling around looking at me. He was swinging me in midair. When Glen and Slim had caught up with us, I was swinging between those two mules. My foot finally came out and I fell to the ground. One of them kicked up and took the top off of my straw hat. The mules ran to the barn scared and we started running after them. If John had started running with me on that chain, he would have killed me.

One year my dad bought a pair of young mules that had never been worked. Me. and my brother decided we would break those mules to work. One time Dad was out working in the field, and we harnessed them up and hooked them to a wagon. We had chained the wagon wheels together where they couldn't turn. They ran for a while and settled down. We never told Dad. Later that spring, he went to hook them up and said, "I believe these mules have been worked." We never told him what we had done.

A mule is more surefooted than a horse. I've worked both of them. We had a couple of horses. A mule is not as crazy as some horses are. Slim was a good-working mule. John was too. We fed them corn and lespedeza hay. Dad kept good stock. We took care of them. My dad would pour a can of Prince Albert tobacco in their feed to worm them.

We worked John and Slim four or five years, then in 1935, we traded them for our first tractor, an old Farmall F-12 on iron. We had to crank it. We cut the tongues out of our mule-drawn equipment and used it with the tractor. We kept one pair of mules for a while to do the planting. Then we finally got rid of all the mules.

 **J.C. Shipman was born July 12, 1920, to James H. and Mary Glenn Shipman. He had four sisters and seven brothers. He was next to the youngest boy. His youngest brother never farmed. His brother John was five years older but never farmed. The brother he refers to in the story was a nephew the family raised, Glenn Pearson (now deceased). He was one year younger than Shipman. Shipman attended Sumach, a one-room school. He and his siblings walked two miles to the school. Shipman was graduated from Holcomb High School in 1938 and was drafted into the Army. He was never shipped overseas due to varicose veins in his legs. Shipman worked 35 years in sales, 15 years at Baker Implement. and 20 years at McClain Chevrolet, both in Kennett, before a heart attack forced him to retire in 1978. In March 2008 he and his wife, Peggy, celebrated 66 years of marriage. The plow Shipman was referring to when he said they plowed 10 acres a day was a one-row, foot-operated cultivator that had a seat on it. "I picked cotton until tractors came out. I started out using a 7-foot pick sack. I had an older sister who could beat me every day we went to the field. I could pick 400-pounds a day, but I had to hustle," he said.**

Ain't That Our Mules. How'd They Get Down There
Curt and Riley
as told by Joe Blackman

Curt and Riley. They were big, tall mules. They were brown, one had a white mouth, Curt. Curt was a horse mule. Riley was a mare mule. We had two mules, two workhorses and one riding horse.

They was friendly to who they knew. And a stranger, they could figure that out in a hurry. They would backup, shake their heads. They wouldn't let a stranger touch them. I grew up with them, feeding them everyday. We were petting them all the time, with the hands, brush or curry comb.

They worked great together. I almost didn't need a line. Just kinda talk to them. You know, "get over, gee, haw." They'd just keep going. You could kinda slow them down, just tighten their lines a little bit and they would slow their steps a little bit. If you wanted to go ahead a little bit, just let the lines go and kinda chat. They were very strong.

I liked harrowing. It was 10 foot wide and would cover four rows. Everything else was one row. We'd stand on the harrow. It had a platform on it and you couldn't hardly fall off.

They almost knew when it was 12 o'clock. They would shake their heads, not want to go at all. No bell. They knew. You could tell lunchtime by the way they act different. If you wanted to make another round, you could tell it was lunchtime. They would kinda shake their heads, want to stop, want to go that way. (At the barn) we'd take their bridle and harness off them, let them drink water and eat hay and corn.

I was two years older than my brother, Marcel. We were together all the time. I worked the mules and he worked the horses. We'd work the field together. I was pretty slender and tall. I could harness them myself.

We'd get up at sunup. Mom would have breakfast done. We'd eat breakfast and cut out. My dad did the feeding in the morning. We had to pump water, morning, noon and evening.

The wagon had a spring seat. My brother and I use to sit in the back of the wagon with our feet hanging down. When we'd get to the east side of town (Poplar Bluff). We'd unhook the mules, and tie them to the back of the wagon. One day they got loose.

My brother and I were going across the river bridge, and we happened to spot them and they happened to spot us. They knew who we were and we were probably three or four blocks away. I don't know if it was what we had on or what. My brother said, "Ain't that our mules? How'd they get down there?" I said, "They must be loose. We'd better catch them or they'll be heading for home." We went around them and came up between them and home to cut them off. They came right up and met us with their ropes dragging.

I got bit once. Curt had a sore on his right shoulder. A veterinarian had put carbolic acid on it. It would boil stuff out. I was petting him and put my hand up there, and he bit me on the shoulder. It kinda hurt, but I knew he wouldn't hurt me.

We used the mules to haul wood to burn during the winter. We'd take the bed off the wagon and pile logs on 8 foot tall. We'd put poles up to hold it.

I think he traded the horses in on a tractor. But we kept the mules. I guess the guy he traded for the tractor liked horses. He would use the tractor for breaking (plowing) and use the mules for planting. And we used the tractor for plowing because it was a two-row and the mules' was a one-row plow (cultivator).

I started driving the tractor and Marcel worked the mules.

Picking cotton wasn't bad. Chopping cotton was. I don't know how I got the job of plowing. My brothers and sisters did the chopping. There was very little cotton I chopped, but I had to help pick it all because time was done for the mules.

We kept the mules in a lot when working them. Holler at them and they would come up. After crops were laid by we had them in a big pasture, they would be half a mile away and you could holler and they would come running. The barn was a block south of the house. The pasture went way back. In the evening, you could go to the back of the lot and holler and you'd see them look up. They would run over you if you got between them and that barn.

I liked working them. I didn't mind that at all. I don't know how I got selected to work the mules.

 Joseph Blackman was born Aug. 7, 1935, to Lloyd Jim and Irene Lucille Blackman in Catron, Missouri. The family moved to the Morocco area in Butler County in 1937, about six miles southeast of Poplar Bluff. He had three brothers and two sisters. His father farmed 40 acres that was owned by his grandfather. They raised mostly cotton, some corn. His dad bought a used John Deere tractor in the mid-1950s. Blackman attended a country school and finished the 11th grade at Wheatley High School in Poplar Bluff and later got his G.E.D. in Southbend, Indiana while working for Rockwell Standard as a press operator. In the early 1960s, he moved to St. Louis where he worked as a lead man in shipping and receiving for Combustion Engineers. He moved back to Poplar Bluff in 1980 to help care for his ailing mother. He was married for eight years and divorced before moving back. Blackman drove a school bus for Poplar Bluff schools for 21 years. In the late 1990s he and another bus driver, Charles Anderson, started Blackman-Anderson Lawn Mowing; which in 2009 continued to do well.

"My brother and I used to go catch them (mules) and ride them down the road. We'd ride bareback. Just me and my younger brother. They'd ride about the same. We'd trot them and run them wide open, going and coming. They didn't mind it. A workhorse is a rough ride. A riding horse is an easy ride. These workhorses we had. They were big. They were rough riding, rougher than the mules. We always had four or five milk cows. I'd milk one, and my brother would milk one. We never milked more than two at a time," he said.

I'd Make Them Go Fast.
I Would Whip'em With The Lines
Blue and Kate
as told by Betty Huffine

I was brought up on the farm. I had an older brother but he didn't farm. My father was always sick. He died when I was 16. I started farming when I was 7. The first thing I done was stalk cutting. They didn't want to go fast, but I'd make them go fast. I would whip'em with the lines.

Dad bought Kate for $15 at the sale barn in Kennett in 1932. A few months later he paid $20 for Blue. Blue was red. Kate was dark brown. They were medium in size. We rented 60 acres, about 15 of the acres was in woods. We raised cotton and corn, and had hogs and five milk cows. I would milk three or four cows two times a day. That's all I knew was work. I was lazy at housekeeping. I still don't like it.

When I got to be 11 or 12, I would harness the mules by myself. I had to stand on a wooden box to harness them. You had to put the harness on, then the collars, then the lines. I cut stalks, disked, used the harrow and planter with those mules. We had little seats on every-thing except for plowing. I had to walk behind the breaking plow. I'd go barefoot. I still like to go barefoot today. I held the lines if I was riding, and put the lines around my back when I was plowing. You didn't sit around on the farm. In the fall we were sawing wood.

After we had had Kate for a couple of years, she got pinkeye and became blind. We didn't know what a veterinarian was. She was the nicest ole mule, just kick her feet and she would move over.

I wore what we called unionalls when farming. You would button them up the middle, kind of like a jumpsuit. They had three buttons in the back for girls, and you could pull them down. I never wore a bonnet. I don't like a bonnet. I would go to the barbershop and have my hair cut short like a boy's. It would only be a half-inch in length.

I would get up early in the morning around 4 a.m. and I would feed my mules before I went to work or to school. I had to lead Kate to the barn. I would lead her by the bottom of the lip because of the blindness. I would go to the house and eat a good breakfast. We had gravy, eggs, bacon and sausage, biscuits. It was all home made. We didn't know what junk food was.

I started out working the mules at daybreak. My dad would say, "You have to have this done and that done." I would work until dark. I would give them a couple of breaks in the morning and afternoon. One lady in the community had a dinner bell. We all listened for that dinner bell. I would take the mules in, water them and feed them corn nubbins.

When I was 15 my younger sister, Carmen, was 3. One day I was cutting stalks and Carmen wanted to ride on the stalk cutter. I helped her up and she sat on my lap. She would try to spit tobacco juice off the cutter and on my foot.

Carmen Jaques recalls: I remember doing that. I did it (spit on her) for pure meanness. Dad would always give it (tobacco) to me. He was sick. I don't remember him being well. I was mean. I would chase guineas until they'd quit running and I could catch them.

Huffine continues: We lived on dirt roads, in the swamp, about a quarter of a mile from the St. Francis River. Driving those mules in the mud the wagon would get stuck. You just had to whip 'em and whip'em to get on down the road.

I think it was in 1937 that we had the big flood. We lived next to the levee. Dad said, "If you hear guns a shooting. You all run to the levee." We sat up all night waiting to hear those gunshots. But the levee broke on the Arkansas side. Later that day we got the mules hooked to the wagon and went to see the flood waters. As far as we could see, there was nothing but water. I had never seen anything like it.

I never thought anything about riding the mules, just working them. I did ride Blue once to school, when it had snowed real bad. School was a mile from where we lived.

It was funny how those ole mules would get scared at a bridge. One evening when I was 8 or 9 years old we had gone to Campbell to attend a tent revival. We were going home in the dark and we were going over the Cypress Creek bridge, and the mules bolted. I was driving and I was pulling and screaming as hard as I could. There were seven of us in the wagon. We all had to pull those lines to stop them.

Close to winter I would go with my uncle along the river looking for honeybee hives. We would listen and look. I covered my head with a mesh-like curtain, wore long sleeves and tied gloves on where they couldn't get up my clothes. I would hold the gallon buckets while he climbed the tree. We would come home with two gallons of honey. It would do us through the winter. I don't remember getting stung.

We kept those mules after we quit working them. I was there when they died. We found them both dead in the woods. Blue lived longer than Kate. We put them on a brush pile and burned their bodies.

When I was 15, Dad bought a used Farmall tractor and I farmed with it for a year. He died when I was 16, and Mom had a farm sale and we moved to town.

I loved working those mules. I enjoyed it all. I think about them all the time. They were my pets. You don't forget stuff like that.

 **Betty Green Huffine was born Sept. 28, 1925, to Floyd and Opal York. Her father farmed in Dunklin County, about two miles east of St. Francis, Arkansas or two miles southwest of Campbell, Missouri. She had an older brother and a sister 12 years younger. She attended Groff School, a one-room school, for six years and was graduated from Campbell High School in 1945.**

Betty has owned and operated Exquisite Beauty Salon in Campbell for 53 years. In 2008, she and her husband, Eugene, had been married 29 years. Carmen Jacques said she quit chewing tobacco after her father died. Huffine said she never used tobacco growing up but added, "The only time I ever smoked was when picking cotton I would smoke corn silks. I would crush them up, roll them in paper."

They Were Big Mules. About as Big as I've Ever Seen
Charlie and Joe
as told by Clemens Deken

I had my first incident with mules when I was 5 or 6. My uncle had a team of mules that would run. Uncle Joe and my dad married sisters. We farmed adjacent to the St. Francis River, and he farmed down the levee from us. One day I was walking down the levee and saw him cultivating some corn, and I took off running towards him.

Those mules heard me coming down a row of knee-high corn and they took off running. He had the lines tied around his back, and when they took off they jerked him down. They drug him 300 or 400 feet. I was old enough to realize what had happened.

It didn't hurt him, just got the seat of his britches dirty from dragging him around. He got up and went on working. They had run away a few times before. They were just skittish.

I was 16 when Dad said it was time for me to get to the field, instead of staying in the house and washing dishes for Mom.

They were older mules, Nig and Jenny. They are what I started out with. Nig was a black horse mule. Jenny was a reddish mare mule. They were medium in size, 1,100 to 1,200 pounds.

We kept them in the barn lot. When I would go out in the morning to the barn and go into the harness room and come out with a bridle, them two mules would come up to you. You didn't have to go after them. They were as gentle as they could be.

I used them to plow with and cultivate corn. That doubletree was always straight. They worked good together. Dad would usually be in another field working the horse team. We were usually in the field by 7 a.m.

They knew when it was time to go to dinner. It was kind of hard to get them to go that last round, if you had a round or two to go. Around 11:30 the dinner bell would ring and when they came to an end of a row, they didn't want to turn around.

When I was 18, Dad got a big team of mules, Charlie and Joe. They weighed 1,700 to 1,800 pounds. They were about as big as I've even seen. Joe was white, more slender and taller than Charlie, who was black to a dark brown, and was more blocky and chunky built. You'd have to sling the harness on them. In the mornings, you had to go after them. They'd usually go to the far end of the lot.

The black mule, you couldn't touch his ears. He'd knock you down. He came close to knocking me down. Dad taught me how to put his bit in his mouth first, then quickly slip the bridle over his ears. In the spring, when the flies and gnats were bad, we would have to put a twitch on his nose in order to grease the inside of his ears. Gnats will drive a mule crazy.

Joe went blind about two years after we had him, from pinkeye. We kept him separated from the others for a while, so they wouldn't get it. He lost sight in both eyes. He worked the same as he always did. You guided him with the lines. A slight touch of the reins and he'd go. If you were plowing, he'd stay in the furrow row. We had no problems with him.

I always had to walk behind Charlie when I was working them. Otherwise he wouldn't keep up, just drag along. Sometimes I carried a stick and poked him. He'd stay up for a while, then lag behind.

They pulled a 14-inch plow. They could pull the 14-inch plow as easy as the older team could pull a 12-inch plow. We logged with the big mules. They pulled some big ole logs out of the woods.

We farmed adjacent to the St. Francis River. One time in 1939 or 1940, one of the Lancaster men had his semi-truck loaded up with logs on the other side of the river. He got stuck going up a 10-foot incline. He knew my dad had mules, and came across the river (bridge) and got my dad to help him out, so he wouldn't have to unload.

Dad took the big mules to where his truck was and hooked them to the front of the truck. Lancaster ran to get in the truck. He was figuring he'd have to start the truck and help those mules. The mules must have figured out what Dad wanted. Before Lancaster could get the truck in gear, those mules had that load on top of the hill. He had about 1,500 board feet and a board foot weighs 6 pounds.

Dad got a big kick out of doing that. He just laughed when Lancaster hurried to get his truck in gear.

 **Clemens L. Deken was born July 25, 1921, to Charles Louis and Thersie Deken. He was the oldest of four brothers and four sisters. His dad owned 40 acres four miles south of Qulin and rented another 15 acres and 40 acres to farm. His grandfather, Louis Deken, ran a ferry across the St. Francis River until Highway 53 was built in 1923. Clemens attended Glennonville Grade School, a parochial school, through the eighth grade. He attended Qulin High School his freshman and sophomore years and Campbell High School his junior and senior years, graduating in 1939. He was drafted**

into the US Army in 1942 and received campaign stars for five European campaigns. He served in an ordinance unit, repairing trucks and tanks. After he was discharged in 1945, he attended the University of Missouri studying ag engineering. He returned home after a year and farmed with his dad some, then did carpentry work with his uncle, Clemens Lampe, for two years, before branching out on his own. He spent 50 years doing carpentry work, mainly in home construction. He and his first wife, Christina, were married for 44 years until her death in 1994. He and his second wife, Ione, celebrated nine years of marriage in 2008. Lancaster owned a trucking business. Deken couldn't remember his first name. "I don't think I've ever seen a bigger or better team of mules," Deken said referring to Charlie and Joe.

Clemens' first wife, Christina Bader (back) and probably her sister Ester (in front). Photo was taken in early 1930s at the Bader family farm in northern Dunklin County. Note cotton and corn in background. "She (Christina) was next to the youngest of 10 kids. Their family had about three teams of mules. They farmed across the river from us. We couldn't see them due to the brush, but we could hear them hollering at the mule teams," Clemens Deken said.

Jack and Jim Were the Best Team He Ever Had
Jack and Jim
as told by Lloyd Payne and Wilma Payne Berger

Jack was born in 1949. Dad raised him from a colt. His mother was a red draft mare named Totsie. I think Dad bought Jim from a brother. Jack was black and Jim was brown. They weighed 1,200 to 1,300 pounds. Jack was 100 pounds heavier than Jim. They were about the same age. Dad broke them to work and kept them until 1968.

You had to stay out from behind Jack. He would kick. I remember my older brother, Jim, one time had taken the mare's collar off, and walked around behind the mare and past Jack who was nursing. Jack kicked out with both hind feet, striking the collar. He liked to have knocked it out of Jim's hands. I guess he didn't want anybody bothering him while he was nursing. I would pet him, scratch his ears, when he was young, but I would always stay away from those hind feet.

Dad broke them by hooking them up with a draft horse for a while. Then he teamed them up together. When he had just started working them, the landowner, Nancy Harper, offered to let him have two years of crops for any woods that he cleared. He and my brother, Bill, cleared out 20 acres using a crosscut saw and axes. They cut down dead trees and burnt the stumps, which left big holes that would become boggy. I would help them out on Saturdays, when I wasn't in school.

The landowner's son, Chester Harper, offered to let Dad use his team of horses, because he didn't think the young mules would work in those stump holes. But Dad told him. "These mules will be all right." Harper told me, "I want to see it when he gets those mules in that stumpy ground."

The first day he took them out, water covered up some of the stump holes and those mules got buried up. They just stood there. Dad would unhook them, take their harness off, so they wouldn't get tangled up, and they'd come out. He'd harness them back up and keep working with them. In two or three days they were calm. If horses got in a bind like that, they would have lunged around and hurt themselves. Mules are calmer. I always felt they were smarter than horses.

Dad always had more patience with an animal. He could get them to do anything he wanted them to. When the mules were out in the pasture, Dad would take a bridle out to catch them. He'd walk right up to them and just when he'd get about to them, they'd wheel around and run off. Then they would go to the gate. Dad would walk up to them again, and they'd whirl and run off. Finally, they'd just stand there and Dad would put the bridle on one of them. Once you had one of them bridled, they would stand there for him.

We used to cut and haul our own wood for a wood stove and heating stove. We would take Jack and Jim out in the woods with a wagon. We would have a rank of wood in the wagon before we headed back. There was a slough or low place about 20 feet across they had to cross over. It would be muddy and the wagon would get buried down to the axle. They'd pull that wagon on across there. They'd go down to their knees. I liked to watch them pull. They pulled even. It was a pretty good match for them.

Dad grew cotton, corn, and soybeans. He'd start out shortly after daybreak and usually work 10 hours a day. They would work steady until lunchtime. He could tell it was lunchtime by looking at the sun, then he would pull his watch out and he wouldn't be very far off. He'd let them rest an hour during lunch.

Jim was a little bit calmer than Jack. I remember the first time he worked Jim by himself in the garden. I wanted to see this. Jim was kind of acting nervous. Daddy just talked to him real easy. Jim walked down those rows and never stepped on a thing. He did a real good job.

Dad was always partial to Jack, but when working single, he always preferred Jim. Jack was a little more frisky. Daddy always said Jack and Jim were the best team he ever had. They never did try to kick him. He farmed with horses and mules all of his life.

In 1955 he bought a used B Farmall Tractor. A lot of times the tractor would be sitting there and he'd be working the mules. One time I asked him, "Dad, why don't you just use the tractor?" He said, "I have to buy gas for that tractor. It don't cost me nothing to work those mules."

Lloyd's sister, Wilma Berger, remembers Jack and Jim:

I was around 6 or 7 when Jack was born. I remember he was kind of mean. When Jack was little they kept him in the barn while they worked in the field. When they came in my older brother, Jim, who was 17, would let him out of the barn. Jack would come out kicking. My brother would hide behind the door. That mule learned to come out, back up against the door and kick at it. After that, Dad wouldn't let my brother turn him out. Jack always minded Dad. Dad wouldn't let us out around him.

Jack and Jim worked real good together. Dad would come in for lunch and take their harness off and they would roll in the dirt. After lunch, he'd harness them back up and go back to work.

Both of them would bite if they got the chance. We had to keep our hands back away from the fence. Jack bit one of my brother Jim's hands, just hard enough to bruise it. My brother, Bill, had a coon dog that had long ears. We came home from town one day and that dog had half of one of its ears bitten off. We figured that dog must have got too close to the fence and one of those mules reached over and grabbed him.

 **Lloyd Payne was born Feb. 15, 1938, to Jay and Pauline Payne. The family moved from Gideon to Glennonville in 1951 and rented 80 acres. He had two older brothers and four sisters. His brother Jim was eight years older and Bill was two years older. Payne attended grade school at Gideon and Glennonville and graduated from Campbell High School in 1952. He farmed until age 24, then moved to Hazelwood, Missouri and worked at an injection molding company. He retired in 2001. In 2008 he and his wife, Dortha, celebrated their 49th wedding anniversary. Lloyd said he mostly chopped cotton while growing up, but started driving the tractor at age 14, and worked Jack and Jim to a cultivator and a disk at age 16. "They'd work all day and still be ready to go at quitting time," he said. In 1968 Jay Payne sold Jack and Jim to a man at Holcomb. Jay Payne died in 2007 at the age of 97.**

 Wilma Berger was born July 25, 1942. She attended school at Glennonville through the fifth grade and then attended Campbell schools, graduating from Campbell High School in 1961. After graduation she moved to St. Louis and worked for six months. In 1960, she met Gerald Berger at John and Nells, an ice-cream place where teens hung out in Qulin. They were married in June 1961. Wilma was a housewife for many years, raising six children. The couple moved to Qulin in 1973. She worked as a cook at Head Start in Broseley for 16 years (1989-2005). In 2008, the couple celebrated their 47th wedding anniversary.

And When I Looked Up, I Was Seeing His Belly
Blue and Red
as told by Louis Wilburn

We raised them from a mare we had, Blue and Red. They were brown mules. I didn't see much red, but my Dad called one Red and one Blue. They were a small team, and he did all light work with them.

We had some larger mules too. We'd do heavy work with them, like plowing and disking. These little ones would do that work also when we needed them.

I was awful small when I first started working Blue and Red. We had a walking breaking plow, two mules to it. When you get to the end of a row, you're suppose to pull it back and pull it around (ready for the next row). So I must have been 8 or 10 years old, because I wasn't big enough to pull it back around. Dad said, "Just pull the mules in there and they'll pull it around." I normally didn't work when I was that small, except when they'd get behind. Dad had eight head of mules. I had an older brother and Dad would hire people to help.

Blue and Red worked good together. We worked Blue and Red until we got tractors. I remember one day I had that little team out in the field, and I seen this cloud come down, and it was looking pretty bad. I was going to try to come on to the house and get out of the rain. I unhooked them and when I bought them out of the field road, and turned towards the house, that rain hit them right in the face with a strong wind. I had my straw hat on. It liked to take my breath away, the wind was so strong. That hat fell over my face and I could breathe then. Them mules, they just started backing up. I just let them go where they wanted to go. Soon it was over. That was the strongest wind I was ever in.

Back during the '30s a lot of people were out of work, couldn't get work. This guy lived down the road from us. He hadn't worked in I don't know how long. Dad got ready to start plowing in the spring and he said, "I'm going to go down and see if I can't get him to work." My older brother would start work early in the spring cleaning out the horse lots, hauling it out and spreading it. He did all kinds of work all spring. We got ready to plow and my brother went down to get this other guy.

They were each using walking breaking plows. Sometime in the afternoon this guy said, "When are we going to rest?" My brother said, "When the sun goes down." This guy thought he was kidding. He didn't stop all evening. It was cool weather and the mules were rested up. The next day the guy didn't show up for work. Later on, we heard his wife couldn't get him out of bed. He couldn't get out of bed. He was middle age, I imagine in his 40s. He eventually wound up over at Sikeston, got a job and worked until he retired.

Dad wouldn't let us ride them. I'll tell you the reason. We had a neighbor one time was letting a boy ride a mule in from the field to the house. Something scared the mule, may have been a quail flew up you know how they flutter. And it scared that ole mule, and they had worked him all day. He jumped and the boy fell off. And his foot hung in that trace chain. It scared the mule, and he started running and kicking. They said after about three kicks the boy just relaxed. It killed him. So Dad wouldn't let us ride at all, and if we did, he didn't want no saddle or anything on them.

Dad would always get up early, and make a fire in the cook stove for mother, and go out and feed the livestock and pump water if they needed it. In the mornings he'd just give the mules corn. They would have hay during the night. He'd give them corn because they didn't have time to eat a whole lot. We'd go out and catch them in the lot, and work them until about 11:30. We'd come in and take their harness off and put them in a lot with feed and water, and at 1 a.m. we'd come out and catch them again to go to the field. A lot of times we'd work three teams in one field.

One time my brother and I had to go back in the field, and we saddled up that Blue mule. He was real gentle. Both of us got in the saddle. We got down the road a little ways, going to the field, but the ole mule wanted to go back. We literally couldn't hardly hold him. Some way or other the saddle started slipping, and he started bucking. And that saddle turned, and when I looked up, I was seeing his belly. We got out from under there without getting hurt.

We had another small mule we called Beck. He was heavy set and muscled up. In fact, we always worked him with a big mule. He'd go along right beside the large one, and do just as much work. He was two or three hands smaller. There are some breeds of horses that are more muscular than others. He must have come from one of those mares.

This Beck mule was the wild one. You couldn't touch his ears at all. He would turn and jump and run. I don't know why Dad didn't put a halter or something on him. He was as ornery as he could be. You'd get them out of the horse lot and take them to the gear shed to harness them, and you'd go in to get the harness, and that joker would turn and run down the road and stop. He done that so many times.

Dad bought a mule from a horse trader, traded one in, with some difference (money). He guaranteed him, broke, and everything. After he bought him, one of Dad's friends, that knew the trader, came around and said, "You want to watch that mule out there with your boy. He's liable to hurt him." That was on a Saturday. On Sunday, my dad and older brother harnessed him up and put him beside a real gentle mule, probably that Blue mule, to a wagon. They put a rope around a front ankle of that mule; that ran up through the harness and back to the wagon. One got the rope, and the other got the reins.

When they said, "get up" that mule started running towards two gates. They hit one of the gates with the wagon and ran out in the field. That mule ran on three legs and made a circle. Dad took the mule back, and the man wouldn't trade back. Dad told him he'd go to a lawyer, and the man said he would trade back even. He traded back, but Dad lost the difference.

In 1940 Dad bought his first tractor, an Allis Chalmers. In 1941 he bought his second one, but he still kept six mules. Dad was old at that time and he said, "You just don't give up something you've worked with a lifetime." He kept them for what they had done, sentimental reasons I guess.

 Louis Wilburn was born May 3, 1923, to Louis "Lou" and Norma Wilburn. He had four brothers and four sisters and was the next to the youngest brother. His oldest brother was 19 years older. During his youth, his father farmed 240 acres in New Madrid County, six miles west of East Prairie. They raised mostly corn and wheat and a little cotton. Louis attended Cade School, a two-room rural school through the eighth grade, and was graduated from East Prairie High School in 1941. He farmed with his dad until his dad retired in 1943, then farmed on his own until he retired in 1988. His son, David, now runs the farm, which has increased to 500 acres. In 2008, Louis and his wife, Wanda, celebrated their 66th wedding anniversary.

Hell, I Wouldn't Have Taken a Thousand for Them Right Then
Jack and Joe
as told by Chalk Givens

I had a pair of mules that I bought from a guy in Bell City, who was a logger. They were horse mules, Jack and Joe. They were little mules, 15 hands tall and in good shape, weighed 1,100 pounds. He was really a teamster. He broke them to log. He'd hook them to a log and have skids up there and them mules would pull the logs on that wagon, and he'd be on the other side.

They were bays, one was more black. They each had a white nose and some white on their bellies. You could see them coming down the road. They were 7or 8 when I bought them.

I would have kept them a lot longer, but people would come around and see them and like them. A neighbor kept after me; he knowed how I traded around. He said, "My brother needs a team. I know how they are and I'd like to trade you something he's got for them."

On Saturday mornings I'd usually go to Sikeston to the sale barn. In the spring of that year I was wanting a good pair to plow with. I plowed all of my property, 200 acres, with mules and horses, mixed them up.

I tried to buy them mules back and he would never sell them. This guy and his wife had a spat. They had two or three Chevy trucks. They'd haul hogs and stuff to St. Louis back then. I went by his place on a Saturday morning. He was there at home and had Jack and Joe in the garden working them. Mules were cheap then. I offered him $250 for them and he said, "No, I just don't want to sell them."

I told him I was the one that priced them and if I could buy them, I was going to buy them. Thought I would scare him into selling them. I went on and that same day he got to worrying about his ole lady being in St. Louis, and him being in Bell City. He took off up there and his nephew came by my house.

He drove up there in one of them ole bob trucks with them mules. He said, "Chalk, I put a chain on each one of them's front legs (to keep them from running) and left it on there." And I said, "I'll turn them out in the pasture with the chains on." They would chase any kind of livestock. They'd paw them, anything they could do.

I remember one thing that was unreal. Me, and Irvin, a hired hand, were shucking corn. There was quite a bit of corn shucking back then with a team. We was back there in that big 40-acre field. I had a big, gray horse and a big, gray mule. The ground was muddy. I had a double-bed wagon and we was loading it and had about two-thirds of a load. The wagon mired down. I had a farm rented across the road and Jack and Joe were over there. I was keeping them away from my barn because people would come and see them and want them. I said, "Irvin, you run over there and get those mules and bring them over here. Come by the barn, get you a chain so you can hook to the wagon, and come on out to the field. When you come out here, go in a circle, so you can drive right up to the tongue in the front of that wagon. Stop and hook them up and they'll pull this whole damn wagon, corn and all, out of here."

That's what he done. Them little mules, he just spoke to them when he got them hooked up. They just took that wagon and drug that ole big team out of there. Hell, I wouldn't have taken a thousand for them right then.

But a year later, I did let another man jew me out and sold them again. He finally had a farm sale a few years later. I thought I would get them bought back on that sale. But there was another ole farm boy there. I knew him. And he wanted that team when he seen them there that day. I didn't make him pay too much. I made him pay enough. I hollered for them but he went ahead and bought them.

They just stayed good all the time. This man took them to my nephew's place and farmed with them some on rented ground. Something happened and he lost one of them and sold the other to an old trader. If I had known about it, I would have bought him back in spite the fact he was alone. Boy! They were a real good pair.

This is the first of two mule stories told by Givens. See also Runaways chapter.

 **Charles H. "Chalk" Givens was born Nov. 18, 1920, to Ancel and Grace Givens. He and his dad farmed southwest of Delta in southern Cape Girardeau County. He had five siblings. Chalk attended Oak Valley, a one-room school, through the eighth grade. He was drafted into the Army in 1942 during World War II and served three years receiving five Bronze Stars for fighting in five campaigns, Normandy, Northern France, Ardennes, Central Europe, and the Rhineland. After being discharged in 1945, he farmed with his dad until 1950, then worked as a heavy equipment operator for 30 years. He traded horses and mules over 50 years, and at age 88 in 2008, still owned two mules. He has been married three times, and he and his wife, Deanie, were married 35 years. Chalk Givens was interviewed in 2008. He died April 4, 2009, from a heart attack. Deanie Givens decided to keep Chalk's 22-year-old bay mules, Molly and Dolly.**

It Was Just Up Good When Dad Left and That Left Me to Take Care of it
Pat and Mike
as told by Rodney Eddleman.

I was 12 in 1941. That was the worst year I had on the farm. That spring my brother, Harley, got drafted and my dad got a job in Jefferson City, a political job. Jobs weren't that plentiful around here. He moved up to Jefferson City and would come home ever couple of weeks. He worked as a guard at the main gate at the penitentiary. When my brother left to go in the Army, my dad had the whole place plowed by a guy with a little Ford tractor, and Dad disked it up and planted it in corn with our mules, Pat and Mike. He figured 38 acres. It was just up good when Dad left and that left me to take care of it.

I wasn't that big of a kid, maybe weighed 80 pounds. I couldn't even get the harness over the top of the mules. Mom would help me. So I plowed corn. I think I plowed that whole bunch three times. Back then they believed in a lot of cultivation. In late summer it turned off dry. My dad had the belief of taking a wheel off the sickle bar mower, hook a mule to one side of it and put a rope to the other side. You held on to that rope and drug that between the rows. That kept the crust broken up and held the moisture in.

We always used Pat. Pat was what they called a blue mule. He was much gentler and slower than Mike, a brown bay mule. It was okay working that wheel except for a couple of places where there was a little slope to the ground. The wheel would want to go downhill and knock over cornstalks. You had to hold on to that rope to pull it off (the corn). It made it worse if the mule was getting him a bite of corn while on that downhill side. That was sheer frustration struggling to try and keep it pulled off. I wasn't old enough to cuss yet, so I stopped the mule, laid down in the cornrow and cried. I had to get up and finish it of course. I got the corn raised that summer.

Pat was the nicest, gentlest thing. Mike was just a mule. You had to watch getting around the south end of Mike. He'd kick you with both feet. I think he got all of us at least once. He just wasn't as tame

as Pat. He was maybe a hand and a half taller than Pat. He might
have weighed 900 pounds and Pat 800 pounds. They were probably 9
or 10 years old. Two things upset Pat. If a truck came down the highway with a canvas over the top of it, and it was flopping, it just drove
Pat nuts. He'd jump and run and so forth if you didn't hold him.
There's a bug we called a knit fly. I think they bothered the mules by
laying eggs in their nose. When one of them came around Pat he had
to be held, or he was going somewhere.

One of my brother, Harley's, friends was drafted or joined the
Army Air Corps during World War II. He was a pilot stationed at
Malden. He flew a C-47 (cargo plane). He used to on flights come up
around here. He knew where everybody lived and he liked to buzz
everybody. One fall day Harley and I were back in the cornfield gathering corn. This guy came over in a C-47 a couple of hundred feet in
the air. Me, and my brother each had to grab a mule and hold on to it
to keep it from running off. We held them till the plane went away
and they calmed down and we went back to work.

I started working early in the mornings after chores and breakfast.
I usually wore jeans, no shirt, and tennis shoes. Pat and Mike worked
good together. When you'd say, "gee or haw" they would both turn.
We always brought our mules in at noon and watered them. We took
their bridles off, put halters on, tied them in the barn and fed them a
little grain, and throwed some hay to them. They knew full well
where the barn was. At about 11o'clock in the morning, you couldn't
turn them away from the barn, so I would have to start at the far
backside and plow towards the barn or I'd never get them turned.
They knew dinner was coming and they wasn't going to turn away
from it. They would want to quit at 5 o'clock. I guess they would
have worked till dark if you could have kept them going towards the
barn.

Pat, he was a very smart mule to my notion. If you hollered
"whoa," he would stop and look around to see why you were stopping. You could do anything with him. He was the easiest riding animal. Don't know that anyone ever rode Mike, because they were
afraid he'd throw them off. A horse when you trot them will bounce

you up and down. Ole Pat was just as smooth, but his backbone was about 3 inches high. If the cultivator was in the backend of the field at noon, I'd just unhook the cultivator, crawl up on Pat and lead Mike, and go back to the house for dinner. I could grab the hames and jump and pull myself up. That was the only fun there was to it. I was 12. I wanted to have fun, go hunting.

I mowed with Pat and Mike, raked hay. That's another strong memory of mine. Most of the good rakes had a foot pedal you stomped down to trip the hay loose. It didn't work on ours. You had to reach back and grab and pull it up and I wasn't heavy enough to pull it. It was heavier than I was. Mom helped me. We got a piece of rope and we made a loop I could stick my foot in to keep me from going over backwards and I raked hay that way. I loved to mow with the sickle mower, something about the "click, click, click" and all of that and the team walking nice. I killed a rabbit once. He jumped back from the bar and I got a wrench from the toolbox on the mower and threw it at him and killed him deader than a mackerel.

That was my worst year on the farm. That fall my brother came home in October. He was almost deaf but he could read lips. That's how he got in the Army, but they found it out and gave him a medical discharge.

We gathered corn that fall with a wagon and the mules. They were so handy gathering corn. I'd say, "getty up" and they would pull the wagon ahead as far as you wanted and I'd say, "whoa" and they'd stop. With a tractor you would have to get up on it and start it up. It sure was handy with those mules. A mule will lean into a load and try it first whereas a horse will dive into it. We'd have a load of corn piled high on a wagon going up a hill. They would pull.

From then on, until we moved off the farm four years later, I was just a farmhand. I drove the mules when they needed driven. If we was taking up hay, I rode the wagon and drove the mules and my brother pitched hay on the wagon.

Dad had a heart attack in 1944 and couldn't work. We had a sale and somebody bought the mules. I was in school when they had the sale.

 Rodney Jerome Eddleman was born Sept. 3, 1928, to Christopher and Barbara Ann Eddleman on a farm near Delta in Cape Girardeau County. He was the youngest of 11 children. His oldest brother, Bill, was 22 years older, and his youngest brother, Harley, was 16 years older. His youngest sister, Gay, was two years older. When Rodney was 2 the family moved to a farm on the southwest corner of Cape Girardeau where now Central High School is located.

Rodney attended Marquette Country School one year, then attended College Training School 10 years, graduating from high school in 1945. When he turned 17, he joined the U.S. Marines and spent time in Europe, but World War II ended one day before his 17th birthday. He was trained as a telephone technician while in the Marines, and when he was discharged he went to work as a lineman for Southwestern Bell Telephone Company, retiring in 1986 after working there 37 years.

He married Glenda Deevers in November 1951. In 2010 their son, Bill, was head of the Biology Department at Southeast Missouri State University. Since retiring Rodney has enjoyed hunting and working outdoors. He hand carved 300 turkey calls from 1975 to 1985 and gave them away. He was enticed in 1990 to make more of them. He made another 150 calls and sold them from $10 to $30 each and quit making them in 2005. "I can remember as a kid plowing along the property line and the neighbor had an M Farmall. He would come up by me and back and make a couple of rounds while I was walking behind those mules. I thought that was so neat. He was sitting up there. He wasn't walking," Eddleman said. "When I first started working for the telephone company, I would make trips down in the Bootheel. On the road between Kennett and Hayti some farms would have tractors, others would have 25 to 30 mules. I would see long streams of black men driving teams of mules, cultivating cotton on plantations. Usually the owner was out there in a pickup truck. On one place they were working, the landowner was walking back and forth at the end of the field with a wrench in his hand. Anytime one of them made it to the end of the field and back, he would stop them and check the cultivators and make sure the shovels were tight."

Well, I'm Going to Hitch to It
Kit and Beck
as told by John VanGennip

Pop bought them for me when I was 17. They were the first team I ever owned. He bought them from Delbert Abernathy, a horse trader from Marble Hill, which was called Lutesville back then. They were both dark bay, and weighed a 1,000 to 1,200 pounds. When I had them fat, they weighed about 1,200.

They were coming 3 year olds that spring. They were supposed to have been hitched up when I got them, but they didn't know nothin. I took them to the logwoods. That's where I broke them, in January 1946. We stopped the loggin, and sewed oats in February. I worked them in the fields, and sewed about 20 acres of oats.

The tractor done the disking. Then we put them back in the logwoods, and finished that log job out. My younger brother, Ed, had a mule team, Jess and Jake. We plowed

Left to right: Junior on Jess, John on Kit, Anna Mae Neels, cousin, on Beck, Ed on Jake. Junior and Ed are John's brothers. Photo taken in 1948.

about 30 acres of ground with the teams that spring. We each had a 12-inch breaking plow.

The next year, Uncle Frank, had a great big pair of black Percheron mares. They had a white spot on their foreheads, real pretty. We'd take the logs about four miles up to the sawmill and come back with lumber. Frank had a brand new rubber-tired John Deere wagon loaded up with lumber. We had to leave the highway, and come across the field, and go up a hill to get to Grandpa's place where Frank lived.

The back wheels of that wagon fell in a sinkhole. His mares, they just shot craps so hard they tore all their harness off, and so I said, "You want me to pull you out." I was ahead of him. And he said, "I bet you $5 you can't pull that out of there." I said, "Well, I'm going to hitch to it." I pulled my wagon off to the side. And I hitched to that (wagon) and put them little mules to it.

The horses had slipped the lumber to the back of the wagon, so I was a little doubtful if they could make it go, but they lit into it. They didn't jerk, just pulled. Kit's belly was getting close to the ground, and I was just about to say "whoa" and I looked back there and saw them hounds (wagon frame) loosening up, and I watched them sneak it out of there. And he owed me $5, see, and I knew he would never pay it.

So I took that load on up the hill and came back and got mine and took it to Grandpa's machine shed, and they had cut a big ole tree down. There was a big ole treetop laying there. Frank said, "Bet you $5 you can't pull that." All I could do was hitch to it. I hooked them little mules to that. They pulled the end up. They knew how to pull. They slung it this way and that way. There was a limb about 18 inches thick stuck straight in the ground. Grandpa and Frank were standing there laughing. I said, "How deep is that limb?" And they said about 4 feet. I said "whoa" or those little mules never would have quit pulling. Frank thought he had won his five dollars back. Those mules were 15 and a- half hands tall, and they out pulled those big mares.

I farmed all summer with them. After planting corn, they went to the cultivator, and I plowed corn with them. Then we went from that to hay making, to the wheat sowing, and then to corn gathering. We counted off five rows. We always gathered corn with three guys. I would step off five rows and call for them (Kit and Beck) to come to me, and they would swing around and come right down that row with the wagon and I'd never touch the lines. They was broke. They was trained.

Pop bought another tractor the next year, a 1937 B John Deere, and said we didn't need four mules. He decided to sell the little mules (Kit and Beck) because they would bring more money. The buyer was looking for a small team. Back then if you could get $400 for a team of mules, that was top price.

They were sleek and fat when the man came to look at them. He went out on that tongue, and sat on that mule's back and looked them over. He said, "What do you want for them?" Pop said $400. The man said, "Well, that's too high." But he told Pop not to sell them. I told him we couldn't sell them for six weeks. We were gathering all of that corn by hand and we needed them to pull the wagon. We tried to always get done picking corn by Thanksgiving.

I told Pop I would use the big team, and I let him take the little team. And when the man came back he said we had let their manes grow out, and they had burrs in their tails. Pop told him, "The boys were suppose to take care of them." He said, "Well look at them big mules. They look better than the little mules when I was here the last time." I had them slicked up. I took care of them. He gave Pop $385. He cut off $15 because they looked rough.

I found out where them mules went. They went to Virginia to plow peanuts. He said they would work them single, and pull a little stretcher plow in the mountains. About 10 years ago my wife and I went through there, and saw where they raised peanuts in Carolina and Virginia. I had the big team, but I really liked these the best. They were easier to put harness on.

VanGennip also has a story in the Mules chapter.

John J. VanGennip was born March 25, 1929, to Martin and Rose VanGennip. He had two brothers, Martin, Jr., 16 months older, and Edward, two years younger, and one younger sister. His father farmed 100 acres six miles south of Leopold off of Dry Creek in Bollinger County. John attended Johnson School, a one-room school in Lutesville, through the eighth grade. He was drafted into the Army and spent two months and was discharged due to having sight only in one eye. John farmed with mules, then horses, most of his life, retiring in 2006. From 1958 to 1963 he worked at the Farm Bureau in Advance hauling fertilizer. From 1964 to 1979 he owned and managed the VanGennip Store in Leopold. In 2009 he and his wife, Wilma, celebrated their 57th wedding anniversary. In his younger years, John stood 6'5" and weighed 230 pounds. "I broke them (mules) all to ride. Just get on them. If they bucked, just stay with them until they quit. We'd pleasure ride them on Sundays, up and down county roads and creeks," he said.

II. Mules

He's the One That My Wife Made Me Get Rid of Mules
Jake
as told by John VanGennip

Jake was a brown horse mule, and stood 17 hands tall. He's the one that my wife made me get rid of mules. He'd run the cows. He'd paw the gate down and push the fence over. He was teamed with Kate, who was black, and was also tall. When I had them fat, they weighed 1,800 pounds.

Jake come from Delmar Abernathy, a horse trader at Marble Hill, when he was 3 years old. Pop traded for Kate from his brother a year later. They were the same age. I was 18 or 19 when I started working them.

We farmed with them from the late 1940s to 1954. They worked good. They could walk off with a big load. I was planting 95 to 115 acres of corn every year with them with a two-row planter. I could take 50 bushel of corn out of the field with them (Jake and Kate) on a big wagon, and they'd come right out with it.

These mules were balky when I got them. We (dad and I) tried to pull a tractor out of a shed. We hooked them to the back end of the tractor. They'd just quit. I got after them though, and they pulled it out. Jake slid that thing about 5 feet by himself, when I had it hooked to the drawbar.

One time we were down in the creek hauling gravel. We had a flatbed wagon, and used it to haul gravel. We had a load and had started up, and Jake balked when we hit that creek bank, and that other mule tried to shoot craps. I got a limb off of a stump, and I kind of worked him over a little bit. He was a young mule. He was a 4 year old. He could pull. My younger brother, Ed, got a blackberry vine and stuck that under his tail. They lifted that load out of there. There was a sinkhole in the bank, and they lifted it out of there.

The families had to haul wood for the church, and I could rig two ranks in a wagon with those big mules. I pulled up to the front of the store with a wagon loaded. They were standing on a slope. We never had a brake on the wagon. I just wrapped the lines up and went into the store, and bought a soda and a sandwich. Them mules never moved. They were broke. When you put them in the harness. They were a pair of mules.

They worked the same. Hitch one single, then the other, and you couldn't tell the difference. Plow potatoes with them, and work the garden, swap them around, put one on one side and then the other, and it didn't make a bit of difference.

I planted corn with them. I would be in the field just before daylight, when I was planting, and work to about sundown. I ate in the field when I was planting. Pop would help me. At noon he'd take the big team out, and feed and water them, let them rest an hour or two; and I would switch to another team, while they were resting. He'd disk ahead with the tractor and I'd plant.

You couldn't catch Jake outside. If you tried, he would run around the barn on you. I'd open the stable door and tell him to get in there.

Ole Jake was a pain in the butt. There were times he wouldn't go in that stable to save his neck. He'd run one way, then the other way. I was getting tired of that crap. I had an old car tire and set that up. I found a couple of sticks and stuck them out of the old tire. I had an old blanket of some kind, and I hung that over the top. And I set it up just far enough, that when he came around the side of the barn he couldn't see it. But when he started around the corner, he saw it, that's when he

Jake, left, Kate, right, with John in summer of 1950. John is 6'5" tall.

flopped back over; and when his front feet hit the ground, he went straight in the barn. He knew his time was up. Then I laughed about it. He was looking at me, snorting. He was tricky.

I never went in the stable to catch Jake. I'd just open the door, and call to him, and he would come right out and put his head in the bridle. Pop always kept two of them (mules) in the same stable. They were big stables.

My younger brother was a pain in the butt. He'd punch them in the belly with a stick or something. He got ole Jess (one of his mules) a kicking. I told Pop, "Jess will kick at you when you open that stable door." He went out there and opened that door and she turned around. He went in there, and she knew it was him and didn't kick. That sure got his dander up. That didn't work with Pop. You worked them, and treated them like a mule. Take care of them and work them like you're supposed to.

When I was at Glennon farming, I borrowed (loaned) them mules to Tony Koenig, a neighbor who lived right across the road. He had horses and a small mule, and was planting corn in what he called his bottom ground. I said, "Take my big mules down there and plant your corn." He said, "By golly, one day he would." He took them down there one day, and a couple hours later came back, and he was aggravated as all get out, because them mules would stop up the shoes on his planter. They just knew darn well he wasn't a teamster, and that I wasn't driving them. He said when he would turn around at the end (of a row), and let his levers down on the shoes, ole Jake would hang back in the harness and rest, and he'd stop up those shoes. That Tony thought he had planted half way across the field, but the planter was stopped up because it had dirt in it. Those mules were tricky. They knew that I wasn't driving them. When I was driving them, they'd walk fast. With Tony, them mules just played hell with him.

Back then you neighbored with people. Tony had this little ole patch up on a (rocky) hill, and he wanted to plant corn and his horses couldn't pull that big harrow of his. He had this old double A harrow. So I said, "Take my mules over there." They'd hit them rocks, and that harrow would jump up and down, and those mules would go crazy. They were just playing hell with him. They'd go so fast that harrow would fly up, and wouldn't hit the ground for 5 feet. They just done that for meaness. Because when I went over there, they knew what to do, because I was behind them.

Turn them loose and they'd (Jake and Kate) play. Jake would push the gate down, just to get out. He just wanted to be free. Then he'd chase the cows, and try to corner them.

Those three jersey cows came from my wife's mom and pop. They were her pride and joy. Jake ran those cows, and that was a bad story. He'd run them through a fence, if he got them cornered. There wasn't any farm in the county big enough for her, and those mules. Jake kicked her shepherd dog.

1954 was the last year I had Jake and Kate. I traded them back to Abernathy for a team of smaller bay horses, and gave $50 to boot. Abernathy said when he got Jake back he tied him up with a log chain. He tied him to a lift with a chain around his neck, where his front feet wouldn't touch the ground (to keep him from pawing).

I liked mules the best, because I was raised up with them. I knew a mule. I started farming with them when I was 9. When I started with horses, they're a completely different story, and it took me a long time to get used to horses. They acted different and trained different.

Jake was as good of a work mule I ever hitched up, and I've worked a bunch.

When John and Wilma owned Jake, they owned 80 acres, mostly pasture, 3.5 miles south of Leopold, in Bollinger County. John also has a story in the Mule Teams chapter.

I'd Just Love to Hit Him With This Stick
Jake, Part II
as told by Wilma VanGennip

We had four or five milk cows. They were our only income our first year (of marriage in 1952). We'd milk them, separate it, and sell the cream. I hated farming, and he liked farming. We first moved to Cape (Girardeau). He didn't like it. Then we moved to the farm at Glennon. We had the cows, and a dozen chickens. I went to work at a shoe factory to pay the bills that fall. That first summer together, we were down to our last pennies.

I hated Jake. He would chase the cows, and try to hurt them. He'd paw them with his front feet and bite them, if he could get them cornered. At that time we didn't have two fields, for the cows and the mules. Later, we got another field fixed, and the mules could run down there.

One time, somehow they (Jake and Kate) got in with the cows, and John hollered at me to come and help catch them. So I had to quit what I was doing, which I didn't like, because I had too much to do. So we chased the mules down the hill, into the field. Finally we got them cornered and caught. We were coming back up the hill, and I was so aggravated I told John, "I'd just love to hit him (Jake) with this stick." I had been dragging this big stick behind me. And he said, "Well, cut down on him." I raised that stick up, and came down with it, and he was gone. John was standing there with an empty hand. So we had to catch him again.

John recalls the incident:

We were getting the mules up one time, and they wouldn't go in the barn, and we went to catch them. I got the bridle, and as soon as they'd get to the gate, they'd turn and run the other way, and finally they ran between the pond and the fence. There was a little strip there. I was at one end, and she was at the other. She had a long stick dragging it behind her. I put the bridle on Jake, and had him by the lead strap. She said, "I'd like to hit him just as hard as I could." I said, "Cut down on him. That's what he needs." She drawed back with that stick. He reared up, and pulled loose of me, and away he went. She hit the ground with that stick, right where he had been standing. And that made her madder yet.

Wilma continues:

We had this ole black and white dog, ole Shep. She was John's dog. She would help us corner Jake. One time we were trying to get him cornered, and Jake kicked her, and he knocked her out. It turned out she was okay. But that didn't set too good with me.

I was off one day from working at the factory, and he (John) was going someplace; and he told me to watch the mules; that they didn't get out of the barn and run the cows. From the kitchen sink I looked out, and ole Jake was knocking out the end of the barn, knocking the boxing (siding) off the barn. He was pawing with his front feet. He was pawing the whole end off the barn. I could see the boards coming loose from the barn. I knew I had to get down there, and keep him in there. So I don't know how I did it. I was scared to death of the thing (Jake). I took an electric fencer, and somehow or other went around the inside of the barn stable. It was a long stable. I knew I couldn't ground the wire. So I hooked it on the bridles that were hung on the wall. I turned the fencer on and the noise scared them. They stayed in there the rest of the day. John said when he came home the mules were standing side by side in the middle of that stable. But I was scared to death of the mule, and I don't know how I had the courage to go in there and run the electric wire around the inside of that stable.

 Wilma VanGennip was born Feb. 28, 1931, to William and Bertha Nenninger at Glennon in Bollinger County. She had three sisters. She attended school at Glennon through the eighth grade, and wanted to attend high school, but her parents wouldn't let her. She met John VanGennip at a Catholic youth function in 1951. She was playing bingo, and used corn kernels, and he flipped kernels at her to get her attention. They were married Oct. 25, 1952. The couple adopted two children as infants and raised them. She worked at the Inman Shoe Factory in Advance for five years early in the marriage, and managed the VanGennip Store in Leopold from 1964 to 1979. After making several moves to town and back to the country, the couple found a home at Leopold, where the front part is town, and the back part country. In 2010, John still kept his two draft horses in acreage behind their home. She enjoys quilting and sewing.

That Swimming Hole Was Too Much To Resist
Roady
By: Dallas McElroy

When I was 8 (1948), my dad moved from central Illinois to northeast Arkansas, four miles east of Supply. He bought 80 acres for $2,400.

When Dad bought the farm, there was an old mule there. He was a brown mule with lots of white hair because he was old. The man told Dad he could have that old mule with the farm. Dad turned to me and said, "You want that old mule?" I said "yeah" so he was my mule.

His name was Roady. I thought he was great. That is, until I rode him. I didn't have to worry about falling off; sitting on his back was like straddling a two-by-four. He had had a mate named Ater, but someone shot him.

I rode him in the spring cultivating cotton with my older brother, Lyle, who was 15. We used a double shovel cultivator. I had to kick Roady just to keep him moving.

One hot summer day, Lyle and I were cultivating cotton. Lyle kept the double shovel upright while I rode Roady. One of our swimming spots was at the end of the cotton patch and that was too much to resist.

We'd make a round, stop, take our clothes off and jump in for a swim. Roady would just stand in the field and wait. After swimming a few minutes we'd get dressed and make another round. We did this for most of the morning. We didn't get much cotton cultivated, but it sure was fun.

Finally Lyle said, "This is more work, taking our clothes off and on, than it is cultivating. Let's just leave our clothes off." It sounded like a good idea to me. We'd get more work done that way. We spent the rest of the morning that way. We'd make a round, then run and jump in the water, swim for about five minutes, then make another round with Roady. We were making pretty good headway on the cotton patch too.

It was getting close to dinner time and we were going to make another round, then get dressed, and head up to the house for dinner, when I heard someone laughing. Startled, I looked up and there was Dad. He was laughing so hard I could tell he was in pain. He collapsed between two cotton rows. I looked at Lyle, and he looked at me, and then we both realized how silly we must look.

We got dressed in 10 seconds. We began to worry about Dad. He was having a hard time catching his breath. Finally he got up and starting walking to the house. We followed about 10 feet behind him. Ever once in a while he'd look back, and start laughing again. We all went to the house, but Dad made us stay outside until he finished eating, because every time he looked at us, he'd start laughing again.

Within days the whole country knew about it. I guess it was just too much to hope that Dad would keep it to himself. Lyle and I were both embarrassed by it, but we learned to smile when somebody mentioned it, and they mentioned it a lot. On Saturday, when we walked into the barbershop, the barber stopped cutting hair, and looked at us. Then he said, "Boys, I'm real proud to see you. It's the first time I've ever met some real down to earth mule skinners."

Later that summer Dad bought a stationary baler. Roady and I
was the motor. I had to lead Roady in a circle to keep the baler going.
Dad wouldn't let me ride him. He said it would make old Roady too
tired. It was the only time I ever really wanted to ride Roady. I was
pooped at the end of the day.

We didn't just bale our hay. We baled all the neighbors' hay too. I
could walk that circle with my eyes shut, and know just when to step
over the drive shaft. I could have done it in my sleep. I think Roady
did. My brothers told me I was lucky, I didn't have to fork hay, poke
and tie wires, or buck bales. I didn't feel lucky.

I had had rheumatic fever when I was 5, and when the weather
was damp and chilly my legs would ache. On those days I had to ride
Roady to school. I hated that. It was only about two and one-half
miles to school walking through the woods, but there were boards
across creeks that Roady couldn't cross. It was six miles to school on
the gravel road, where I had to ride Roady. If I was late getting
started, too bad, Roady never went faster than a walk. I got to where I
would lie, and say my legs didn't hurt, just so I wouldn't have to ride
Roady.

We all knew Roady wouldn't go faster than a walk, and that was
why Lyle made a bet with one of the neighbor boys. He bet Tom
Woods that he couldn't make Roady run. Tom said he could make
him run all right. Lyle put up his blue-handled Sears and Roebuck
pocketknife. Tom put up a brand new can of Velvet tobacco.

I thought it was a sure bet. Nobody could make old Roady run.
But I didn't know what Tom had in mind, until the day came.

It was an exciting day, and some of the neighbor kids were there,
Tom's sister, Alice, I had a crush on her but I wasn't about to let her
know it, Mary Lou and Buck Kimbell, me, Lyle, and our brother
Dean. Tom led Roady down in a ditch, backed him up to the bank. I
thought he was going to jump on him and surprise him into running.
But instead, he reached into his back pocket and brought out a bottle
of turpentine. He dosed Roady up real good. Roady came out of that
ditch like his rear end was on fire! He wasn't running, but he was

walking mighty fast. Lyle got his can of Velvet and everybody was laughing.

I felt awful. I didn't know Tom was going to do something like that. I don't think Lyle did either. But he was my mule, and I'd let something like that happen to him. I was just sick. I hated riding Roady, but I didn't hate Roady.

When I got home from school the next evening, Roady was lying down in the barn lot. Dad was standing by him. I asked what was wrong with Roady. Dad said Roady was old, and it looked like he was giving up; that when a horse or mule got down like that, they'd just lay there until they died. I knew that it was my fault. He couldn't die now, not this way.

I prayed for him all night long. I didn't get much sleep. When morning came, I took him some hay and a bucket of water.

When I came home from school he hadn't touched the hay or water. I started crying and sat down by him, and stayed with him until dark, when Dad made me come to the house. I wondered if Dad knew what was really wrong with Roady, but I didn't say anything.

When I came home from school the next day, Roady was on his feet; he was being held up by two ropes tied around him, and the other ends were tied to a tree limb above him. Dad had pulled him up with a neighbor's team. I knew he was going to make it now. I took him more hay and water. He never touched them, and he died while I was at school the next day.

Dad bought a little Ford tractor to replace Roady. I finally told Dad what we'd done to Roady. He said that he didn't think that had much to do with it. Roady was almost 28 years old, and that's really old for a mule. But he hoped that I'd learned to treat my friends better.

Roady was just a sad looking old mule, but I didn't know how much I liked him until that day. I guess there are some things in life you just have to learn the hard way. I've always been sorry that Roady had to pay for my lesson.

Dallas McElroy was born on Sept. 26, 1940, to Kenneth and Mary McElroy. He was the youngest of six siblings, four brothers and a sister. His parents divorced in 1941, and his father remarried prior to the family moving to Arkansas in 1948. McElroy didn't get along with his step-mom, and he lived with his uncle in Illinois for a while and attended high school at Nokomis, Illinois. In 1955 , he lied about his age and enlisted in the Army. After being discharged, he worked various jobs including as a forklift mechanic for Caterpillar in California until loss of hearing forced him to quit. He moved back to Tunas, Missouri, in 1987 and spent several years working in construction and doing home repairs before retiring in 2002. He was married for several years, raising five children, before divorcing in 1992.

That Son of a Gun Had Sense
Frank
as told by Wyman Hampton

My favorite mule was Frank. Frank was born May 13, 1920. My brother Sodie was born on his birthday. Sodie was born on that date in 1928. Ole Frank was born to a nice mare, that dad had we called Puddin. She was part Clydesdale, coal black, with four white feet. Kids could ride her from her ear to her tail. There were nine of us boys and four sisters. We would load her down, and she wouldn't hurt any of us.

We played with Frank. My older brothers would wrestle with him when he was a colt, but he would never hurt us. That thing became a pest in a way. We (kids) would be working in the field chopping cotton, and Frank would slip up behind one of us, grab a straw hat, and run off with it and bite the top out of it.

As he grew up he became our favorite mule. Frank could open any door in the barn. He would nibble at a latch until he got it open. He even learned to slide the latch back. He might stand there for hours. He would open the crib door and stick his head in and eat all he wanted.

That mule could almost talk. He would watch us as we opened a door or gate. That son of a gun had sense. If there was a gate he couldn't open, he would put his head over it, and break it down by pushing it with his front end. He would rear up a little if it was necessary. He would let all the livestock out, cows, mules, horses and pigs. They would follow Frank. We learned to take one-by-fours and drive nails in them, and nail them to

Mules crossing bridge. Frank in foreground. Painting by Wyman Hampton.

the gates with the nails pointed to the inside, which kept him from opening them. Inside the barn we used chains to keep him from opening them.

Frank was a medium-size black mule. He was a good riding mule. I rode him a lot. He could do what we called a cat lope (short lope), but he couldn't run very fast. If we were with a bunch of boys on horses and they started running. Frank couldn't keep up, so he would stop, and try to throw whoever was on him. He threw my older brother, Walter, that way. I learned to slide up around his neck and lock my legs around his neck to keep from being thrown. He wanted to throw us to get the weight off his back so he could keep up with the others.

We raised cotton. Cotton was the money crop. We also raised corn, watermelon, and hay. We teamed Frank up with Beady, a mare mule. She was a bay mule, smaller than Frank. She would stay right with him working. They were good pullers. We used them as hay hauling mules. They weren't very big, but boy they could pull. They would pull anything. We had a big International stationary hay baler that was self-feeding. We had to feed hay into the hopper. It was powered by a team that circled the baler. Frank and Beady did that. When we set the baler up we took the front wheels off and dug a hole for the back wheels to make it solid.

When we had finished baling and got ready to go, we took a jack and jacked up the front and put the wheels back on, then we would dig out the hole for the back wheels. People would find out when we were going to move it and would come out and watch Frank and Beady pull that baler out of that hole. Boy! They would get down on their bellies, almost to the ground. She was quicker than he was, and would set herself. Frank was the one that did the pulling. He would grunt and groan, but they would bring that baler out.

Neither one of them liked crossing bridges, especially Frank; they were always pushing against each other going across a bridge. I knew someone where one mule pushed the other off a bridge (see Joe Hillis story in Mule Teams chapter).

Frank was full of mischief. One time we had plowed all day with him. We came in tired, unhooked the teams, watered them, and put them in their stalls. Frank got out and ran into a pasture. Walter and I called him but he wouldn't come. We walked out to catch him, and he ran circles around us, teasing us. It made us angry. We were mad enough to teach him a lesson.

We took a railroad tie, dug a hole, and set it out in the pasture, and tied Frank to it and didn't feed him, and left him in the pasture all night. He could hear the other mules and horses eating, and he wasn't getting anything. We worked him the next day until noon without food or drink. Frank didn't do that anymore.

In the early 1940s Dad went into real estate and did good. He sold Frank and his full brother Slim. Dad told the man about Frank opening doors. The man had put rat poison in the gear room by the corncrib. Frank opened it and ate the oats intended for rats. That was the end of Frank.

 **Wyman H. "Jim" Hampton was born on April 10, 1914, and died at age 93 on July 1, 2007, about two weeks after he was interviewed for this story. His parents were Felix and Fletie Hampton. He was the eighth of 13 children. Hampton farmed with mules over 25 years in Dunklin County, roughly three miles northwest of Malden, from the mid-1920s to the late 1940s. He**

opened the Hampton Insurance Agency in Poplar Bluff in 1960, where he was recognized as an outstanding agent in the industry and retired from the insurance business in 1980. He and his wife, Ruby, were married 58 years until her death in 1995. Hampton was an ordained General Baptist deacon for 60 years. Hampton painted the picture of the two mules crossing a bridge. The mule in the foreground is Frank. "I picked cotton over 35 years until 1960, when I was 46. Usually a field had to be picked twice. You would reach in and pull the cotton out (when picking), then we would pull bolls. We used gloves to pull bolls. I never was a good cotton picker. If I could pick 200 pounds a day I was doing good. There were people who could pick twice that. We would pick with whoever we could get. Cotton picking began in late August or first of September and would go into December when we pulled the bolls out," he said. Hampton was interviewed in June, 2007. He died 3 weeks later.

He Would Get Down on His Knees for You to Ride Him to the Barn
Rock
as told by Johnny Williams

Dad had a team of mules; one in particular was unusual. He was called ole Rock. He was grayish with little black spots in the gray. The other mule was named Kit. She was brown. They were average in size. We used them to farm about 40 acres, mostly cotton and corn. We farmed in the Bacon Pasture area, about four miles south of Poplar Bluff. Dad bought Rock at the Poplar Bluff Sale Barn when I was 15 (1953).

The nature of those two mules was very opposite. Kit was one that would do an average day's work. Ole Rock was very conscientious on what he would do.

In the mornings, after we'd feed them, we'd hitch them up, and take them to the field. Rock was a very good worker unless you'd go over quittin time, or noontime. He seemed like he knew when it was a quarter till 12 better than we did looking at the clock.

At quarter till 12 when we would get to the end of a row, he would stop and wait for you to unhook him. If you decided to do another row, he would drag to the other end, go as slow as he could, but when you got to the far end and headed back, he would walk as fast as he could. You almost had to run to keep up with him.

When you'd unhitch him, he'd be eager to get back to the barn. If you hesitated on getting to the barn, he would get down on his front knees for you to ride him to the barn. At the barn we fed them corn and hay.

After lunch when we would get ready to go back to the field, ole Rock wouldn't let us ride him. He would swing his back end around to keep us from getting on him. If we managed to get half way up on him, he would reach around and grab you by the britches's leg, and jerk you right back off. He was determined not to let you ride him back to work.

When 5 o'clock came around, he'd start to get antsy. He'd come to the end of the row, stop and look at you, and wait for you to un-hook him. I imagine if he could talk, he would have said, "Dummy, don't you know it's time to quit?"

At the barn I would feed them and pump water. We had a hand pump at that time. I made sure the water trough was full. We also had five or six milk cows, some calves, and eight or 10 hogs. We raised our own feed and meats.

When the corn would get 3 foot high, Rock was determined to get out. In the middle of the night, he would jump the fence, eat what he wanted, and jump back in the lot.

One night the moon was shining bright, and Dad heard the steps of a mule. At first he thought it was a neighbor driving by, then he re-alized it was about 2 o'clock in the morning, and that struck him as funny. About 45 minutes later he heard the same steps coming back by his bedroom window.

After a couple of nights, he decided he would investigate it fur-ther. Sure enough that night he heard the same steps. He put his clothes on, and waited to see if the steps would return. He looked in the lot and didn't see ole Rock. He still wasn't sure it was him, be-cause there was no place in the fence that was broken down; but the more he thought about it, he was pretty positive it was Rock.

So he watched him come back and walk up to the fence, jump the fence, and lay back down in the lot like nothing had taken place. The fence was 4 or 5 foot tall. Kit never did join him.

The next two nights, Dad observed to see if it happened again. On the second night, Rock jumped the fence again, and went out in the corn for 45 minutes. When he came back, and was walking towards the fence, Dad had loaded the shotgun with salt in the shell. Just as he went to jump back in the lot, Dad lowered the boom on him. He was shot in the rear as he jumped the fence. After that he never got back out anymore.

One Sunday morning when I was 15, a man showed up in our community. He and his lady friend had parked in an old driveway at the edge of the woods, about a half-mile from where we lived. It had rained that week and the ground was soft. They sat there in the car and the ground was softer than it appeared to be. The more they sat, the more the ground gave way.

After they had sat there for a while, he decided to leave, and soon realized his car had sank into the mud and he was unable to move it. That's when he started searching the area to find someone to pull him out. He later knocked on our door, and asked me who the mules in the pasture belonged to. I told him they belonged to my dad (who had already gone to church).

He asked me if I could drive them, and if I would pull him out of the mud. I told him that my dad didn't usually work his mules on Sunday. That's when he turned them out to pasture.

He said he would pay me to pull him out, and offered to pay me $5, and when I refused to hitch the mules up without permission from my dad, he then offered to give me $10. Still I refused.

That's when the tears begin to fall, and he said, "I'll give you $15 if you will pull me out." After seeing the extra urgency of the man on being released from the mud, I decided to try and give him some help.

I caught the mules and hitched them up and walked them down the road to the area where he was parked. I hooked the mules to the rear bumper of his white Chevrolet, and it was pretty easy for them to pull him out.

When he went to pay me, I told him I wouldn't charge him anything, that I was glad to pull him out even though it was against my dad's will to work on Sunday. He insisted that I take the money, and said he couldn't have gotten out without me and gave me $15.

I had never seen him before, and I've never seen him since. When I told Dad and gave him the money, he hesitated for a moment, then he quoted a scripture that said if an ox was in the mud, you would pull it out.*

There was times we would take Rock out and ride him. He was very good for riding; sometimes as many as three would be on him bareback, me, one of my brothers, and a neighbor kid. When you'd go in the pasture to get him to put his bridle on, if his ears were forward, he was okay to ride. If he had his ears back, and a little hump on his back, we knew he didn't want us to ride him. Sometimes we would back off. When he'd get stubborn like that, we didn't want him to bite anyone.

Dad kept Rock and Kit for five or six years, and then sold them.

Luke 4:5: And he said to them, "Which of you, having a son or an ox that has fallen into a well, will not immediately pull him out on a Sabbath day."

 **Johnny Williams was born Feb. 18, 1938, to Jethrow and Mary Williams. He had four sisters and six brothers. Two of the brothers were younger. Johnny attended White Oak, a one-room school, for eight years and Wheatley High School in Poplar Bluff through the 11th grade. He then worked for the Poplar Bluff Hospital 13 years, 10 of those years as an orderly. He worked for the Poplar Bluff Police Department for 25 years, the last 20 as a detective. He retired in 1995 and went to work as a security guard at the Poplar Bluff Junior High School and was working there in 2008. Since 1989, Williams has been the pastor at True Believers Baptist Church in Poplar Bluff. In August 2007 he and his wife, Hattie, celebrated their 49th wedding anniversary. The man he befriended by pulling his car out of the ditch was white. This story took place at a time when there was a lot of segregation between the races.**

I Don't Know What Kept Me From Killing That Mule
Kit
as told by Ping Davis

I started mule skinning when I was 5 years old (1934). A neighbor, Reed Walton, let me drive his mules, Kit and Joe. They were black with white noses and were well matched. Walton's folks came from Indiana and settled the Walton Chapel Community. He would go from his home to Chapel Hill to pick his daughter up. She taught school there. He drove over and back. It was about five miles each way. We lived about two miles from where he lived. He would stop and pick me up and let me drive the mules. It was an iron-tired wagon with a spring seat. Sometimes we would stop under an apple tree and pick an apple.

In 1938, when I was 9, Daddy bought a team of mules from Leo Wisdom, who lived at Broseley. Dad had an aunt who lived in Poplar Bluff and he went to visit her. While there he went and looked at the mules and bought them. He paid $150 for the team and a wagon. He drove them back to Poplar Bluff and spent the night. He drove them home the next day. He didn't get in until after dark.

They were named Kit and Toby. They were black mules. Toby was a horse mule, and was 100 pounds heavier than Kit, who was a mare mule. He weighed 850 pounds and she weighed 750 pounds. Kit was lazy and smart. He was real high strung.

The next morning he told me, "Don't let that little mule get you hemmed up. She'll kill you." They (the previous owners) had trained her that when you went to the barn and approached her, you would say, "Come around here." And she would turn around, and you could put the bridle on her. After you put her bridle on she was all right.

That's when I done my first farming with a team. Daddy was sick, got gassed in World War I. I did what farming we done. We had 25 acres. We raised four or five acres of corn, hay. and pasture. We had free range. The cattle and hogs would run outside. We kept those mules until I went in the service in 1950.

You could work her (Kit) 50 minutes. If you didn't stop, and let her rest, she'd do something to mess you up. I don't care if you just had one row left. She might step on every third or fourth plant. She might jerk the plow, which caused the plow to throw dirt over plants. Or she might put her front legs on one row, and her back legs on another row, and tromp down two rows, if you didn't let her rest.

But if you let her rest 10 minutes, she was fine. A mule is a very intelligent animal. You could force her into working. But you'd lose time by doing it. I think she spent all of her extra time thinking how she could mess you up. She was a fascinating mule.

She knew when that time was up. She'd work another 50 minutes fine and dandy. After a hard day of plowing, come around 5 o'clock, the horse mule would bray. He wouldn't miss it 10 minutes either way. He'd bray before you got to the end of a row. He was telling me, "I'm tired. It's time to quit."

Sometimes I would start working them at 7 a.m. It depended on what we were doing. I broke ground with them with a 13-inch plow, cultivated, cut hay, harrowed, and planted, ever facet of it. I used to plant corn in checkered rows, where you plant from both ways. That way you could cultivate from both directions. Dad would help me what little he could. He would work when I took a break. But he couldn't work long. The gas settled in his kidneys. He died in 1944.

Kit could open a gate and could jump about any fence she wanted to. She'd just do it for orneriness. I would open the gate, walk out, and get around her, and drive her back in. We had to fasten everything on the opposite side from where she was at. Dad made a (U-shaped) yoke out of hickory, which he put over her neck. It had a throatlatch where it wouldn't slide off. She wouldn't jump a fence with that on.

They ran away with me one time. I was probably 12 years old. I was hauling some water in an iron barrel from the creek that divided our property line. I picked the barrel up and loaded it in the back of the wagon and leaned it on the sideboards. It rolled towards the front of the wagon and when it hit the end gate it busted through. It hit the ground by Toby, and went "Boom!"

It sounded like someone hollering in a barrel. They bolted. The rear wheel of the wagon hit my leg and knocked me down. They ran about 70 feet and got astraddle a tree. They didn't move. They stood there until I got them all unhooked. Then I led them right out.

They could pull hard. I used to haul pitch pine for the school at Walton Chapel, and get paid $5 a load. Pitch pine was good for kindling. I had stopped and loaded some pine on. It was a full load. I started them up a bank, and it was steeper than I thought. They started up it, stopped, and let the wagon roll back. I started them over again, made a run for it. They lay too, gave it all they had. I grabbed a front tire, and gave it a push, and they made it over the bank.

I used Kit when plowing the garden. She was a good worker. Toby was touchy around his ears. You had to work around him quiet. He wasn't a mean mule.

When we sold them. They were getting to be around 25 years old. They were very durable until the end. We sold them to Mr. Julian, a peg-legged man at Ellsinore. Everyone called him "Peggy." I never knew what happened to them after that. That was near the end of the horsepower era. Everyone went to tractors and autos after that.

As far as I know Dad never owned a horse. He had a pair of log mules before I was born, and sold them to a man in Poplar Bluff. Dad really liked mules.

You can take a team of mules in the logwoods, and work them all their life, and they will never step in a stump hole, but a horse will. The hole can be covered up, and a mule will never step in it. How they know, I'll never know.

Horses are smart, but mules are smarter. If I had to work a team today, it would be mules. They are something to reckon with. I don't know what kept me from killing that Kit mule. If I had it to do over, I probably would.

Edmond "Ping" Davis was born Jan. 10, 1929, to Fred and Dovie Davis. His father farmed six miles east of Ellsinore in Butler County in the Walton Chapel area. He had four brothers and eight sisters. He was the seventh child, middle boy, and had four sisters older and four younger. His older brothers died at a young age from pneumonia. He attended Walton Chapel School, a two-room school, for eight years, and attended Ellsinore High School two years.

When age 2, he started hammering nails into the interior walls of the log house they lived in and was nicknamed "Peen" for using a small ball peen hammer. Later at high school, girls changed it to "Ping." He worked various jobs and was drafted into the Army in 1950 and fought in the Korean Conflict, where he was shot in the neck and chest by a Russia-made 31 cal. machine gun during a skirmish and spent six months in a Tokyo hospital. He received four major battle stars and the Purple Heart.

A few of the many jobs he has worked include farm work, airplane mechanic, carpentry, sawmill, and driving a livestock truck for six years. He retired with full disability in 1980. He has been married twice. He resembled the actor Randolph Scott so much that he was nicknamed "Sugarfoot" in Korea from a movie Scott made.

Davis was interviewed February 18, 2008. He died July 17, 2009.

Her Ole Ears Would Flop and She'd Just Pace Along
Jane
as told by Paul Vance

Ole Jane was a red mule about normal height, and she probably weighed 800. She had big floppy ears. Uncle Jeff Thomas raised my mother. He lived about a quarter of a mile up the road from us. He had mules and horses. She was his mule. My dad farmed some and we worked together with my uncle a lot and we used his team.

Ole Jane, she was the one I would ride most of the time. The other boys rode horses. I found out that Jane was the best riding horse because she was gaited. She was easy to ride. No one seemed to know she was gaited but me. I got on her and started riding her and said, "Man, this is great." Her old ears would flop and she'd just pace along. She was easy to handle, responded well. You didn't have to get a club to make her move.

I was 8 or 9 when I rode her. I weighed about 50 pounds. I'd jump on her and ride for hours. I'd ride to houses that was five hours away, which was a pretty long ride. Uncle Jeff's daughter married Hadley Mouser. They lived on the river. It had to be 10 miles and I'd ride her up there. They'd always say, "Here comes Paul."

We rode across the Castor River a few times. Sometimes I'd have to get a stick to make her go across. She apparently didn't care too much about that.

Jane was easy to catch, once you got her penned up. I had to chase her once in a while to get her in the barn. Once you got her caught, she was really good.

We didn't have a saddle. I rode her bareback. Her ole long ears would flop. You'd just get her in that pace and she'd go all day. They (cousins) always laughed at me, even after I got grown up, about riding that ole mule. She looked so funny.

I thought she was wonderful. I loved her dearly. I used her as a riding horse, probably only a couple of years, but it was a lot of riding. We moved to St. Louis when I was 10.

Jane was a work mule. They worked her with a brown mule. They were similar in size, but she would work with any of the mules they had. They worked her all the time to the harrow and drag.

Uncle Jeff was a barber in town and his boys did most of the work at the farm. They had about 150 acres I guess, and we had 80 and they worked together and shared everything.

The other boys, frankly, they laughed at me, because they had some nice horses. They were beautiful. I don't know what kind they was. I always thought it'd be awfully nice to have one of those, but after I got used to Jane, I didn't care if I rode one of those or not.

We'd all ride together and I remember them laughing at me, those ole floppy ears. She was just a better horse for me to ride. She liked me and I liked her. She'd come to me, but she would run from those other guys. If they wanted to catch her, they'd say, "Go get that damn mule." That's why I liked her most I guess because she liked me.

I worked her to the harrow and drag and some plowing. When we were plowing there were a lot of rocks and stumps. My job was to drive the team and my two brothers would hang onto the plow. I was always riding them into a stump or something and they would start beating up on me. They were older than me. There was just a year and a half between us.

I didn't work Jane very much because the guys used to give me a bad time. They'd call me "Speed" because I was slow. I would take a little more time because I liked to think about what I wanted to.

My cousins teased me for years. They used to needle me. "Get ole Jane. How's ole Jane doing?" or something. They'd get such a big kick. She was the ugliest horse we had. Her ole ears just flopping like a hog almost. She was my pet horse.

They had her a long time, but I really don't know what happened to her.

 **Apostle Paul Vance was born July 22, 1919, to Benjamin Lloyd and Adelia Cullison Vance on a farm about a mile northeast of Zalma in southern Bollinger County. He had four brothers, two of them older, and six sisters. They farmed mostly corn and hay. In 1930 the family moved to St. Louis. He married Sue Elizabeth Humphries in 1938. She passed away in 1999. Vance received a bachelor's degree from Southeast Missouri State University in 1942 along with a commission into the U.S. Navy as a pilot. He piloted a transport plane during World War II, mostly hauling prisoners and wounded out of North Africa.**

After the war he returned to St. Louis and worked at Monsanto in product development for 17 years. Then in 1965 he started his own company, Aviation Fluid Service, which is now run by his son, Robin.

Vance moved to a farm off of the Castor River, east of Fredericktown, in 1986 and constructed a three-story log cabin, where he still resided in 2009. He owns 1,500 acres and during a shear windstorm in April 2009 he lost 10,000 trees and his Cessna 175 airplane, which he had had since 1985.

In 1988 Vance drove a team of mules, Kate and Allie, 1,100 miles in three months, from Red Clay, Tennessee, to Tahlequah, Oklahoma, as lead wagon in a ride that marked the 150th memorial to the Trail of Tears.

Here He Came Home a Buckin and a Snortin
Pete
as told by Isaac Nesler

I was born in Arkansas in 1924, and we moved to the farm at Parma in New Madrid County in 1925, when I was a baby. I had two brothers and six sisters. I was the sixth child. My dad died of pneumonia in 1931 when I was 7, and for a while we rented the farm, which had about 40 acres of tillable land, out to sharecroppers. We farmed cotton, corn, sorghum cane, peanuts, anything you could raise to eat. We moved from there in 1936.

My favorite mule was named Pete. He was teamed with Jack, a female mule. He was black and weighed about 700 pounds. She was about the same size, but Pete would push her all around. We'd be driving them down the road and come to a pool of water and Pete would go this way or that way around it. He didn't want to get his feet wet. He was the mischievous one. We worked them to about everything, plowing, disking, harrowing, and the double shovel.

I rode him everywhere while I was growing up. I'd catch him down in the woods, lead him to a stump, and jump on him bareback without a bridle or halter, and he would take me to the house. When I was 11, I started working Pete and Jack to the harrow. I would have to walk behind it. I've walked many a mile behind that harrow.

Pete would get out and wander down the road. One time he went over to a neighbor, Al Parker's. They lived about a mile and a half down the road. They caught him, and put tin cans on his tail, and here he came home a buckin and a snortin! They liked ole Pete. They just did it as a prank.

We lived across the ditch from a one-room school (O'Callon), but my older brother, Edgar, went to Risco High School, and had to go two miles to meet the bus. Edgar rode Pete the two miles to the bus, and would turn him loose, and Pete would go back home.

I don't remember the whole story, but one time when Edgar was about 16, he walked behind Pete, and Pete kicked him between his right eye and right ear. I don't know if Edgar scared him or not. He just missed hitting the temple. If he had hit that, it would have killed him. Edgar carried that scar with him to his grave.

I think it was June 1936, when Edgar and I rode Pete one night to Al Parker's house to hear the Joe Louis and Max Schmeling (heavyweight) fight on a battery-run radio. We could always count on Pete getting us home.

My brother traded Pete for a mare in late 1936, the year we had leased the farm to sharecroppers.

 **Isaac Nesler was born July 4, 1924, to Bob and Martha Nesler. He attended O'Callon School in New Madrid County through the seventh grade. He spent 15 years working in oil fields in Illinois and New Mexico and moved to Poplar Bluff in 1963 and ran a lawnmower shop out of his home for over 30 years. He and his wife, Ailene, were married 58 years until her death in 2003.**

She Was a Good Stepper
Gin
as told by Troy Hartle

I started farming with mules when I was 11 (1938), breaking ground and harrowing with an ole mare mule named Gin, and a mare named Daisy, while Dad worked another mule team. We worked from sunup to sundown. I wore overalls. We didn't know what a T-shirt was back then. If it was cool, I would wear a jacket. I went barefoot until I got to using a cultivator. Then I wore shoes. A cultivator will catch shocks and roots and you have to trip it with your foot.

Gin was a bay with a white nose and stood about 15 hands high. Daisy was shorter. Dad traded for Gin before he was married (1924). She was just a colt, probably a year old. He got her off of a Mr. Clark. Dad trained her to work.

She was a good ole work mule. But sometimes when you went to hook her up, she'd balk. We would throw a shirt over her head, and she'd go on. Once she was working good, we'd take the shirt off.

She (Gin) was the best mule that Dad ever had. She had long legs and was a good stepper. Dad would brag on her. Most of the other mules, you had to whip them to keep them moving. He didn't have to punch her along.

Mom used to work her (Gin) by herself with a one-section harrow. Dad would be disking with a team. Back then you had to double cut. Mom would work Gin to the harrow, and she would keep up pretty well. Us kids were too little to work. I remember one time going to the back of the field with Dad, and him saying, "I don't know why I ever started a farm with a woman and a bunch of babies."

It was hard times. One time Mom was helping Dad put up some barbed wire fence. They were stretching the wire, the wire snapped, and Mom was holding the wire, and it tore her hands up.

Dad done about all the plowing in the garden until the kids got grown. That was my job. I'd take the ole Gin mule, a one-horse plow, and plant potatoes. We planted 150 pounds of potatoes. We took a team to a lister plow to dig them out. We planted pumpkins in the corn, and when we'd gather corn, we'd pick the pumpkins up. We'd keep them upstairs and have pumpkin pie in the winter. Mom would fry it down, season it and we'd eat it like applesauce.

I don't guess she (Gin) was ever broke to ride, don't remember anyone ever riding her. Dad would work her in the garden with a double shovel. I used her to a double shovel, and to a one-horse sled hauling manure out of stables.

I remember coming back empty from unloading manure in a pasture, and the gate wasn't open as much as I thought it was. I was sitting down on the front end. I just got her stopped in time to keep the gate from mashing my legs.

Gin was initially teamed up with a mare mule named Kate. She developed heaves, and he had to get rid of her. About a year later, Dad bought a bronco mare at a farm sale up the road. She was brownish black and he named her Daisy. She was shorter than Gin, 13 to 14 hands. She'd woller in the mud just like a hog. You'd have to scrape her an hour to get it off. We had a hole in the back of the pasture

where she'd go and woller. Dad and a guy named, Albert Riddle, broke her to work by hooking her up to a wagon with a gentle mule.

Daisy and Gin worked good together, a good planting team. Dad used them for planting from the time he got married (1924) to when I got big enough to plant at age 13 (1940). We also used them for putting up hay, cutting hay with a John Deere 5-foot sickle mower, raking hay with a horse rake, and hauling hay to the barn. Stacking loose hay on the wagon was my job. Dad and an older brother would fork it up to me. I would stack it 8 foot high. I only lost a corner off a load one time and that was when the wagon twisted when crossing a slough.

When gathering corn, my job was the down row. Dad would be on one side picking two rows, and my brother would be on the other side. Dad gave the team voice commands. Sometimes he would get aggravated, and throw an ear of corn at them. It's a good thing he didn't hit them. They'd liable to have runaway.

One time (1947) me, and my older brother, Delmar, were breaking up the right of way with breaking plows. I was working Gin and Daisy. He was working a horse team. That mare mule (Gin) fell in the mud, got mired down. I reached down to get the doubletree pin out. About that time, the bronco mare (Daisy) fell over on the mule and was choking to death. Delmar yelled for me to cut her hame string. When I cut it, she got up and knocked me into the fence. About that time the mule got up. That's when we quit for the day. Dad hated it I cut the hame string. He didn't want to buy another one.

I don't ever remember Dad losing a mule or a horse, until Gin died in the back of a field, probably in 1947. She was 23 or 24, and had lay down in a plow furrow to woller, and got on her back, and couldn't get back up. When I found her, she was laying on her side dead. She was a good ole work mule. I think we just drug her off in the woods.

Dad turned Daisy out in the pasture. We had tractors then. A couple of years later Daisy died in a barn stall. She was getting up in years, close to 20.

 **Troy Lee Hartle was born Nov. 30, 1927, to Elmer and Carrie Hartle. His dad farmed 70 acres in Powe, east of Bernie, in Stoddard County in the early 1930s and purchased an additional 160 acres in the late 1930s. Hartle had two sisters and was the middle of three boys. He attended North White Oak School, a one-room rural school, through the eighth grade. Hartle was a member of the Missouri National Guard from 1948-1953. He was married in 1948 and farmed with mules until 1957, when he bought his first tractor. "I farmed all of my life, until 1989 when I had bypass heart surgery," he said. Nina, his wife of 51 years, died in 2001. He and Charlie Jennings (see Jennings' story in Farming With Mules chapter) grew up together, attended school together, and were lifelong friends. Troy Hartle was interviewed for this story in Jan. 2008. He died Aug. 20, 2008, at age 80.**

If We Had a Job for a Single Mule, Ole Kate Was the Mule
Kate
as told by Joe Sifford

I started farming with mules when I was 12. Dad had this big ole mule, Kate. She was brown and stood about 15 to 15 and a-half hands. In the spring, when plowing corn, we'd hitch her to a double shovel, or if it was real dry weather, my dad would cut the spokes out of an old mower wheel. We'd hook Kate to that mower wheel and use it to drag the middles, to hold the moisture in during dry weather.

I would walk behind the wheel. It had a rope tied to it, where we could move it around. With Kate pulling on it, I could handle the mower wheel pretty easy.

Mom usually had lunch ready at 11:30 and that's when we'd quit. We'd bring the mule in and feed her. Sometimes she'd let me ride her in. She'd be slow going back to the field after lunch. I'd have to use the lines on her a little bit.

If you were coming down a row going away from the barn (around noon), she'd go slower, and when you'd go towards the barn, she'd go faster, a fast walk. She'd just speed up. I had trouble keeping up with her. She knew she was going to get something to eat.

We worked her by herself, and as a team. We had another ole mule we worked with her when we were breaking ground, or plowing corn with a one-row cultivator. If we had a job for a single mule, ole Kate was the mule.

Dad had three teams, a horse team and two mule teams. I worked with them all. I had two older brothers who worked in the fields. Kate was just a good ole mule, gentle, about anybody could work with her. I'd just as soon work her as anything.

When using that mower wheel or cultivator, we did a lot of walking. After you'd work an hour or so, you'd stop and rest a few minutes; if you could keep the ole mules from eating the tops out of the corn. When the corn got high, we put muzzles on them.

We'd try to plow the corn at least twice, then use the mower wheel, then lay it by. When we'd lay it by, we'd use the same cultivator, only turn the shovels in where they'd throw the dirt on the corn, and make a ridge around the corn, and cover up any grass around the corn (stalk). We'd plow from April into July.

I only worked with mules from age 12 to age 14. Once I started high school, I helped Mom with chores, and my brothers helped Dad with the farming.

Joe T. Sifford was born June 26, 1919, to Tilman and Jane Sifford. He had two older brothers, an older sister, and a younger brother. His father owned and farmed 70 acres seven miles northeast of Puxico in Stoddard County. He farmed corn and a few beans. Joe attended Puxico schools, graduating from Puxico High School in 1937.

He was drafted into the U.S. Navy in 1942 and was discharged in 1946. Sifford said he was on a boat in Tokyo Bay when the peace treaty was signed. Sifford worked in grocery stores in his youth, and owned and managed the Joe Sifford Grocery in Puxico for several years, then worked as a rural mail carrier, retiring in 2000. He lost his wife, Verna, in 2000. The couple had been married 52 years.

Neighbors Were Always Saying How Pretty He Was
Red
as told by J.D. Patton

I grew up with mules. Dad had three teams of mules. We farmed 200 acres. He bought a B John Deere in 1942, and sold off two of the teams.

We had one mule we raised from a mare we had. He was born in 1941. He was a red mule, with a white mane, very pretty mule. He had a black streak that went down the middle of his back and a black tail. He was really a pretty papa. Neighbors were always saying how pretty he was. We just called him Red. He was red all the time, born red, and I guess he died red.

His mother was a white mare. She was wild. We never could work her. She was a nervous type of mare. You could hardly even catch her. Dad bought her at a sale somewhere.

There was 11 of us kids. We played with Red as a colt in the barn lot. We would chase him around. He was very playful as farm animals generally are. We petted him and rubbed him. He became very gentle.

We started working him when he was 2. At first we worked him with a mare mule named Rhoda. She was sort of a blue mule. They each weighed around 1,300 pounds. They worked good together. I plowed with them, cultivated, harrowed, mowed and raked hay, about everything there was to do on the farm.

I also worked Red with a horse. Dad had this horse he had raised from a colt. He called him Ben. Ben was a bronco. We had to break him about every spring. He wasn't ready to go to work, but he was ready to run away. He always wanted to run. He'd take me, the plow, and the mule, and go on. I remember one time he jerked me, Red, and the plow across the field and back. I just took the mule loose, and put Ben to the plow by himself.

He soon got tired when he had to pull that plow by himself, because it was a two-mule plow. I'd bust his hind end with a whip when he slowed down, to make him go.

No matter where you were in the field, when that dinner bell rang, Red wouldn't stay in the furrow. You had to make him stay on the row to the end. If not, he would cut across to the barn.

One time Dad had me plowing water furrows with him. We used a middle buster that threw dirt both ways. I would go where the water was, and try to run a ditch to a nearby creek, so the water would drain. Red was real good at that, because he was a steady mule and worked good by himself.

I remember one Saturday in 1952, we had plowed water furrows all morning, and we came to the end of the row around 3 o'clock. We were about a half-mile from home. I wore wading boots, which made me tired and wore out, and Red was too from slopping in the water and mud. I said, "Ole mule, you know you've never been ridden. Red, you are going to give me a ride, because I am too tired to walk." I led him up to a (field) lane, and jumped up on him.

He turned around and looked at me on his back, then he bowed up, and I said, "Get up Red." And he wouldn't move. "Go on Red, let's go." He wouldn't move. I took the rein and pulled him around in a circle. When I got him in the position to the direction I wanted to go, I straightened him out, and he just walked on to the house.

My dad was sitting on the porch and saw us coming. When we got to the house he said, "J.D., don't you know that mule has never been rode before?" I said, "Yeah, I knew it and he knew it." I don't think anyone ever rode him after that.

Most of the time we were in the field by daylight and worked until dark. We raised mainly cotton, corn, and soybeans. Dad and I would trade off working the mules and the John Deere. There were certain jobs I was better at and jobs he was better at. He did most of the planting with the mules.

I was better at making straight rows with either the mules or the tractor. I remember Dad was sick one time, and my older brothers made rows, and they didn't satisfy him, so I said, "Let me try it." My brothers made fun of me wanting to try it. One was four years older and the other was six years older. Finally they agreed to let me do it. I run just as straight of a row as you can imagine. From then on, I had the job of putting in rows. I guess I had a knack for it. Usually on the first row, I would look at something on the other end and look straight at it. The main thing about getting a straight row is not looking back.

Red was a general-purpose mule. If there was anything on the farm you could use a mule for, usually we used Red to do it. We fed him corn three times a day and if we were late he would bray, wanting to be fed. If we were out in the field and the dinner bell didn't ring, he would turn around and look at you. He knew when it was 12 o'clock as well as I did. It's surprising how well they learn.

James D. Patton was born Aug. 30, 1927, to Walter and Lucy Patton. He had five brothers and five sisters. His father farmed in Pemiscot County in the Hayward community, about four miles southeast of Portageville. He attended Hayward School through the 10th grade. In 1945, Patton was drafted into the U.S. Air Force and served two years stateside. When he was discharged, Patton spent 10 years working for a friend in plumbing, heating and air-conditioning. In 1958 he opened Patton Plumbing, Heating and Cooling in Portageville, and retired from the business in 1998. In May 2008, he and his wife, Priscilla, celebrated 60 years of marriage. "We kept Red into the mid-1950s. Dad took him to a sale barn. I still think about him, and the things we did, plowing the water furrows, and that time I rode him when he had never been ridden before," he said.

I'll Learn You to Act Like a Cock-Eyed Mule
Red, Part II
as told by Kenneth Patton

When I was 5 or 6, never will forget, I walked through the barn; one of my brothers was in the crib getting corn out, I walked behind ole Red. That bugger kicked me right in the forehead. I rolled out of that barn like a ball. I was a small boy. I don't know why he did it. They had to put a-half dozen stitches in my forehead. That was the only time I was ever hurt by a mule.

I was 10 when I started working the mules. J.D. is 10 years older than I am. He got married when I was 10. I can barely remember him being at home. I remember when he joined the service. Dad had a fit about it, but it didn't do any good.

Dad had Red and an old mule named Rodie, and later on he sold Rodie, and bought a mule named Blue. He was a big mule, bigger than Red. I'd say he weighed 1,400 or 1,500 pounds. He was taller than I was at that time. I worked Red and Blue together to a breaking plow, cultivator, and harrow. When corn got taller, I would plow with a double shovel on both sides of the row.

Red was a stout bugger. He worked real good by himself. Put him and Blue together and he was lazy. Blue did all the work. I'd tap him (Red) ever once in a while, and he'd perk up for a while, then he'd slow back down. As long as he was working with Blue, he let him do all the work. He'd limp along. He could put out when he wanted to.

I remember one time me, and my brother, Alfred, were gathering corn. Alfred was older than I, between me, and J.D. He was the kind of guy that would give you the shirt off his back, but he had a real high temper.

We were gathering corn and had Red and Blue. In the beginning he'd (Alfred) holler "getty-up" and they would get up and holler "whoa" and they'd stop. He done that two or three times. We had about a half load of corn, and they got to where they weren't whoaing too often. Of course he was hollering too loud.

All of a sudden they took off and ran right to the barn! They got to the gate and stopped. Alfred went up and took their harness off, took them into the stable. He got a line, and he gave them both a good whippin. He told them, "I'll learn you to act like a cock-eyed mule."

He put their harness back on. We took them back to the field. And when he hollered "whoa' after that, they whoaed. He'd say "getty-up" and they got up. They learned to mind.

I can remember working them in the field to the cultivator. If you had rows that turned to the barn all the time, they done pretty good. They didn't want to turn the other way at all. I'd have to hit them with the lines a couple of times across their tails to make them turn.

Anytime Dad worked one mule, he always worked Red. I don't know why. He said he could always get more out of Red. I can remember Dad clearing new ground. He'd take ole Red out, and hook him to a big log, and Red would pull it. Dad would talk to that ole mule, he would say, "You can do it. Come on boy, you can do it. You know you can." Pretty soon ole Red would get down and almost straighten out to pull it.

Dad bought a B John Deere in the late '40s, and a Fordson in 1950. Dad quit using the mules in 1957 or 1958. The last four or five years they didn't do anything but eat. In 1963 he took Blue and Red to the Malden Sale Barn and sold them.

Kenneth G. Patton was born March 19, 1937, to Walter and Lucy Patton. He had five brothers and six sisters and was the youngest boy. When he was growing up, his Dad farmed five miles north of Portageville in New Madrid County. Kenneth attended Marston schools and was graduated from Marston High School in 1956. He worked as an auto mechanic at Delta Auto Parts in Portageville for 48 years. He lost a leg in 2007 due to complications from diabetes. In 2008, he and his wife, Sharon, celebrated their 37th anniversary. "When pulling a cultivator, Red would want to lope a little bit. He was one stout mule," he said.

My Gosh A Mighty! The Dirt Was Flying
Dave
as told by Buck Farmer

Dave was the fastest mule I ever saw. You had to work him with a hitch rein to the other mule to hold him back. He would go like the devil. He was a black mule with a white nose. He probably weighed 1,100 pounds. He was a pretty good-size mule. We bought him with Rodie. They worked together all right, but Rodie worked better with Rock.

He'd walk fast, looking back. The reason he (Dave) was looking back is because we had a hitch rein connected to the other mule. If we didn't do that, he would walk off and leave the other mule.

We brought a mule named Rowdy and worked him with Dave. We worked them together, and would hold Dave back. Rowdy was a hinny. He was a good mule in the field, but he wasn't good at pulling a heavy load. He'd balk in a minute. Many a time, I'd have to take Rock and Rodie, put a pair of stretchers (to pull with) on the front of the wagon, to help them pull the load, because a load of watermelons was pretty heavy.

Dave had a big blemish on his right thigh, right below the flank. We had a big male hog that had big tusks. I guess Dave got to close to him, and he laid that thing wide open. He had a scar about three-inches long that had a hump on it when it healed.

You can kill a mule. There was a pharmacist in town (Charleston). He and Dad were talking one day about this fast mule, and the pharmacist said, "Charlie, I got a mule you need. He'll leave your mule." Dad said, "I doubt that." He said "Go ahead and try him. I want you to, and if he suits you, I'll sell him to you."

He was a much smaller mule than Dave. A pilot disk cultivator is about the hardest work that you can have a team of mules do; it's what we used to knock cotton ridges down. The disk blades came together, and it was hard on mules.

So Dad bought Tom's mule over to try him with Dave. And I sat in a lot watching them. My gosh a mighty! The dirt was flying! And I could see my dad grinning. He thought he had found a mule that could match ole Dave. And the little mule wouldn't let Dave get ahead of him. They were moving out.

All of a sudden I heard a mule snort and throw up its head. It killed this Dave mule. Blood just threw everywhere. I think he busted a blood vessel in his head. I'd never seen anything like that, but I'd never seen a team of mules go through the field like that either.

We brought him to the barn and un-harnessed him, and he fell down in the lot and never got up. We buried him in the field he was working in, when he had the hemorrhage. The year he died was 1938. We had Dave about four years.

This is the final of four mule stories told by Farmer. See also Mule Teams chapter.

He'd Scare the Living Daylight Out of Them
Jim
as told by Alex Cooper

I had my first experience with mules with Jim and Slim in 1943, when I was 10 years old. My dad bought a farm through the Farmers Security Administration, and part of the program was that he buy two mule teams. Slim and Jim were the older pair.

Jim was 15-hands high. He was a big brown mule and had been well trained. He was the single mule you could use to run water furrows with. That made him special. If a water furrow had been run the previous year, all you had to do was get him started with the middle buster, and he would follow the old trail.

Another thing that made Jim so special, he was the best night watchman we had on the farm. On any strange occurrence at night, he would snort. That sound would carry a quarter of a mile. If a cow or hog would break out of a pasture, he would snort. That would alert us in the house; it was such an unusual sound. When he snorted between midnight and daybreak, you knew something was unusual, because that was an alert system. If anybody was coming down the road, he'd scare the living daylight out of them.

Jim was very gentle. We had 20 acres of wood pasture in the back of the property, where we kept the mules when (after) crops were laid by. You could call his name in the wood pasture; and Jim would come up, and he would be the lead mule for the others to follow.

His working mate, Slim, was entirely different. He was contrary. During spring plowing, Dad had to rectify him to get him to go to work again. We had a small two-team disk, and Dad would hitch Slim by himself to it, until he got to the time he would follow his mate.

They were excellent workers together. When you were working the team, if you would call "gee" or "haw" Jim would move one way or the other. If you turned over a root or something, just say, "whoa" and they would stand still. We didn't use what you called a full harness. We used a collar, hame strings, the back band, and the traces.

The reason Jim was my favorite is I had an experience with him. In the barn we had a side for cows and a side for the mules. Dad had a young bull he used with the stock cows, and the bull and mules didn't get along together. There was a side with stalls that we used for both the mules and milk cows. On the other side (of the hallway) was the corncrib, and the seed bin where we kept oats, barley, and cottonseed. And we had a calf stall that had an open space (facing the barn aisle).

This one particular night, it was early in the fall; my two older brothers had gone on to college. I was 13. I got up early when it was dark and walked by the side of the barn with my bucket. When I was walking down the barn aisle, feeling my way down the side, (I couldn't see him) Jim had his head out in the aisle way, and as soon as I came in close proximity to him, he snorted, "Ooooh! Ooooh!" And I cleared a 5-foot-6-inch gate, bucket and all.

When I got to the house, Dad asked me what had happened. I said, "I don't know. I think someone laughed at me." He told me to go right back out there and find out what that was. I had to go by myself. This time I took a lantern. Then I found out what it was. My brother, Mike, had gone and changed them around, and left ole Jim in the calf stall.

You could cultivate five or six acres a day with them. You watch them. They had to be conditioned like you did. When you first started working them to a breaking plow in the spring, you'd work them until you saw acceleration in their breathing or if they were perspiring. You used that as a signal. We were always told, "Don't over extend them."

When they (mules) got out they had a route. They would go south to the end of 80 acres, run to the east along a fence line. Along this line on the north side of the road there was a cemetery. It's still there.

One night they got out, and we kind of knew which way they would be going, and my brother, Joel, who was just younger than I, he took across the field to cut them off. In his movement, someway he went through the cemetery. But luckily enough, they had dug a grave that was lined with funeral grass (grass mat). He stumbled in the grave and that funeral grass got around him, and he beat the mules to the house.

The neighbors to the left had a chow dog, a big dog. This chow was known to be brave. When he saw this fellow with a strange wrap running down the road, he tucked tail, turned, and ran. He couldn't stand it either. Joel ran the whole way home, about three quarters of a mile.

 **Alex A. Cooper was born Feb. 15, 1933, to Roy Cooper, Sr., and Louise Cooper. He had 10 brothers, three of them younger, and one sister. His father farmed in Pemiscot County on Ingram Ridge, about six miles northwest of Hayti. Alex attended Hayti schools, graduating from Hayti High School in 1950. He attended Lincoln University in Jefferson City from 1951 to 1955, graduating with a degree in biology. He was drafted into the Army's Corps of Engineers as a second lieutenant and served two years during the Korean Conflict, helping to make floating bridges that were the longest the Army constructed at that time. After being discharged, he served as principal at Reeves School District in Dunklin County from 1959 to 1965. He worked for Delmo Housing Corporation in several programs from 1968 to 1993. In 1982, he lost, Louise, his wife of 25 years.**

Jim Would Bow His Head Down Ready to go to Work
Jim, Part 2
as told by Mike Cooper

My favorite mule was Jim. Jim was a big old brown mule that was so gentle you could just talk to him in their language. He's the one that was bigger and older. He was just as gentle, and you could ride him. He was teamed with a mule named Slim. Slim was darker and slightly smaller than Jim and wasn't as strong.

If you got ole Jim, and put him on the top of a row, and he begin to walk off, if you'd say "gee" he'd go right, "haw" and he'd go left. He responded very patient. If Dad would say, "It's time to go to work," Jim would bow his head down ready to go.

When we had rain that would fall on crops it would create what we called water furrows. Dad would take ole Jim and he would follow the flow of water using a middle buster.

Slim had lost sight in one eye in the latter part of '45. We don't know what caused it. When you went to his blind side, you had to let him know, "Slim! Slim!" Then you could go and put the bridle on. You hollered to Jim first. He knew you were coming with the bridle. You'd bridle him, and carry him to a post and tie him; then you'd have to go to Slim, respond to the language. When he responded, you'd go up on the left side, kind of caress him a little, before you put the bridle on. Then you were ready to lead them to the post by the gear shop to put their harness on.

We had 20 acres of wood. Sometimes we'd have a lot of big logs, 3 feet in diameter, on a wagon. Jim was our strongest mule, so Slim and Jim had to be worked in the woods. Jim was on the right side. We would shorten Jim's trace chain, so he could pull more. They'd go across the ditches, and the Slim mule would just stop. Once a wagon stops, it's difficult to get it going again. We'd shorten the traces some more. I'd take the line and click it on Jim's back and he would go with it.

In the fall of the year, we'd take the mules down to the woodland. I'd ride ole Jim, and someone else would ride Slim. We only rode them to and from the wood lot. When we'd bring them back, we'd race them. During lay by time in July, when we weren't using the mules, to save on hay we'd take them down to the woods.

Sometimes someone wouldn't close the gate, and the mules would get out. When they'd get out. They'd just run. My mother never did sleep sound. She'd say, "Lord, the mules are out." That meant we all had to get up, and get our clothes on. They'd run down the road. They might go across a field and everywhere. We could hear them. We'd cut across the field, not our land, to catch them, corral them. When we'd get close to them, we'd begin to call their names, and they would recognize us.

Those are fond memories when they'd break out of the lot. Sometimes it would take hours. Funny thing about a mule, after he exhausts himself, he'll kinda do like a rabbit, he's going to come back home. If you got exhausted, you don't have to worry about it. He's going to come back home, then you use the mule language, "Jim, Jim, Slim." They will perk up and stand still, where you can put the bridle on them.

Dad sold Jim and Slim in 1948 to an individual, and I believe he got $100 a piece. At that time a lot of people were still mule farming. Cotton was still king.

Mike also has a story in the Farming With Mules chapter.

 **Mike M. Cooper was born May 28, 1931, to Roy Cooper, Sr., and Louise Cooper. He had 11 siblings and was the third oldest of nine boys. He and Alex are brothers. Mike graduated from Hayti High School in 1949 and then attended Morgan State College for two years in pre-dentistry. He transferred to Lincoln University in Jefferson City in 1951, and was drafted into the military. He worked as an instrument technician on B-47 airplanes while serving in the U.S. Air Force. After being discharged he worked at Boeing Aircraft in Wichita, Kansas for a year, then re-entered Lincoln University and graduated with a degree in civil engineering in 1958. He worked for the University of Missouri's Special Programs from 1966 to 1990, when he retired. He and his wife, Octavia, celebrated their 50th wedding anniversary in 2009.**

She Was a Family Heirloom. She's Done Gone to Mule Heaven
Red
as told by Talmadge Gann

I started plowing with mules when I was 9 or 10 years old. I made a hand in the field when I was 10 or 11 years old. (We would) go all day long, sunup to sundown. That's the way we used to work. You'd put your water in a jug and wrap it with a gunnysack. It wouldn't stay cold, but it would be cool. If you're a mile from the house, any kind of water will be good.

I used to plow barefoot as a kid. I wore bib overalls and a 49-cent shirt from J.C. Penney. The hardest part was walking behind them all day. Your feet got tough. We plowed old ground. If a root hit you in the belly; man, that would hurt. If you got some good stout mules out there—they'll keep a going.

Cultivating cotton 1938–40. Gann is in white hat.

My dad owned 30 acres and rented 400 or 500. We had four or five teams of mules and Dad used day laborers. We raised corn, cotton, and soybeans. We had Ole Bird, Ole Blue, Ole Dan, Ole Dick. We didn't have any small mules. They had to weigh 1,000 pounds to work that black gumbo. Back then mules were the common thing. Ever body had two or three.

We didn't keep mules too long. We traded mules pretty often. A mule sleeps just before daylight. We used to get them up right after daylight to go to the field, so they lost some of their sleep. Four or five years was a (work mule's) life, so we traded. We kept them until they were 7 or 8 years old.

We always traded for young mules 3 or 4 years old; used to get mules out of Illinois. They'd come in here on a train. Hatch Doan had a mule barn. Bob Harris had a mule barn. Leo Adams had a mule barn. All of them were in Blytheville. They'd usually break a team before they sold them. Most of the time they were pretty well broke. Once in a while you'd get one that wasn't broke too good.

We kept corn and alfalfa hay in the troughs all night. A mule will eat all night. He'll eat most of the time and sleep just before daylight. An ole horse will kill himself if you leave a bunch of feed in the trough.

We had one ole mule we didn't trade. We kept her for years and years. She was as smart as you and I. She could open that crib door with her nose and go in and get what she wanted. Ole Red, she was probably 15 hands and weighed a 1,000 pounds. She'd work with any of the other mules.

She could foxtrot like a horse. We'd ride her to town or wherever we had to go. Ole Red, she'd catch a cow by the back of the neck. She enjoyed doing that. You couldn't keep a (milk) cow in the lot with her. She'd kill a calf. She was a mean ole girl.

When we first started raising soybeans, we took enough out for seed from the field, and let the hogs have the rest of them. You'd have to go down late in the evening to get the hogs and cows, and drive them back to the barn. Most of the time we used ole Red. Dad would ride her too. But Mom wouldn't get around a mule.

I don't remember where Red came from. She's the only one I remember that would foxtrot. You could catch her anywhere, walk up to her with a bridle and put it on. Sometimes you had to get her in a corner to catch her. She was a family mule. She was a family heirloom. She's done gone to mule heaven.

Talmadge Gann was born July 22, 1922, to Buddy and Eddie Gann near Gosnell in Mississippi County, Arkansas, about three miles south of Blytheville. He had a brother who was three years younger and a sister who was three years older. Gann attended Reece Elementary School and was graduated from Burdette High School in 1941.

After high school he was drafted into the U.S. Army and spent 36 months in Italy and Africa during World War II. He was assigned to the 1659th Ordinance-Heavy Maintenance, which was part of the 12th Air Force. "There were a lot of mules here when I left in 1942, when I came back in 1945 they were all gone," Gann said. "I didn't like working with them. Most of the time it was from the sun coming up to the sun coming down, all that in between." He farmed for 20 years after being discharged from the army, then sold farm machinery for several years for Ford, Allis Chalmers, International, and John Deere. He never married.

Jake Was the Meanest Mule Ever Born
Jake
as told by Floyd Howe

Jake was the meanest mule ever born. We couldn't keep hogs with Jake; he would lay his ears back and go after them. He'd paw them and try to bite them. He got some pigs one time. We couldn't keep calves with him either. He'd bite and try to kill them. You just couldn't keep him around them.

You had to keep a pitchfork in the stall to bridle him. If that pitchfork wasn't there, he'd turn his rear to you. He'd kick the fire out of you. He knew when it was in the stall. What learned him so fast, was when he'd turn his butt, he was hit with that pitchfork. If it was there, he'd snort, run around and poke his head around, ready for you to put the bridle on. Once he was bridled, we would tie him in the stall and put the harness on him. He never liked it. Never did like it.

Jake was a dark brown mule with a white nose, muscular, not all that big, probably weighed 1,100 pounds. He was a working dude. He was fast-gaited.

Dad had a western bronc, a wild mare that came from the wild herds out west; he bred her to a jack. That's where Jake got his meanness from. Broncs are hard to tame, hard to break. We worked Jake with a deadhead mule called Sam. Sam was longer legged, a lighter brown, raw bony type of mule.

You had to let Jake run down a little bit before you could work him, otherwise he'd run away with you. My cousin, Donald, used to hook Jake to a locust tree log, that he had cut the limbs off of. I've seen him get the front of the log stuck in the ground, and Jake would squat and lunge until he got that out of there. He'd run him over that bank two or three times with that log until he was ready to go to work.

I used Jake and Sam to turn the soil with a 14-inch breaking plow. When working them, Sam would lean back on the doubletree, and ole Jake was out there getting it.

Jake loved to work. If they were getting up on a row with their feet, you'd pull the line and Jake would get over. Ole Sam, that hard-headed son of a gun, you had to have a whip on the cultivator handle, or he'd walk right down the middle of a row. If it wasn't there, I would say, 'haw' and instead of turning left, he would continue walking on down the row. He knew when you had that whip. They get smart.

We would then disk it, and harrow it down, to make a seed bed for our two-row planter. We started plowing in early April, sometimes in March, and we would plant around the 10th of May. When working them, Jake would usually lead by 2 or 3 feet. He was a hard-working mule.

When crossing a bridge, Jake would try to push Sam off. He would move his shoulder over on Sam while they were walking across. We had to get a pitchfork after him to make him stop. He'd bite and kick if you didn't gouge him.

In the off-season they would get out. Jake would jump the fence, and Sam would put his shoulder against it and push it down. They would take off in the open range. We might not see them for a month, then someone would tell us they saw them around Knoble, which was six miles west of us. Everyone in the country knew ole Jake. He would be in their pasture at one time or other. Some of the neighbors had dogs they would sic on him. There wasn't any fence he couldn't clear. Jake would jump a railroad fence, which was 6 foot tall. He would back up 30 feet or so, ring his tail a couple of times, and run and jump that fence to get to some grass on the other side.

A Missouri Pacific train came by in the evenings about an hour before sundown, which was usually the time we quit working. It would bring the mail, and drop it at a drop off at a post office called Stonewall, which was about 400 yards from our home. A steel arm reached out and got the mailbag. The mules would hear the train coming before we could. Once they heard that train they would start twitching their tails, almost trying to run away to get to the barn. They would go fast so they could get to the end of the row and quit.

We always knew when that train was coming before we could ever hear it.

Back then you needed a good stock dog, a heeler to run livestock in from the pasture. Our Collie Cork loved to heel that mule. One time Jake got loose in a neighbor's field, and I walked out barefooted to catch him. I was about 12. Jake jumped the neighbor's fence into their yard, and their Airedale (terrier) took after him and got Jake by the nose. Our collie had him by the heel. Jake bawled like a cow. When the Airedale let go, he jumped back over the fence and took off running for his stall. I've never heard one before or since bawl like that.

To tell you how smart a mule is, when we would take Cork towards him and say, "Go get Jake." Jake would jump back over the fence to keep Cork from heelin him. We could whisper to the dog, "Where's Jake?" and he'd take off looking for ole Jake. He loved to run that mule down and heel him.

That mule would stop and snort, look around behind him, and take one foot behind and try to strike that dog with it. About the time he lifted one back leg; Cork grabbed the other one. Then Jake would head for the barn. I've seen blood pouring off those legs.

My Uncle George Howe ended up with Jake. He had the same problem we had; no fence would hold him.

Floyd Howe was born April 13, 1928, the oldest son of Jeff and Balcus Howe. He had three younger brothers and a younger half-brother. He was raised in rural Hooker in Greene County in northeast Arkansas, which is located between Paragould and Corning, about 10 miles west of Missouri's Bootheel. He said his Dad raised Jake and then sold him as a 2 year old to his brother George, who broke him to work with Sam. Jeff Howe kept the mules from 1942 to 1945, when George was in Michigan.

"My first job was harrowing off cotton ridges with a team of mules when I was 11. I was paid 50 cents a day," Howe said. "Mules could stand the heat better than horses, and they were tougher and smarter. During World War II, they stopped the production of tractors and fuel was scarce. In 1947, there were only two tractors between Poplar Bluff and Neelyville (which are 15 miles apart). Back then a good matching pair of mules would bring $500, and you could buy a team of horses for $250. The only cash crop people had back then was cotton. Hogs didn't bring nothing. Things didn't start picking up until 1941. Cotton came up, hogs came up a little. In 1946 we got 40 cents a pound for lint cotton and $100 a ton for the seed. That was the highest I had ever seen it. Rice started up in 1944-45.

"We used horse teams when shocking rice, because they didn't mire as bad. That was before combines. We had to shock rice, bind it in bundles like wheat, and let it dry out. Once it dried we would go back with a horse team hooked to a flat wagon and pick it up, then haul it out to a thresher. I got $5 a day for that. We would pay a man $10 a day if he had a horse team and a wagon."

Although Howe was never injured by a mule, he nearly lost his life farming with a Farmall tractor when he was 12 years old. "I was disking and the disk breakers hit a stump. I was looking back, thought I could run through it. The seat went down, and the front end went up. I clutched it just in time. When the tractor went down, it busted the radiator cap. If I hadn't of clutched it, it would have come back over on me," he said.

Howe was graduated from Lafe High School in 1947. He missed a year of school due to working in the field. At age 19, he went to Flint, Michigan to work for GM. He worked there 30 plus years, the last 24 years as an overhead bridge crane operator. While there, he started buying some cheap wood lands south of Poplar Bluff and kept adding to it. At one time he owned 1,000 acres, and in 2008 he owned and managed 740 acres. Howe cleared and leveled the land for rice farming; and the land is now considered some of the best farmland in Butler County. Howe and his wife, Marvella, have been married for 31 years. They have resided in Poplar Bluff since 1977.

He'd Mind You With Just Saying a Word Once
Jake, Part II
as told by Wallace Howe

Wallace and his brother, Donald Howe (1930-1992), who was a year older, were double cousins to Floyd Howe. Floyd was two years older than Wallace. Their mothers were sisters and their fathers were brothers. The boys grew up in northeast Arkansas in flat Cache River delta country, about 10 miles west of Missouri's Bootheel.

Donald and I grew up at Stonewall, which is two miles north of Hooker. We were working with mules by the time we were 9 or 10.

We moved to Michigan from 1942 to 1945, where Dad worked on an automobile assembly line.

When we moved back Dad had two mules, Sam and Jake. Donald and I took turns a lot. We started out working one mule to a harrow section. Sam was the gentle mule. We started with him.

Jake, you had to break him twice a year, in the spring and in the fall. When we first hitched them up in the fall, we would hook them to a loaded cotton wagon that was parked in the hay field. We would let them run in circles, until they run themselves down, then we would take off towards the cotton gin. You'd work Jake down one day, then you could do anything you wanted to after that. Sam was a slower mule, one we worked by ourselves.

When I was 15 or 16, we'd come home from school, harness the mules, and hook them to a mud boat (flat bottom sled made of wood planks) and head for the woods. Dad would hew railroad ties and we'd meet him in the woods, and haul the ties back home. He could hew out eight or 10 ties a day, depending on what kind of timber he had.

To harness them, we would rub them on their heads and they would hold their heads down. We would slip the bridle on over their ears, then unbuckle the side of the bridle and put the bit in their mouth. Then we would lead them to a trough and one of us would get on it and put the harness on.

You could have a good fence and Jake would breast it, then back up a ways, and take a run and jump it. Some of the fences were 4 foot high and he'd sail it. Anytime we wasn't working that son of a gun, we had to pen him, or he'd get out. Sam never would get out. We had a yellow collie dog named, Corky, that would heel him. When you'd call that dog, them mules would head for the barn.

If Jake was out and Corky couldn't see him, we would hold him up high, and say "get him," and he was gone. You could squirrel hunt with Corky, do anything with him.

Back then the Cache River would flood several times a year, and people would go out in a boat and use a tree stand to cut cypress trees about 6 to 8 foot from the bottom. Once they were trimmed and cut into logs, they would float them down the river to a sawmill at Stonewall.

We lived about 100 yards from the sawmill, and Donald and I would hire out to drag the logs from the river to the sawmill, about 400 yards. The smaller logs, 2 foot and under diameter, we would only use Jake. For the larger ones we had to hook Sam up with him, and work them as a team.

One of us would stay at the river and hitch him to a log; the other would be at the sawmill. At the river, we would hook Jake to a log and turn him loose, and he would go to the mill. The other would turn him loose after the log was dropped off, and he would go back to the river. If he was pulling a heavy log, he would stop and rest a minute, then he'd get down and go again.

He worked so long at it he wouldn't pull (a log) straight. (He) always cut it (pull at an angle) so it will start easier. Daddy never took a penny from what we made hiring out. We'd buy clothes and stuff with it. After we'd get out of school we'd go over and haul logs for someone, and on Saturdays, we'd work all day to get the logs. He (Jake) never wore down. Some of the wood was sold to the Dr. Pepper plant in Paragould for $15 a 1,000 foot.

We owned 40 acres, and grew lespedeza, cotton, and corn. Dad bought another 40 acres in 1940 that was not cleared and his first tractor in 1946.

There was always one mule one was more partial to, just the difference in them. Jake never did quit jumping as long as we had him. We would plant cotton with a one-row planter, and we would make the top of the bed higher. Jake would get on that high layer, and he'd really streak though the field. He'd mind you with just saying a word once. He'd really mind you. We'd ride Sam, but not him (Jake). We were always afraid to get on him. Daddy always fed those mules good, took care of them. That team of mules was our bread and butter.

Wallace was born Dec. 4, 1930, to George and Vester Howe. He had one brother, Donald, who was 1 year older. Wallace graduated from Lafe High School in 1949. After spending four years in the U.S. Air Force as an airplane mechanic, Wallace returned to Hooker and farmed, mostly rice, with his brother until 1986. "Donald and I were always together. The only time we were apart was when we went to the service. He was with the mules more than I was," he said. Wallace retired from farming in 1992; and he and his wife, Maire, celebrated their 52nd wedding anniversary in 2007.

III. Farming With Mules

If You Could Go and Catch a Pair of Mules. You Had Passed the Threshold
as told by Mike Cooper

In 1939 my mother and father purchased a farm through the Farmers Security Administration. There was 11 boys and one girl. Before that, we had sharecropped with my grandfather five miles north of Hayti. They (FSA) came out and interviewed Mom and Dad. They wanted to know if Dad knew anything about mules. My grandfather had 20 sharecropper families, and Dad was the foreman. He was the one who would break mules.

They were approved (by FSA) to buy a farm; that had 68 acres of cultivation, 12 acres of new ground, and 20 acres of heavy wood, hardwood, oak, hickory. Dad said he loved the farm because he could use the wood as fuel.

The FSA bought two pairs of mules, a younger pair and an older pair. I think they got them at the Crow Mule Barn on Highway 84. The older pair, called Slim and Jim, had been broken (see Jim stories in Mules chapter).

The younger pair of mules were named Rat and Rodie. Rat was a dark charco black. Rodie was a mare mule and was more brownish. They was so mean. Dad had employed a man 19 years old named

Perk. He wanted to help Dad break these mules. My dad knew he could, but he had other things to do. He employed him for a dollar a day. That was big money in that time. He was able to work with Rodie, but it took him several weeks to train Rat. Perk broke them to the plow and harrow and also to respond to language.

Rat was a highly intense mule. When he heard any noise he was like a thoroughbred race horse, he wanted to run away. Perk would have them to a harrow or a one-row disk, and if Rat would hear a noise, regardless of what it was, he'd just take up and go to running. You couldn't control him with the disk at all. Dad decided he would put a weight that went in his mouth, that he could pull on and quiet him down.

Both teams of mules responded to language. Everybody of my generation learned the language of mules. The older team was easier to work. They had been used to the language.

We had a one-row stalk cutter. That's the first thing you learn. We'd do that in the first part of the year. When it got up to 30 degrees, you'd start cutting stalks. After that, we had a one-row disk that we used the mules to pull. We had a seat on it, but Dad didn't want us to get on it.

We (my brothers and I) learned to disk and harrow when we were 9 or 10. At first we were introduced to their language. Then we would go out in the lot and catch them. For the generation born in the '30s, that was just part of who we are. If you could go in a lot and catch a pair of mules, everybody thought you were a man. You had passed the threshold. Once you were able to work a team of mules; the young ladies, the teenage girls, they would just be thrilled to death. They would tell their dad, 'That's someone we would love to marry.' And the mothers of these young ladies would watch young men doing that. And we'd get so much praise.

Dad would work the young pair, and my oldest brother, Roy Jr., always worked the older pair. We (my brothers and I) did the hoeing. Roy, and Charles, my second oldest brother, left to go to college in 1946. After that my brothers and I would alternate working the mules.

When working a one-row cultivator, you carry the lines around your shoulder and back. Working the middle buster, you carry them around your waist. Learn the mule talk. Give his name and be very gentle to him. If you want to go left, you say, "haw." If you want to go right, "gee, haw, get up, whoa." Just talk to them. If you want them to step up, "get up, get up, move, move."

Rat ran away with me a couple of times. One day I was working them fairly close, 10 acres east of the house. Somebody came up in a loud car. Rat got excited, and he just run away. You let the lines go. He'd be running around the field with a plow or harrow. Finally they'd head to the lot, and that's when my dad would get them.

Depending on the temperature in June, when we got to the end of a row, we'd let them rest for 10 minutes. Most people that had mules let them rest. We fed them alfalfa hay and corn.

In 1948, my dad bought a Ford tractor, and he sold Rat and Rodie for a pretty good price to a farmer. He kept Jim and Slim. My dad was a real good farmer. He bought that farm in 1939, and we had it paid for in 1949. The first year in 1940, we planted 30 acres in cotton and made 27 bales. The next year we increased the acreage to 40 acres, and we made 50 bales. Later on some acres were making two to two and a half bales an acre.

All of us kids started picking cotton when we were 6 years old. When we were grown we could all pick 300 pounds of cotton a day. On some days, we'd pick 300 pounds, then go help others pick.

This is Mike's second story. He also has a story about Jim in the Mules chapter.

You'd Soon Learn to Jump Working a Breaking Plow
as told by Jay McCurry

In southeast Missouri and northeast Arkansas I don't remember horses being used. Mules were all of it. One of the big reasons was you could take eight, 12, 20 or any number of mules, and turn them together and they will run up and smell each other and its all over. You can't do horses that way. You put new ones in and they will try to kill one another.

We fed all the mules together. We put out corn once a day in the evening. We'd put out enough corn on the cob in the wagon bed there would still be some out in the morning. It (the wagon) stayed there year around. Every night we'd put more corn in it. There'd better be a little corn in there the next morning. If you did that with horses, there would be some foundered horses.

What you could do. You could go to the mule sale barn and get you a pair of un-broke mules. You could break them, take them back to that same sale barn, trade them for a pair of un-broke mules. You'd get about $300 for broke mules and you could buy un-broke mules for $100 each.

Three trades you had you a free team. They done the work the same. Buying un-broke mules you knew you were going to have some trouble, some of them more than others. Usually Dad got them from the Bucy brothers at Rector, Arkansas. The sale barns at Kennett and Malden, they kinda got the scrubs of the country. But the Bucys handled good mules. You'd pay a little more for them.

You've heard the old saying "a mule is contrary." If you know anything about them, you know the type of mule you've got pretty quick. Some of them catch on faster than others; you've got to be patient; they're a very smart animal.

When I was 13 (1939) Dad bought two mules and rented 80 acres of land in Peach Orchard. We brought one team with us, and Dad bought Joe and Red (un-broke) at the Bucy Mule Barn. I think he paid $100 a piece.

I worked Joe and Red for two years. Red was a sorrel mule, Joe was a brown mule. They weighed about 1,200 pounds each. They was in the neighborhood of 4 or 5 years old when I made a crop with them.

They had been hitched a few times before he got them. I took them myself and by the time the crop was laid by, they'd gee and haw and whoa and back up and all of that stuff. In other words they knew what they were doing. I trained them. I'd say, "back, back, back," and pull the lines and they'd catch on. I didn't do it overnight. It took awhile.

They were both nice mules. I'd work them to a breaking plow, middle buster and a cultivator, section harrow. We didn't have no disk. We raised cotton and corn. That was before the days of soybeans. We gathered corn by hand. We had too many stumps, we couldn't of got a combine through it if we had had one.

You'd soon learn to jump working a breaking plow. That plow would break a root and it would come back and hit you across the shanks. You'd jump up while holding the handles. If you said "whoa" the mules would stop. Sometimes you'd hang them so big, that they would stall. They couldn't go further. Sometimes it would be bad trying to pull your plow out from under that root.

I would work one team and Dad would work the other. We'd bed it up, take a middle buster, which would throw it up both ways; and you come back down with a harrow, which makes a bed to plant your crop on. I worked the bed down with a harrow, and he'd come down it with a planter.

It was loam soil. The ground wasn't packed then. There had never been a tractor on it. It had been under water since the earthquake of 1812, until the Little River Drainage District was formed. It was what had been the old Gray Horse Lake. The drainage district put five floodways right through there and came through the Gray Horse Lake. It had stayed under water for history. It was drained around 1917 to 1920 and was put in cultivation.

We could do eight acres a day with a middle buster. We'd work six days a week. Unless we were really behind, we took off noon on Saturday, but we never worked on Sunday. I can only remember working one Sunday, there was hay on the ground and a rain was coming, and we hauled in that hay.

We'd be up at sunup and work until 11:30. We went back at 1 o'clock and plowed till sundown. We might work in the garden or repair harness or fix a plow or something, but them mules got to rest and hour and a half at dinner.

I liked Joe the best. He wasn't no better. We'd make a big sweep down the middle with one mule. We used what they called a single-stalk plow. Most of them were shop made. Mr. Johnson, at a blacksmith shop at Peach Orchard, made ours. It was wide enough it would take the whole middle at one sweep. It was a wide plow that dug down about two inches. The corn would already be laid by. The corn was too big to get through with a team and a cultivator. But you could get through there with one plow after it had tasseled. It would be 5 feet tall. That was the hot job.

If it was 100 degree or 95 degree weather, you'd use one mule for two hours. You'd take him out under the shade tree and tie him up, and use the other one two hours. You'd be wringing wet with sweat. We'd wear a turtle shell hat; if we had enough money to buy one. It had a band around it and air holes. The band would let air go up under it and out the air holes in the hat. I always wore overalls, a light shirt, and shoes. I never went barefoot. I was always tender footed.

We'd have storms come up and we'd be a quarter of a mile from the barn. It got pretty exciting sometimes. We'd either get under a tree for protection, or if we knew it was coming, we'd head for the barn.

Most mules know the guy that treats them well. I fed them good corn on the cob and good hay. We raised a little patch of red clover, three or four acres. We bought hay. We bought lespedeza out of Crowley's Ridge at Dexter or alfalfa at Steele and Hayti.

They worked good for us. When we were pulling heavy loads with them, like working a middle buster or a big section harrow, when it would get 5 o'clock and you'd get to the end closest to the barn, they'd go to braying. They'd bray. If it had been rainy and you were behind in your work, you didn't let them rest that much. Usually we'd let them rest a lot.

During two winters I hauled corn nine and a half miles to an elevator at Gideon. Let me tell you, when you put a pair of young mules to a load of corn, when you got back from that 19 miles they were work mules. They'd go fast when you first started, but when you got a load, they'd get in a good gait, and when you got to Gideon they were still in that gait.

The road had a little gravel in it at places, but most of it was mud. There were a lot of places that were real boggy. There was one place south of Peach Orchard the water would get over the road, axle deep to a wagon, and stay there half the winter. We'd put extra sideboards on a wagon and put on 30 to 35 bushels of corn. I think corn is 72 pounds a bushel. And that was a load in those bad places. They would just stretch out and get through it. I didn't whip them.

 **Jay McCurry was born Oct. 18, 1926, to Luther and Birdie Mc-Curry. He had two brothers and three sisters. One brother was 15 years older; the other 20 years older. His parents moved six times by the time Jay was 10, from Texas and across Arkansas before finally settling down in Peach Orchard in Pemiscot County. He attended elementary school in Lapanto, Arkansas for four years and quit school to help his Dad. McCurry was drafted into the Army at age 17 and served 18 months in the Philippines.**

He was a lifelong farmer, retiring in 1983, after the land he had been renting became unavailable. At one time he and his son, Bud, farmed over 1,000 acres of cotton, soybeans, and wheat. He and his wife, Mildred, celebrated their 63rd wedding anniversary in 2008. "I was always partial to my dad. When I seen him out there doing two-man work, it made me sick. So I quit school at an early age. He wanted me to stay in," McCurry said. "Them big stumps (cypress), after they sat there for several years, you could pull them over with a team of mules. Then when you got them pulled over, you had to roll them on what we called a mud boat and take them to the ditch and roll them off. You could burn on them about five years. They would burn so deep and go out. The next year they would burn so deep and go out again. There would be 18 to 24 big stumps per acre. We'd work with them in wintertime when it was easier to pull them. It wasn't easy back then, but nobody complained. I loved them (mules) then, and I still love them. I sold my last team in April 2008. The last several years I skidded logs with them and took rides on the wagon."

If Hired Hands Were Working Them, Dad Preferred Mules
Rolling Shoals Farm in Wayne County
as told by James (Jim) Becker,* and **Fritz and Gabe,** as told by Artie Hillis

My dad (Coulton Becker) always said mules were smarter than horses. We had a lot of hired hands. We had six to eight mules on the farm in the 1930s. Mules were used to plow, drag, disk, plant, cultivate, and harvest corn.

Dad had six to eight men working for him, and if one of them left the feed room open, horses would overeat and founder themselves, whereas a mule won't. Back then if people did their own work, they preferred horses. If hired hands were working them, Dad preferred mules.

In 1936, when I was 6, we were harnessing a mule to take us to the river, and the mule stepped on my toe. I screamed and my older brother, Ed, picked me up and put me in a manger, and pulled my sock off, and my big toenail came with it. I was disappointed I didn't get to go swimming that day.

We had one mule that when you put the harness on him, he would take his left front foot and feel for your toe. When he found it, he would put his weight down real easy, then his whole weight. He did it to my dad, when Dad had a three-quarter-inch drill bit in his hand, and Dad jabbed him in the ribs. From that time on, he never did it to my dad, but he would do it to others.

Until 1944, the farm used mules and hired hands to put up loose hay in a 60 by 80 foot, two-story barn; that had a hayloft that would hold 200 tons of loose hay. There was a big outside door at the top, and a rail ran along the top of the roof from one end of the barn to the other. We used a U-shaped hook to hook to a wagon load of loose hay, and a mule team on the opposite side of the barn would pull the hay up 42 feet to the loft, and then down the rail on the inside of the

Beckers' putting
up hay in June
1929 on Rolling
Shoals Farm.

William, John, John O,
Edward Becker. May 1933.

loft. We had a trip rope, and when it was pulled it would drop hay.
We would drop the first loads on the end of the barn nearest the feed
bunks. In the winter, a man using a pitchfork would pitch hay down
from the loft to the mangers,where cattle and horses would eat the
hay.

One day when I was 12 (1942), I was handling the trip rope on
the wagon being unloaded, and the rope wrapped around one of my
legs and drug me off the wagon. When the hay load got up to about
30 feet I realized it was going to carry me up with it, and I tripped the
rope. Rube Keasling, a hired hand, was on the wagon. When he saw
the hay coming down on him, he somehow slid down under the

wagon. The wagon had spaces between the wooden planks that made up the wagon bed.

We always rode mules bareback when working cattle. One year the cattle got out across the river, and cleaned out the owner's corn patch. The man locked them up in a corral, and Dad paid him the settlement they agreed on. He didn't like Dad much and told us we could pick the cattle up at dusk. It was dark by the time we got them. On the way to the river, my brother, John, was on a mule and got into a grapevine, and he slid off the mule on to the river bottom. We drove them across the Black River at night.

Dad was one of the best corn planters around. He continued using mules (Fritz and Gabe) to plant up into the 1940s after he had tractors. He planted checked corn, and would put a chain down the length of the field and plant a row ever 42-inches. He drove the mules along side the wire, and dropped grain ever 42-inches. That way he could cultivate corn from both directions.

Artie Hillis worked for Coulton Becker as a hired hand for two years, starting in 1940, when he was 12. Coulton Becker assigned young Hillis his planting mules Fritz and Gabe. Both were black horse mules. Becker had raised Fritz, and purchased Gabe. Hillis recalls:

That one old mule (Fritz) if he took a notion to tear up things, you might as well forget it, because he'd tear it up, and after he got it tore up, he'd stomp.

(One time) when mowing uphill, Fritz decided he didn't want to go forward and went backwards. By the time we went backwards about 20 feet, he would have the mower tore up by hitting a rock or stump on the tongue or mower blade. It didn't scare me. I would stay seated until they stopped. Before I got off. I would have to unhook them, and it would have to be fixed. Mr. Becker never said anything to me. They (mules) were good when working them on bottomland.

Mr. Becker told me to take Fritz and Gabe and clean out some ditches with a dirt mover. Gabe was supposed to be the good one. A dirt mover had a curved blade with handles. You'd lift the handles to dig in. When I drove them down the ditch to clean it, I couldn't do anything with Gabe. He'd try to get out of the ditch. I never had a bit of trouble with Fritz. I would lift the handles to dig in, and Gabe would try to get out of the ditch. He would get up on the bank, and fall back on his side. He even fell over on his back a couple of times. We didn't get anything done. Gabe didn't like being in that ditch.

Fritz didn't like you riding him. A manure spreader only has one seat; William Strange (hired hand) would be on the seat, and I would climb on the tongue, and walk out on it and mount Fritz. He'd do a little bucking, and then start running. We'd spread manure a lot wider and unload it a lot quicker. When we got unloaded, I would get off. Becker would tell us, "It's okay to ride him, just don't get hurt."

*Jim Becker was interviewed by the author in 1998 and again in 2008. Parts of this story were previously published in a story in the *Daily American Republic*, a newspaper in Poplar Bluff, MO.

Rolling Shoals Farm, primarily a cattle ranch complex, consists of 2,800 acres near Williamsville in Wayne County. Prior to 1935 the farm consisted of about 210 acres in cultivation, all of it in the river bottom with 13 fields ranging from two to 30 acres. James T. Becker was born Jan. 11, 1930, to Coulton and Grace Becker. He had three older brothers and two sisters. Coulton Becker worked mules on the farm from 1916 to 1946. He bought his first tractor in 1935, and young Jim Becker spent most of his working childhood driving tractors. In 1935, Coulton Becker purchased additional farm acres and rented ground to local farmers. The rule was 10 acres to a farmer with one mule or horse team, 20 acres if they had two teams. The renter got half the crop and picked his half first. One of his renters was Artie's dad, Pearl Hillis. Hillis rented a low spot that is still referred to at the farm as the Pearl Hillis pond. Jim attended Williamsville schools, graduating from high school there in 1947. He graduated from the University of Missouri at Columbia in 1951 with an engineering degree. Becker was drafted into the Army in 1952, and spent a year in the Korean Conflict. While stationed there he spent six months as part of a 144-piece 10th Army Division Band. After being discharged in December 1953, Becker returned to the farm and co-managed the farm with his brothers Bill and John, until John died in 1988. Coulton Becker died in 1947 at age 58. In June 2009, Jim and Patti Becker celebrated their 55th wedding anniversary. Jim's grandfather, Edward C. Becker, owned the St. Louis Cardinals for two months in 1899, the year the team joined the National League. He sold 51 percent in-

 terest in the team to the Robinson Brothers and retained 49 percent interest in the Cardinals until 1917. Since 1989, Jim and Patti's son, Bob, has managed the farm. Jim continues to do the bookwork and drive trucks for the farm.

Artie Hillis was born March 7, 1928, to Pearl and Mary Hillis. He had nine siblings. Artie attended school through the third grade and quit to work for his dad. During most of his working life he owned and operated a sawmill. He quit that in the 1960s and farmed for 10 years. In 2009 he and his wife, Julia, celebrated 63 years of marriage. Julia has a story in the Nubbins chapter.

You'd Stand Up and Grab the Lines
as told by Ralph Higgerson

I grew up 10 miles east of New Madrid. My dad put me on a stalk cutter to cut corn stalks, on an old pair of gentle mules when I was 8 years old. The first team I drove as a boy was Ole Flora and Alice. They were real gentle mare mules. They knew more about what they were doing than I did. One was gray the other was a bay mule. They were normal size and weighed 800 or 900 pounds.

I worked them to mule equipment, one row at a time. I'd plow with cultivators, harrows and disks. I started out at 8 and I plowed with mules up until I was 20 years old.

Dad had to hook the old team up. He'd go off some place and do something else. I'd cultivate or plow. Come quitting time, I'd come in. I'd have to lead the mules up to the barn door steps to take the collars and harness off, because I was so small. That's how gentle they were. Now, I wouldn't put a kid out there with cultivators, but then, they just started you pretty early. I'd go barefooted sometimes. And if I had shoes, I'd wear shoes.

I didn't run the planter. They had a special team to do the planting with. They had a two-row planter. They had a team that could step out and they could drive them straight. Grown people done the planting.

I remember when Ole Flora and Alice both died. We had what they called the 'Blind Staggers.' They would be apparently in pretty good health, then they would fall through a fence or something and die. It was some sort of disease we had back in the'30s.

Later on we lost our mules with anthrax. Anthrax will kill horses and mules quicker than it will anything. We lost five or six mules with blind staggers and we lost six or eight with anthrax. Anthrax hit the mules after World War II. We were still working mules after World War II, but many farmers were going over to tractors. They were phasing out mules.

Dad had a pair of mules called Blue and Bob. Blue was kind of blue colored. Bob was red. He raised ole Bob. I didn't work these mules because they were a little spirited. I was young then and worked the older mules. Dad worked the younger mules. They died with blind staggers. They wouldn't be sick very long. You go out there in the mornings and they just fall through a fence or something. You'd hardly know they were sick. My dad would go out and come back in and say one of them died last night. That was back in the '30s. We didn't have much veterinary work then.

I plowed with mules till I was 20 years old. They were still plowing with mules back in the early 40s. I've worked a lot of different mules. I can't remember all of their names now.

I was caught out in a rainstorm many a time. It was a wonder I hadn't got killed by lightning. We'd see a cloud coming. We'd know it was going to rain. But we'd always work right up to when it was pouring down, and we'd start to the barn. The mules would want to run or trot. They wanted to get out of the storm too. If you got a rain, that ended the plowing for that day.

Dad farmed 50 to 60 acres. About 40 acres was all you could handle with a good pair of mules. I worked with my dad and my grandfather. We'd sometimes work the same field. Whatever field needed to be plowed. Whatever needed to be done.

We'd get up at daylight, have a breakfast about the time the sun's coming up, and we'd work till about 5 o'clock in the afternoon. You'd get in a full day all right. Our family usually took a two-hour lunch. We'd take off about 11 or 11:30 and go back about 1 p.m.. That would give the mules time to rest. They didn't worry about a man getting rest, but they'd worry about the livestock. We didn't work Saturdays unless we were behind. We didn't work on Sunday unless we had a wet spell and were behind our work.

Most of the time we had riding equipment. But you had to walk behind a plow. You'd really get tired. We had a one-row riding cultivator and sometimes you'd ride a harrow. We'd have a board mounted on it. It's hard to stay on that rough ground. I've had to jump off several times. You had to stand up. You couldn't sit down. There were usually four mules to a harrow. You'd stand up and grab the lines! You'd have a weight on it to help hold it down and bust the clods up.

Disks had seats on them, but it took four mules to pull it. The first hay baler I ever saw was when my grandfather had a horse-drawn stationary hay baler. The bales looked just like they do now. A mule would go round and round to bale the hay, the same way they would with a sorghum wheel. They'd hook a mule to a pole and go round and round and squeeze the sorghum out. We used whatever mule was handy. The mule would get lazy too, going round and round. It'd get monotonous.

I was never kicked by a mule. You had to let them know you're behind them. When I was a kid, they rang a dinner bell. They always had a dinner bell at my grandfather's. On a windy day, you couldn't hear that bell. The mules would hear it. They've got better hearing than a human does. When they would get to the end of the row closest to the barn, they'd want to come in fast.

Most of the time fields were divided up where you had about a quarter of mile rows. We didn't have long rows like they do now. It would take too long to plow them. Mules were very vital. I can remember as a kid, mules were very expensive. Back in the Depression when there wasn't any money, a good pair of mules would go for 300, 400, or 500 dollars. That was a pile of money then.

They had mule dealers just like they have car dealers now. There were mule barns in New Madrid, mule barns in Sikeston. They'd get mules off of Kansas in the plains or from Missouri. Breeders would raise them to sell. You could trade off an old pair of mules for a younger pair. Sometimes they'd be broke and sometimes they wouldn't.

Back in '43 before I went in the Army we had some young mules and they'd never had harness on. We had a small stall we got them in and put their harness on. We had a pair of old mules. You put one (unbroken mule) between them, and they've got to go then. That's the way you break them. In a month or so, you could put the two young ones together. A young mule don't know what work is and they're wild, maybe right off the range someplace.

I was raised on horses and mules. You get to where it's just a day's work; like going out to start a tractor. If you don't know anything different, it's all right. I don't think I liked any of it. It was a day's work. It's like anything else. You have to do what you have to do. It's a lot more responsibility than going out and starting a tractor. We had two or three teams. We all chopped cotton, baled hay, whatever needed to be done. I could pick 200 (pounds of cotton a day) but I had to work awful hard. It's a knack for some people. I've picked for 75 cents a hundred. Sometimes they'd pay a dollar a hundred. I never picked any after 1943, after I was out of the Army.

 **Ralph W. Higgerson was born Feb. 17, 1924, to Andrew and Lena Higgerson. He was the oldest of six brothers and one sister. Higgerson attended country schools through the eighth grade and attended East Prairie High School through the eleventh grade at which time he was drafted into the Army and served as an infantry sergeant in the 42nd Infantry, part of the 3rd Army under General George Patton during World War II. He fought in Germany, France, and Belgium.**

After his release in Jan., 1947, he was married; attended a barber school in Memphis, Tennessee, for 18 months, and worked as a barber 40 years, 35 years in New Madrid. He owned Ralph's Barber Shop from 1960 until he retired in 1987. He enjoys gardening, fishing and doing volunteer work. He and his wife, Cuba, celebrated their 60th anniversary in 2008. Higgerson also has a story in the Mules That Worked Without Lines chapter.

Higgerson was interviewed April 22, 2009. He died on March 11, 2011.

My Brothers Were in the Service, and I Got Stuck on the Farm
as told by Walter "Dub" McGhee

McGhee is featured on the front page in 1941, at age 14, cultivating corn with a brown pair of mules.

There was 10 kids in our family, four boys and six girls. I was the youngest of the four boys. My brothers were all in the service, and I got stuck on the farm.

My parents were Guy and Ida McGhee. Dad tenant farmed on land owned by Metropolitan Insurance three miles north of Qulin. He later purchased a farm in the Morocco area, east of Poplar Bluff, where the photo was taken. Dad had a team of horses, and two teams of mules, a large red pair, and a medium-size brown pair, and a John Deere A tractor. He always kept the horses and mules groomed.

The team in the photo are the brown pair, Pete and Peewee. They were gentler than the red pair, and were always reliable. We used them for cultivating and pulling a harrow. We used the larger team for plowing and disking. I farmed with them five years from the time I was 11 to 15. Then I started driving the tractor. Dad still used the mules to drill plant seed. Back then you couldn't purchase a drill for the tractor.

Peewee, the mule on the right, was kind of silly. You can see it with his head slightly cocked in the photo. He's got his ears up. He was always unpredictable. I was always careful harnessing him when moving around his hind legs, especially when he would shift his weight to one leg. In the photo, I have the reins behind my back and my T-shirt hanging on the cultivator. They understood my commands, gee, haw, whoa and get-up.

Dad and I would get up before daylight and go to the barn to do chores, milking, and feeding the mules, while Mom cooked breakfast. After chores, we would go eat breakfast, then head to the barn to get the mules to take to the field. Mother would have lunch for us around noon. I would either ride or lead the mules to the barn. The mules were taken to their stalls and fed five or six ears of corn, and there was always hay in the manger. We took a good mid-day break usually an hour to an hour and a half. We would go back to the field and work until dark. Peewee would be the first to get tired. I would see his traces start to get slack and I would take the lines, and flip him once to get him going.

Back then everyone had a large garden. Mother did a lot of canning. Dad always used Pete hooked to a double shovel to cultivate the garden. Mules were better to use in the garden than horses, because they didn't do as much damage to the garden vegetables. Horses have larger feet and are more clumsy.

On the farm was a learning process for kids. We saw breeding and birthing of animals first hand. Mules won't reproduce, but they would show signs.

When I was younger, I learned a lot from my older brothers. We had a problem bridling Peewee. When you approached him from the side, he would sling his head any direction. He hit one of my brothers and made him angry. He picked up a pretty good size rock and hit Peewee on the side of the head. That mule expelled a lot of gas, which I thought was funny.

One time I went to the barn with Dad, and one of our milk cows was down, trying to birth a calf. The calf had turned. They are supposed to come out headfirst. This one had his back legs out. I was pretty strong for a kid, and Dad and I pulled with all of our might, and we couldn't get the calf out. The calf's shoulder blades were caught. Dad lubricated his hands and arms and reached inside with one arm on each side of the calf, and pushed its' shoulder blades together, and the calf came right out. It had suffocated, but he saved the cow.

There were several dairy farmers in the area, and they didn't want their bull calves, and would sell them to Dad for $2 or $3. Dad would put two calves to a milk cow, and he would later sell them for veal.

When I started driving the tractor, most of the time I was in the field by myself. I would do the preparation of the soil for planting. He'd do the drilling with the mules. After the planting was done, we would put the cultivator on the tractor.

There were a lot of black families in the area. They farmed 10, 15, or 20 acres. I did a lot of custom work for them with the tractor, mainly plowing and disking. I played with the black boys close to my age. In the summer, we would go to the Black River and swim in the nude.

Walter McGhee was born Nov. 14, 1927. He was graduated from Poplar Bluff High School in 1946 and enlisted in the U.S. Navy and served briefly in the Pacific during World War II. After he was discharged he lived in Los Angeles with his wife, Yvonne, and worked at Goodyear Tire and Rubber for 27 years, retiring in 1979. After retiring they moved to Medford, Oregon. Yvonne died in August 2000, and McGhee moved to Poplar Bluff in 2001.

Mules Do Have Some Sense
as told by Marvin Kesterson

We had two mule teams and a horse. Kate and Jude, both were mare mules, was one team. They were gray/black and weighed about 1,000 pounds each, a standard mule size. Kate in particular was the problem mule. When you would hook the team to a wagon or piece of equipment with the harness on, she would turn her head in towards Jude. I would jerk the reins and in the process also jerk Jude. I'd have to run them in a fence corner, whip her and she would straighten up for a few days.

I plowed, disked, cultivated corn and put up hay with those mules. We also used them to plant and cultivate cotton, and we also grew watermelon. My brother went off to college in 1935, when I was 11, and from then on, it was Dad and me working the mules.

We would get up before dawn, milk the cows, feed and harness the mules, eat breakfast, and then go to work after that. Dad would work a team, and I would work Kate and Jude. We would work until noon and come in for lunch. How long we worked them depended on how much we had to do. We would turn the mules loose in the barn-yard and feed them.

Kate and Jude would do pretty well what you wanted by voice, mostly 'gee' for going right and 'haw' for going left. In the sandy soil, we never did have to shoe them.

We had a gate in back of the barn. If that gate wasn't to, Kate would get out and go to the back of the farm and get in the brush. It was about a half-mile walk back there, and you would have to look for her. When you found her, she would be looking to see where you were. Usually you could get her in a corner and catch her. Jude (and Dad's team) wouldn't get out. They would stay in the barnyard.

Dad grew up in Oxly (Ripley County) working in the timber business making ties. We would be plowing corn with cultivators and he'd say, "Let's let the mules rest a while, and while they're resting, let's go out and cut some wood." That didn't set well with me.

Later when I was 16 or 17, Dad had a gray mare he would breed to a jack, and we raised a couple of gray mare mules. The older one was better built. If they were hooked to a big load, the younger one would jump out, get the singletree set, and hold ground until the other one started pulling the load. Mules do have some sense.

In 1943 Dad was able to buy an Oliver 60 tractor. He sold the gray mules to Zack Henderson, Doniphan, a trader, for $450. The tractor cost $950. Henderson sent them down to Tennessee where they were used by a sharecropper.

Marvin Kesterson was born July 30, 1923, to Joe and Pearl Kesterson. He had one older brother. He was raised on an 80-acre farm 2.5 miles southeast of Naylor in Ripley County. Twenty-five of the 80 acres were tillable, the rest were wetlands. He was graduated from Naylor High School in 1941 and served in World War II. Kesterson graduated from Arkansas State University in Jonesboro, Arkansas in 1953 and earned his master's in elementary education at the University of Missouri in 1956. He taught in elementary schools for 22 years. He then worked in vocation rehab covering Ripley, Oregon, and Shannon counties for 11 years and retired in 1983. He and his wife, Sondra, celebrated their 39th wedding anniversary in 2009.

I Would Walk About 27 Miles a Day
as told by Charlie Jennings

I still live on the same place I was born, one mile east and two miles north of Powe in Stoddard County. I started out farming with my dad when I was 12 with a team of mules named Sam and Jack. They were brown mules and were pretty good size, weighed about 1,100 pounds. They were pretty mules. We kept them fit, looking good all the time. We used them to pull a one-row cultivator, and a two-row planter.

It was a full day's work to plow (one-row cultivater) 10 acres with Sam and Jack. I would have to work hard to plow two and a half acres a day with a 12-inch breaking plow. I've broken ground many a day with knee boots on, because the ground would be wet and muddy.

We'd be up by 5 o'clock, and start farming by daylight. Sometimes it would be so hot at noon, we'd take a couple of hours off for dinner, then we'd plow until dark. I usually wore shorts, a T-shirt, and be barefoot when working the mules. Mom would cut the legs off of blue jeans for the shorts

Rows were a quarter mile long. There were 11 rows to an acre. I would walk about 27 miles a day with the one-row cultivator. I would be tired at the end of the day, but didn't pay no attention to it.

When I was a kid, my dad used to breed mares for six or eight of our neighbors. He had a jack, and a black Percheron stallion that was as pretty as a picture. I think he was paid $10 (stud fee). My dad raised six or eight mule colts each year, and in the winter my older twin brothers, Edgar and Eddy, would break them to work, and Dad would sell them at crop time.

They used a sled with a log on it for the young mules to drag. One of them drove, the other walked beside the mules, in case one of them would throw a fit. I've seen them rear up. Once in a while they'd wreck a harness.

We owned 280 acres, and farmed 200 acres. I had seven brothers, and we averaged having 10 mules. They were different sizes and different colors. There would be four teams working at a time. My brothers and I would be plowing and disking, and Dad would be out there with a double shovel. A disk will leave a streak in the middle, and it would take a double shovel to break it up.

When I pulled a disk, I used four mules. I had to borrow Dad's mules. We hooked the four together using their bits, and the outside mules each had a line. I had to have a switch in case one of them lagged behind, so I could bust his rear. Usually when working four mules, you'd be riding, and if working two, nine chances out of ten, you'd be walking.

We used what we called a regular cultivator for the first plowing when the crop had just started to come up. For the last plowing (cultivating), when corn was about 3 foot tall, we used a disk cultivator, which had round blades, and you could angle the blades to throw a dirt ridge that would wrap around the corn, and make a real good cover. We called that "lay it by."

The first plowing went pretty slow because you were walking (with regular cultivator). But when we would lay it by (disk cultivator), you were riding and we'd go pretty fast then.

I only went to school through the eighth grade. When I was 15, I bought 40 acres for $10 an acre, from McFall Land Company. I paid cash from money I made from pulling a crosscut saw, working in a sawmill, and picking cotton. I would pick beside my brothers and beat them by 100 pounds more a day. The most I ever picked in one day was 414 pounds.

The land was about three-quarters of a mile west of our home. I bought Sam and Jack from Dad to farm with. I farmed mostly corn. Our land wouldn't grow cotton very good. The cotton would be 5 foot high, but had small bolls. I farmed with them for five years, then got me a tractor. I sold Sam and Jack to a neighbor, who used them for farming. Mom died when I was 18. I took care of Dad. He died in 1952 when I was 23.

Charlie E. Jennings was born March 30, 1929, to Bill and Vida Jennings. He had seven brothers and four sisters. His twin brothers, Edgar and Eddy, were 25 years older than he was. He attended White Oak School, a one-room school, through the eighth grade.

Jennings was the Stoddard County surveyor for 28 years. He served as treasurer for 30 years and tax assessor 10 years for Liberty Township. He served on both the Dexter Hospital Board and Bernie School Board for 12 years. He farmed for 46 years, retiring in 1994. In 2006 Jennings had open-heart surgery. His wife of 54 years, Doris, passed away in March 2007. "The worst job I hated when I was a kid was making sorghum. Neighbors would come over. Yellow jackets would be on the cane and sting the tar out of you," he said. Jennings and Troy Hartle grew up together, attended school together, and were lifelong friends. "We were born and raised about a mile apart. Our daddies grew up together too," he said. (See Hartle's story about Gin in the Mules chapter.)

Pete and Joe, Mutt and Jeff, and Dan and Bill
Mule farming in Dunklin County
as told by Bill White

Dad had sharecropped for about eight years, and in 1936 we moved from Coldwater to Hornersville, a distance of four miles. With the wagon loaded down with oak furniture and the knee-deep sand, it took us four hours to go the four miles. Dad bought 120 acres. He also bought six head of mules and all the equipment, cultivators, wagon, and planter. A buddy of his drove a truck to Searcy (Arkansas) and hauled them home.

When they arrived, I jumped on one of them to see if he would ride. He just stood there, didn't buck or nothing. Guess he'd already been ridden.

Pete and Joe were my favorite team. They were medium-size brown horse mules, weighed around 1,400 pounds. They were good little mules. They'd mind you. Just say, "getty-up" and they'd go. They worked good together. We'd go to town with them because they would stand still when you tied them up. The others would move around and fight like other mules do.

Me, and my twin brother, Jewel, worked them to a breaking plow and cultivator. We would fight on which one would get Pete and Joe. We would get up at 4 o'clock in the morning and work until sundown. I always looked forward to the weekend, would get to sleep. I used to ride Joe four miles to Hornersville every night for two weeks, until I learned how to use a movie projector.

The other two teams were named Mutt and Jeff and Dan and Bill. Mutt and Jeff were smaller, weighed about 1,200 pounds. They were spotted black and white. I called them polka-dot mules. Dan was black and Bill was brown. They were bigger, around 1,500 pounds. But they were slow workers. Dad always said you had to get culls when you bought them all at once, and these two were culls. They'd lag behind. You had to keep using lines to pop them, yell "getty-up." They moved slow. Mutt and Jeff they pulled together like Pete and Joe.

Pete and Joe were a little older and more friendly. When they were in the barn lot, they'd walk up to you, hold their heads down for you to pet them. They were 9 years old. Mutt and Jeff were 5, and Dan and Bill were 3. We kept them all together. They got along pretty good. They'd fight and kick each other while playing.

Dad did all the hair and tail trimming, and he put shoes on them. We had gravel roads and they needed shoes. We raised cotton, corn, and watermelons.

We'd be plowing for a month. It was so hot, we'd have to stop and let them rest, get a drink of water. Sometimes it would be 115-120 degrees out in that field, wide open, no trees. We took water to the field with us in a tank that sat in a wagon. We'd unhook the wagon and go back and get equipment. Dad would work a team, and me, and my brother would work a team. Rows were a quarter mile long. We always worked the same field together. We were anxious to get that first 40 acres done.

When we came in from the field, it seemed like it took two hours to pump water for them. They'd drink as fast as I could get that trough full, pumping it.

Dad bought two sulky plows (with seats) in 1939. It took three mules to each plow. We thought we were rich. We farmed with mules until 1944. Dad bought a Super M Farmall. It would plow four rows and plant four rows. We sold all the mules at once. They weren't worth much by then.

 **Bill White was born April 17, 1927, to Hardy and Gerdie White. Hornersville is located about 18 miles southeast of Kennett in Dunklin County. In addition to his twin, White had an older brother and a younger sister. He attended Coldwater School, a three-room school, through the eighth grade. He walked a half-mile to school in knee-deep sand. After leaving the farm in 1948, he worked in shipping and receiving 25 years in St. Louis, retiring from Fisher Body in 1972, after having worked there 10 years. He and his first wife, Ruby, were married 55 years until her death in 2000. He and his wife, Betty, celebrated their 7th anniversary in 2008. "I liked to farm with the mules. I was about 17 when Dad got rid of them. By that time I was tired of walking with them. We were proud to get that tractor," he said.**

I Didn't Like It. It Wasn't No Fun
as told by Pete Snider

Dad had horses and mules. When I was a kid, I farmed with Kate and Jude, and we also had a mule we called ole Diner. She was the one always getting out. She was an ole mare mule, and when she would come in heat, she would jump the fence and get in with the neighbor's horses.

Dad would sic our farm dog, Brownie, after her and she'd come home fast then. Dad got his shotgun out and stood behind a tree. As the dog ran her back across the fence and towards the barn lot, Dad shot her as she ran past him. He just shot her one time. It kept her from doing it again.

Kate and Jude were brown and weighed about 1,100 pounds. Kate was a little bigger than Jude. She was the one we used to drive in the furrow when breaking ground. She was a little stronger.

I was 10 when I started farming with mules. Dad would be at work with me with another team. I broke ground and cultivated with Kate and Jude, and used them to gather corn in the fall. I didn't like it. It wasn't no fun. My legs would hurt, and I would keep on going.

It was boring, and horseflies would be after the mules. They would cause the mules to switch their tails a lot. They would bite me too. Sometimes you could hit a horsefly with one of the lines. The mules would go a little faster when you did that. I would say "gee" and "haw, whoa." and "getty-up." If the mules didn't respond, I'd slap them a little harder with the lines.

Dad and I usually worked together. If he was planting corn with mules, I was harrowing ground. I walked behind a plow and cultivator, and he rode the planter. We'd get out in the field by 7 o'clock and stay until 11:30, come in you'd feed the team, eat your dinner, take a 30-minute nap, and go back to work. Usually we'd quit about sundown, because we had to come in and milk (cows) and feed the hogs.

I would stay with him (work as much) in the summer. In the fall, I'd go to school. I'd get up and feed the mules and hogs, and feed and milk the cows, eat breakfast, go to school, come home, and do it all over again.

When I was 12, Dad bought a used 1020 Farmall tractor. He paid $200 down, and we used it to cut wheat for the neighbors. It would burn out a valve about once a week, and Dad took it back and paid $939 for a new F-20 Farmall.

We used to think we had to plant with mules, because a tractor took a lot more room to turn. Dad used the mules to plant with five years after we got the tractor.

The mules gradually died off. There were six, then four, and then two left. One of them (Kate or Jude) lay down in the lot and died. We had been working them. After they died, we'd pull them to the back of a field in a gully.

We lost our (160 acre) farm in the Depression (1929) to foreclosure. We didn't move, stayed there. We had a little orchard. Mother made a big garden and canned. We had our own meat, and we lived that way.

In the late '30s, we started paying back interest and making payments, and eventually paid it off in the '40s. There was pretty good money made during the war. Farm products sold higher.

 **Pete Snider was born July 24, 1925, to John and Emma Snider. He had 12 siblings and was the middle of five boys. They grew up in Stoddard County 11 miles southwest of Dexter. Snider attended Ivester, a one-room rural school named after his grandfather, for eight years and was graduated from Dexter High School in 1943. He was drafted into the Army in 1944, and after being assigned and trained to be a paratrooper, spent 18 months in Europe during World War II, which included going in as a replacement during the Battle of the Bulge.**

He ran his own Holstein dairy farm for 35 years. "I once milked cows day and night by myself for 13 years in a row," he said. "I tried to milk 30 cows all the time. I didn't do more than that because I also farmed 240 acres." Snider quit the dairy in 1968, and was a Stoddard County commissioner for 10 years. He was married to Georgia 30 years. They divorced. He and his wife, Mabel, have been married 26 years in 2008. "We had a small dairy of 10 cows. I could milk a cow before I went to school. We had an old cow named Bob, because she had a bobtail. I would take an empty Coke bottle out in the lot; and she would let me milk her anywhere, and I would drink the warm milk," he said.

Somebody Would Jerk the Chain and Turn Them Loose
Breaking mules in New Madrid County
as told by Louis Jones

Young mules are hard to break. They were just wild, ran out on the range and came in, in boxcars. It's a wonder I didn't get killed. You had to corral them down, put a bridle on them, just woller with them and finally get them broke down, get a harness on them, turn them loose; get an old mule hooked to a wagon, prop the tongue up on a pole, tie it, put that old mule to the wagon, and try to get the young one around by the traces and hooked up.

Somebody would jerk the chain and turn them loose and let them go. If you could get them circling in the woods and get a log behind that wagon. Well, that evening he was broke. He'd let you take the collar off him.

I had a pair of black mules we called Nig and Coalie. I broke 'em. We used an older mule to break them one at a time. They came from Texas in a boxcar in 1943. They probably weighed 800 or 900 pounds.

They were a fine little team. I guess; I thought they was. I worked them five or six years, worked ground with a 12-inch breaking plow, I still got the two-row John Deere planter. It takes a good pair of mules and a good man to plow 10 acres of cotton a day, one row at a time.

That's the reason I can't hardly walk now. Sometimes when I get off the tractor I go down and just lay there. I bought this tractor (Jones was interviewed while seated on a John Deere tractor). It's a 1967 model, bought it new. It's been overhauled three times and still has the same crankshaft. That was the best tractor ever made, a 4020.

I've been kicked (by mules) a few times, hurt me, but didn't break any bones, right in the side; it hurt, had them hooked up to something. They were gentle and would let me walk up and pet them.

We'd go to work at 6 o'clock in the morning , work 'till 11:30, come in to the barn. We'd feed the mules, then eat dinner, and at 1 o'clock we'd go back and get the mules and work till 6.

Me, and my dad came on this 400-acre farm in 1943. We had 12 head of mules and two horses. Worked it all with two-mule breaking plows, planted it with a two-row planter. Men worked for a dollar a day. We raised about all cotton, maybe 300 acres. Cotton was our cash crop. We only raised enough corn to feed the mules, the livestock.

At one time there were six houses on this farm and six families made a living on this farm. They sharecropped. Workers would come and go. We didn't try to keep them. They'd do what they wanted to. If they didn't want to work, they'd leave. And lot of them did. They were coming and a going.

 Louis F. Jones was born July 27, 1924, to E.D. and Thelma May Henry Jones. He has one sister seven years younger. He was born and raised five miles southwest of New Madrid and has farmed there all of his life. He attended Dawson school, a one-room school three miles down the road, and was graduated from the eighth grade in 1939. Jones rode a horse for two years to high school, at New Madrid and Scott streets. He was drafted into the Army during his junior year, and was released about a month later due to a rupture, which Jones had corrected later. He married Dorothy Cobb in 1948 at age 24. She died in 2003. In 2009, Louis resided on the farm helping his son, Tony, with farm work.

Somehow That Harrow Got Standing On End
as told by Naomi Ross

When I was growing up, Daddy grew corn and when gathering it, we had what we called a down row; the row the mules and wagon would go over. I was 11 or 12 when I started driving the mules. I would drive them 20 feet or so, stop them, then get down, and pick corn from the down row, while my mom and dad each picked two rows. Once the row was picked, I would jump back up in the wagon, grab the lines, and drive them further up the row again.

Daddy had six mules. I would hold their reins, while Daddy trimmed their hooves. Sam was more gentle. I wasn't afraid of him. I was afraid of the rest of them. I was even afraid of cows.

I tried harrowing when I was 12 (1942) with Sam and Toby. It was my dad's idea. He didn't have any sons, and he needed help. I got to the end of the row and tried to turn them around, and somehow that harrow got standing on end, so I just stood there and cried.

Daddy saw me and came stomping across the field and told me to go to the house, and he took over. I didn't do anymore mule farming, but that didn't get me out of choppin cotton.

I always had to pump water and put out feed for the mules and cows. I remember how boring it was to stand there and pump water. Kids don't want to be still.

I remember the first tractor Daddy bought in 1942, a new B Farmall. He was very concerned if it would do as good of a job as a team.

 **Naomi Ross was born Jan. 18, 1930, to Hiram and Daisy Ross. She had two older half-sisters who had left the house by the time she was born. Her father farmed five miles southwest of Kennett in Dunklin County. She attended Two-Mile School, a three-room school, through the eighth grade, then attended Senath High School graduating in 1947. She worked at the Bank of Kennett for four years out of high school, and married Jack Rollins, Sr., in December 1949. She was a housewife for many years, raising four children. The couple divorced in 1970. "Daddy said I wasn't a good cotton picker because I ginned it. I couldn't stand to put leaves in with the cotton. I would pick 100 pounds, and my older half-sister could get 400 pounds. I hated farm work," she said.**

He Got a Stalk, Put a Match to It, and Stuck It Under Their Tails
Mule Farming in Pemiscot County
as told by Ancil Robertson

I was 10 when I first started working with mules. My dad had four mules and two horses. The oldest team, Red and Nell, were over 20 years old. My dad had them when I was born (1923), and still had them when I went to war in 1942. He sold them during the war.

Red and Nell were brownish. Nell was reddish brown. They were both medium-sized mare mules. We knew they were old, and we never pushed them. Nell was real easy going. Red was the kind to spook a little bit. Even though they were old, they would run away at the drop of a hat.

The other two mules were named Tricksie and Fritzie. They were about the same size, but younger than Red and Nell, and they could work a little faster. My two older brothers worked them, while me, and my younger brother worked Red and Nell.

We had two one-row cultivators, each with a seat on the tongue. One of us would sit and drive the mules, while the other one walked behind guiding the cultivator. We kept a little toolbox on the cultivator. If a plow would get loose, we'd tighten them up.

Dad would mix tobacco and sorghum and put it in a RC bottle, and feed it to the mules to get rid of bots (botfly worms). He would tie their heads to a rope and pull their head up, so he could pour it down. He broke Red's teeth trying to get it down her. Ole Red couldn't keep her head still. Ole Nell was a little older, and she would drink it down.

When working them, they would get their shoulders sore with the collars, and it would get raw. I felt so sorry for them. We would put powder on it.

When cultivating, my brother and I would take turns. When the other would get tired, we'd trade. I preferred riding. Because walking you'd get a big ole vine with roots that would jerk you up. I'd have lines around my back, and it would jerk your back.

Red and Nell were good about getting to the end of a row. They would turn around and head back down the next row. They would balk sometimes. I had a cousin who had a team of mules balk while they were gathering corn. He got a stalk, put a match to it, and stuck it under their tails. They ran off and tore the wagon up.

We used all four mules to a disk. One time we had them tied up and someone shot off a firecracker and away they went. We thought the disk was going to tear them up, but it didn't. They stopped after about 100 yards.

We would get up before daylight and feed the mules. They had their own stall. They wouldn't eat unless they were in the one they were used to eating in. After breakfast, we would curry them down to get cockleburs out, harness them, and go to work. We'd work from 6 to 12 o'clock. Dad would let us know when it was time to come in. We'd take an hour off for lunch, and then work from 1 to 6 at night. Dad would say, "Let's go blow awhile," and we'd take morning and afternoon water breaks.

When working behind the levee, going to the field those mules would walk through water four or five feet deep on the other side of the levee. We'd take our lunch. While we had lunch, the mules would stand in the (Mississippi) river. It kept their hooves soft and probably made them feel better.

I didn't care too much for it (farming with mules). They were too slow for me. I'd have plenty of energy, and want to move, not follow behind them all day. They had one slow gait. You'd whip them, and they would move a little bit, then go right back where they were.

They never kicked or tried to bite. I've had my bare feet mashed a few times, when they were stomping their feet to get rid of flies while I was harnessing them.

I would rather chop cotton. I didn't like picking cotton. I started taking a row by myself when I was 10. I didn't do very good at picking cotton. A good cotton picker could pick 400 to 500 pounds a day.

When my older brothers left home for the war, I started working with the younger mules, Fritzie and Tricksie. I think they were 15 years old. They were faster and stronger. My younger brothers took over Red and Nell.

We never shoed any of them. We would take a chisel and hammer and cut their hooves off. Then we would take a big file and smooth it off.

One time my young sister came out to the field, and my older brother put her on one of the mules. Then he slapped Fritzie, and she fell off backwards. My granddad saw her fall off and came running out. I think if she had been hurt, he would have killed my brother.

 **Charles Ancil Robertson was born Sept. 4, 1923, to Charles A. and Ada Robertson. He had two older brothers and one younger sister. The family farmed 60 acres in the 1930s and 1940s in what is now part of the southern edge of Caruthersville. Robertson attended elementary school in Caruthersville and was graduated from Caruthersville High School in 1941. He served in the Army Air Corps from 1942 to 1944 and in the Merchant Marines 1944-1946 in the Philippines.**

He worked as a car mechanic five years, and as a service manager for a Buick-Cadillac-Pontiac-GMC dealership in Caruthersville 30 years. He and his wife, Mary Alice, celebrated 67 years of marriage in 2008. "I have been in the American Legion longer (since 1943) than anyone else in Missouri," he said. In February 2008, at the time of the interview, Robertson was managing Robertson's Garage in Caruthersville. Robertson said when he was 12 or 13, one of the old mules was reaching through the fence, eating some flowers and a big boy walking along the sidewalk, ran up and grabbed the mule's head in an arm lock and pummeled him repeatedly. A couple of years later when Robertson was bigger, he saw the kid in town, confronted him about it, and Robertson said he did the same thing to him.

He Would Have His Head Down Almost Touching the Ground
as told by William Cato

From the time I was 9 (1949) to the time I was 12, I spent six to eight weeks in the summer helping my best friend, Bobby Singleton, farm with his dad's mules.

Sometimes during school, I would take the bus to his place, and we would farm two or three hours after dinner, and on Saturday. During the summer, I would ride my bike or walk out there and come home in the evenings. Sometimes I spent the night, and he would spend the night with me. But when he did, he had to get up early to go home and do chores. He was my best friend. If you saw one of us, you saw the other.

They were medium in size, brown mules. One was nearsighted. He wouldn't work by himself. You couldn't use him to pull a garden plow. He only worked as a team. Bobby's dad farmed 50 acres, mostly row crops, beans and cotton, grass and hay. We plowed and cultivated with them and used them to cut hay and rake. We stacked the hay with pitchforks.

When it came quitting time, it didn't matter if they were in the middle of the field, they would turn and go to the barn, where they each would be given one ear of corn, some oats and hay.

Bobby and I worked the mules together. He would harness one, and I would harness one. One of us would drive them, and the other would walk behind, and we'd talk. His dad helped occasionally, but most of the time he was doing some other farm work. We were always under his watchful eye. He made sure we didn't mistreat his mules.

When we worked them all day, at lunchtime we brought them to the house, and took their bridles and harness off. They would run in the lot. After lunch when we came back out to where the harness hung and grabbed the harness, here they'd come. They were ready to go back to work.

On Sundays, we took the mules to the creek that ran in the middle of the farm. We'd put the mules in the water, and wash them down, clean them up. And ride them the half-mile back to the house. That was the whole thing. That ride made the whole weekend worthwhile. We'd get to ride the mules.

We jumped on them bareback. I rode the nearsighted one. He would trail the other one. He would have his head down almost touching the ground, where he could see the ground. If Bobby would run the other one, he was right beside him, almost touching each other. I would have both hands on his mane trying to hold on. At times he got to running a pretty good speed. Then Bobby would stop (his mule), and the other one would stop——- I'd go flying out across there. This happened several times. Sometimes I would belly flop. Sometimes I would go rolling. It was always on plowed ground. I never got hurt. Bobby just did it to watch me roll in the dirt in front of a mule.

His parents had rules. After we got through working, we took the mules and put them up. We put their harness up, and gave them their ear of corn and hay. Then we fed the chickens, and went to the house for dinner. I remember his mom saying, "Did you feed the chickens?" If we said "no," she'd say, "Get up and feed the chickens, then you can eat."

In the evening we would set by coal oil lamps and do homework from school. I enjoyed it, because I was away from Qulin. I remember it was fun.

 **William Cato, Jr., was born Jan. 13, 1940, to William and Lorenia Cato. He had two sisters and one brother. The farm he worked on was located three miles southeast of Qulin in Butler County. After graduating from Qulin High School in 1957, Cato joined the Army and didn't move back to Qulin until the fall of 2007. Cato spent 21 years in the Army in nuclear weapons, retiring as a sergeant in 1980. He then obtained a law enforcement certificate from Southwest Texas State University at San Marcos, Texas, and spent 12 years as a police officer in Guadalupe County, Texas. Ella, his wife of 29 years, died in 2007. Cato said when he was in the sixth grade, Bobby Singleton's dad sold the farm, and the family moved away. He never saw Bobby again. He found out in 2006, after Bobby had died, that the family had moved to Greenville, about 45 miles north of Qulin. Cato could not recall the mules' names. Cato was interviewed February 27, 2008. He died August 30, 2010.**

My Older Sister, Loeta, and I Had to Put in the Crops
as told by Curtis Ashby

When I was 11 (1944) my dad was down in his back that year, and my older sister, Loeta, and I had to put in the crops.

We had two teams of mules, Kit and Kate, and Nig and Coalie. Coalie was black, the others were brownish black. I worked Kit and Kate. They were young female mules. They were good sized. I had to stand on a manger to throw the harness on them. You didn't have to hardly have any lines. You'd holler, "gee" and they'd get over there.

I harnessed all the mules and hooked them up. We had two breaking plows. Loeta, who was two years older than me, would go first plowing and I would follow. I was barefooted breaking ground. I remember Dad wasn't out there, just me and my sister.

We raised cotton and corn. We put in about 35 acres, 12 acres of cotton, rest corn. We raised a lot of hay. Dad had eight or 10 head of cattle and a lot of hogs.

If I got hung up on a stump and couldn't get it out. I had to take a chain, and unhook the mules, put them at the back of the breaking plow, and pulled it out that way to get it out.

If we got in trouble Dad would come out. We were plowing on the side of a hill one time in the spring and my team went belly down. In other words, they went completely down. It was soft and they just went down. We had to go get Dad. He helped us get them out. He let them rest a while, took their harness off, except for the bridles. They finally got out themselves.

After we got the plowing done, we hooked on to a disk. One would disk and the other would harrow. We had a one-row planter. Everything we had was walk behind. Both of us planted. The rows weren't the straightest.

One of the mules, believe it was ole Kate, when you'd hook her to a tongue of a wagon, she'd nip you on the arm or shoulder. It wouldn't bring the blood, but it sure would pinch hard.

I remember one morning, I was probably about 12, I was hooking her up and I wasn't in the best of mood that morning. When she bit me, I grabbed her ear and pulled it down, and I was chewing on that. Then all at once she hit my head with her head. I saw stars for five minutes. It didn't knock me down, but I saw lots of stars.

The workday would start at daylight when I done the feeding. I fed the mules hay and corn. Mom and I milked the cows. I milked three and she milked two. We had one jersey, most of them were white face. We used a cream separator. She'd sell the cream. Milk, no one wanted it, so we'd give it to the hogs.

Mom always fixed breakfast. We killed lots of hogs. We always had salt pork. We canned our own sausage, put it in jars. We always had sausage or some kind of pork for breakfast. She'd make biscuits three times a day. We'd go to lunch when the sun was directly over our head. We'd go to the house, un-harness the teams, and feed them corn and hay while we ate. An hour later we'd go back and work until just about sundown. We'd bring the mules in and feed them, then I would start milking cows.

I remember Dad got kicked by a mule one time. He had them in the barn. They were separated where they couldn't get to one another. He went around the back of one with some hay, and it penned him against the barn and kicked him. He got a pitchfork and stuck her with it. That's the only time I ever heard my dad say a dirty word. He said, "You dirty bitch."

Me, and my dad worked with mules until 1950 when I was 16. I never was afraid of them. If they didn't get over when I'd holler "gee" or "haw." I'd holler a little louder and they'd step over then, either right or left. Dad never wanted me to get them too hot, when you're out there in the hot summer. Dad said when they'd start alternating moving their ears back and forth you knew they were getting tired. I never did have to stop them. They'd just keep on going. We never had shoes on them. I don't ever remember them getting sick. Dad never liked for me to ride them. A lot of times, I'd jump on one and ride it to the field. He'd always get on to me, "Don't ride them."

I remember one time it was raining and I took the mules from the field and Dad said, "Why'd you come in for?" I said, "It's raining." He said the next time unless it was pouring straight down, I didn't need to come in. A few weeks later it started raining hard, and it was coming down sideways. I got soaking wet and kept breaking ground. When I came to the house Dad said, "Why didn't you come in from the rain?" I said, "You told me not to come in unless it was coming straight down."

We cut our own wood from our timber. We cut wood all the time because Mom burned wood in her cook stove, and in the wintertime we had a wood heater. If Dad couldn't keep us busy cutting wood, we'd cut posts.

For a winter or two, Dad would go to the logging woods and work for someone else. On Fridays after school, I'd walk down there. It was only about two and a half miles. I might find him down in the woods loading logs. One time we were riding on a wagon load of logs, and we got about halfway to the mill, and Nig and Coalie got stuck. They started seesawing. They wouldn't both pull at the same time.

Dad said, "You stay up on the wagon and hold the lines. They can pull that. I know they can." He got out and got a log chain and whipped them a couple of times. They squatted down and pulled that out, no trouble at all.

In 1950, when I was 17, Dad bought an Allis Chalmers tractor, a one row job. I didn't like it at all. I liked riding the tractor, but it broke down so much. He kept the mules for a couple of years and used them for logging. Then he got a larger tractor.

 **Curtis Ashby was born Oct. 29, 1933, to Amos and Lucy Ashby. His mother had 15 children but lost three of them as infants. He was the 14th child and had a brother six years younger and one six years older and two sisters in between. His dad owned 100 acres one mile south and four miles east of Broseley in Butler County. Curtis attended Slough School, a one-room school, through the sixth grade.**

At age 16, he moved to Michigan where he started working in a laundry room at a hospital. He worked at General Motors for 30 years, retiring in 1982. He worked 10 years on an assembly line, and the last 16 years as an automotive electrician. In 2008, he and his wife, Georgia, celebrated their 55th wedding anniversary. "The reason I didn't get past the sixth grade is because I didn't get to go much. Dad would keep me home to work," Ashby said. "I didn't get enough time in to pass the grades. He wouldn't let me bring a book home. He said I come home to work.

When I decided to leave home at 16, Dad said, "I thought you would be my first son to be a farmer." I said, "You have one more after me, but it won't be me." I had a brother and a sister in Michigan. I got a job that winter. The next spring (1951) Mom wrote me a letter and said for me to come home and help get the crops in. Dad told me if I came back I could have my pick of 10 acres and plant anything I wanted and it would be mine. I picked the 10 acres I wanted and planted it all in cotton. I finished up on July 24th, when I laid by the crops and went back to Michigan. I came home to visit in September, and the cotton looked like it was shriveling up. I told Dad he could have the crop and the 10 acres. He said, "But that's yours." I said, "All I had to do was make a living for myself. You can have that 10 acres. I don't want it." When they started picking cotton, Mom wrote me a letter that said, "Son, your cotton is doing real good. It's getting a little over a bale an acre." That was something unusual at that time. I told her, "You guys need it more than I do. I'm getting a check every week."

I Had Two Older Sisters, and We Took
Turns Harrowing
as told by Willie Velma Whitney

All I was allowed to do with mules was harrow the ground. I thought it was fun. I was 9 years old, and I guess I thought I was pretty big to get to work the mules. I was the youngest one working at that time. I only did the harrowing one summer for maybe two weeks.

I had two older sisters, Ora Lee, and Wandara, and we took turns harrowing. After I would make a round, each of my sisters would make a round. The rows were almost a quarter of a mile long and sometimes they seemed longer. The harrow was wide and covered three rows. When I was really enjoying the harrowing, it seemed as if the round was over before I knew it.

My older brother, Charles, was overseeing our work. I think he must have made the harrowing resemble as much fun as Tom Sawyer did the painting of a fence. He would always take his turn, and then watch us to see that we were harrowing correctly. Daddy would be working in a field nearby, with our other mule team. He worked the middle buster and the cultivator.

Our black mules were named Rodie and Kate. They were good gentle mules. All I had to do was to guide them as I held the lines in my hands. When I would get to the end of the rows, I would pull back on the lines and say, "whoa." Then I would say, "gee," or "haw" depending on which way I wanted to go.

Since it was a mile or more to the field, we'd sometimes ride the mules to the field. Often, we would put a bridle on Rodie or Kate and ride around the pasture. To get on a mule, we would lead it to the steps at the fence. Dad built really sturdy steps over the fence so that we could carry buckets of milk into the house without having to open the gate.

Each day as we went to work in the fields, my sisters and I would leave home wearing overalls, bonnets, and long-sleeved shirts. We soon pushed our bonnets to the back of our heads and rolled up our sleeves. The sun was so hot that we would get sunburned, but it didn't take long for us to get a tan.

We went to the fields early and came home late in the afternoon. Then we all had to share in doing the chores. We had to feed (often mixing cottonseed and sorghum) and milk the cows, feed the horses and mules, pump water for the cattle, feed the pigs, grind the chops, feed the chickens, and gather the eggs.

We also worked with baling the hay. There was a stationary baler near the barn. My job was to poke the wires through. We used Rodie and Kate when it was time to gather the corn. Because I was the youngest, I picked the down row. As we went down the rows, I rode the coupling pole at the rear of the wagon. The others walked along the sides to gather two rows. With each round, we gathered the corn from 10 rows. My brother usually took care of guiding the mules.

Sorghum making time was really a fun time on the farm. After the cane was cut, the mules would pull a wagonload to the mill. The mules were used to walk around and around the mill to squeeze the sweet juice from the cane. The juice was poured into long hot pans to boil and make the molasses. All of the Carey and Waddell children (there were also eight of the Waddells) loved taking a piece of cane and eating the hot molasses.

I started chopping and picking cotton when I was about 6 years old. Mom always made the little ones cotton sacks from the tow sacks. While we were small, we received 50 cents a day for chopping cotton. We would make a lot more money picking cotton. It was great when we were paid $3 dollars a hundred for picking cotton. I could make (as I grew older) $8 or $9 dollars a day. We used our cotton-picking money to buy school clothes and to spend at the Mississippi County Fair at Blytheville. We would order our first new clothes ready made and hope the order would come in time for us to wear them to the fair. Then we would study the Sears Roebuck catalog to order pretty dress material. Our mother made us beautiful clothes. Sometimes she entered dresses in the fair and would win the coveted blue ribbons.

 Willie Velma Whitney was raised in the Black Water Community in Mississippi County, Arkansas, which is about 16 miles south of Dunklin County. Her parents, W.W. and Opal Caery, raised four boys and four girls. Willie had one older brother and two older sisters. She attended Black Water School through the 10th grade and was graduated from Manila High School in 1946. She married Guy M. Whitney, Sr. They lived on a farm in the Black Water community until Guy had served his time in the Navy. Then they moved to the college campus at Walnut Ridge.

Willie earned an A.A. degree at Southern Baptist College at Walnut Ridge and bachelor and master's degrees at Arkansas State University at Jonesboro majoring in English. Her husband was a minister for 40 years throughout northeast Arkansas. The couple raised five children: Judith Ann; Guy, Jr.;, Marv; Dawn; and Leah. Willie taught high school English for 48 years at various locations, including Cooter, and Arbyrd, Missouri. In Arkansas she taught at Oak Grove, England, Piggott, 15 years at Rector, Leachville, Knobel, De Soto at Helena, Manila, and Marvel. She retired in 1994 but was still substitute teaching in 2009. Guy Whitney died in 1991. "Dad owned 40 and was farming 80 acres when I worked the mules. Later on it was 120, then he got up to a section of land, but he didn't farm with mules at that time," she said.

IV. Robert "Uncle Bob" Boyers Family of Butler County
Uncle Bob Boyers Brand Was a Big "B" on the Right Hip

Robert J. "Uncle Bob" Boyers was born March 4, 1864, and died Nov. 11, 1944. He married Cassie Miller July 6, 1884 and the couple raised seven children, sons Chester, Hannibal, Byrd, and Ira, and daughters, Effie, Agnes and Katy. Cassie died in June 1931 at age 65. Uncle Bob married Maggie Nichols in May 1934 when he was 70*. She was 36. This union produced four children. Nichols had worked as a housekeeper for Boyers. She had three children before she married him.

Bob and Cassie Boyers started farming 80 acres in the Lone Hill Community, and over several years expanded their land to 623 acres.

Robert Joseph Boyers and
Cassie (Miller) Boyers at their
home in the Lone Hill area.

At some point, probably 1912, they purchased a 300-plus-acre farm in the Hvam area near Coon Island, located about eight miles south of Poplar Bluff and about eight miles northeast of Neelyville. They moved there in or after 1915. One reason he moved to this farm was because it had open range, whereas the Lone Hill area didn't. Kelly Boyers said his grandpa moved cattle back and forth between the two farms for 20 years or longer. The farms were about 15 miles apart.

At Hvam the livestock was turned out on open range. Each owner had their own brands, ear notches, etc. for identification. Boyers' brand was a big "B" on the right hip. His cow bells had a large "B" on the leather strap. Boyers was believed to be the first person to bring Hereford cattle to Butler County.

Cassie Miller Boyers and her sisters inherited the 220-acre Ezekiel Miller farm located eight miles west of Poplar Bluff with the understanding they could buy each other out. Bob Boyers eventually owned the whole farm and he and Maggie moved to the Flatwoods Place, part of the Miller Farm, in 1943. This is where he spent his final days. When he died, Boyers owned the three farms plus some other tracts that totaled about 1,400 acres.

The following is from an interview with John Barker, son of John and Effie Boyers Barker:

Grandfather Bob lived on Coon Island (Hvam). They had open range there. Everything was pretty much in the woods. There was very little cleared land. He didn't farm but 20 to 40 acres. They raised cattle, hogs, and mules. He always had 150 to 200 head of cattle, and they run on this open range.

He (Grandpa) always rode a bay mule. He could trust that mule. He went to the woods a lot of times on weekends, on a Sunday afternoon. He liked to go in the woods by himself. Sometimes he would be gone three or four hours.

He had a certain spot he went to, to leave salt. And that's where they (cattle) would come to for salt. He'd either ring a bell or call the cattle. If he saw a baby calf that was having problems keeping up, he'd get down off his mule and catch the calf, put it on the saddle in front of him, and haul that calf to where he wanted it to go.

In the wintertime, Grandpa would put a beef up in a pen and fatten it out. Of course they didn't have refrigerators, no ice. He had a large barn with a hay mound 30 to 35 foot high and a hayfork. He'd kill the beef. He'd dress it but wouldn't cut it up. He'd take the beef to the hay mound, run the hayfork down and tie it to the beef, and get a mule to pull this beef to the top of the barn. He'd leave it hang there. It would freeze and when he wanted some beef, he'd go down there, lower it down, and cut off a piece. He'd just cut off a big chunk. He'd get his mule to pull it back up to the top and let it hang there.

In winter months, my dad got unbroken mules from grandfather. I was riding in a wagon one time with my dad when they (young team) run. You can't get a mule to hurt themselves. He'd (Dad) get one check line and pull them into a fence or something. Them mules would stop before they got there. They would not hurt themselves. A horse is different. They will.

There are many family stories about Uncle Bob. A few are as follows:

Grandpa was driving stock from Lone Hill traveling down Roxie Road and Maud Street to J.R. Hogg's Market at 16th and Maud (Poplar Bluff). A woman, who lived at Roxie and Maud, came out and said to Grandpa, "Have you seen my cow?" and described the cow. Grandpa told her "Yes, and she since has had a calf." And then ordered them cut out of the bunch and put in the woman's pen.–Kelly Boyers

******

One time he (Bob) drove some big steers to a buyer at Taft. The steers with their horns wrecked the scales. The buyer and Dad both agreed on the weight of a medium-sized steer, and used the weight as an average of the rest.–Ira Boyers.

Kelly Boyers at Hvam farm in 2010.

******

One time when Uncle Bobby was moving stock between the Lone Hill farm and Hvam farm, Cane Creek was out at the Frick Bridge (County Road 472 off of M Highway). Some of the cattle crossed the bridge, some the creek. Uncle Bobby was on his horse "Old Tim." The horse reared and he and the horse ended up in the creek. He stayed on him while the horse swam to the other side.–Ed Nichols.

******

One time a new employee kept pulling a team of mules out to a shade tree to rest them. Uncle Bobby went hotfooting across the field and asked him what was going on. The man said, "I'm shading the mules." Uncle Bobby told him, "Push them mules. That harness will fit another team."–Ed Nichols.

******

One time Grandpa followed a neighbor's dogs home that had been in his sheep. The neighbor denied the dogs did it. Grandpa said, "Call them out from under the porch and check their teeth for wool." The neighbor obliged, then proceeded to club the dogs to death.–Kelly Boyers.

******

Grandpa was in Harviell one day. When he was ready to go home a boy named, Jimmy, was in his wagon. He had run away from a circus that had been in town. Grandpa took him home with him and raised him for a while. One day he was gone, the same way he was found. –Ira Boyers.

******

He (Bob) had a load of (railroad) ties to take to Harviell. He asked Grandma Cassie if she needed anything from town. She said, "Yes, coffee." When he returned she said, "Bob, did you get the coffee?" He said, "No Cassie, I didn't. The money (for the ties) came out even dollars. You'll have to boil the grounds."–Bob Boyers, grandson.

******

Robert and Cassie Boyers deeded land for the present day Revival Time Tabernacle Church at Lone Hill. –Kelly Boyers.

******

When Grandpa was elderly, a neighbor, Acel Wilson, observed him cutting sprouts and said, "You're not able. Why don't you go home" and helped him on his horse. Later in the day while heading home, there Grandpa was. He had stopped at another field and was cutting sprouts. When he died, the doctor said he was just wore out. – Ira Boyers as recalled by Kelly Boyers.

******

Uncle Byrd got after Grandpa about him having all those kids when he was in his 70s and Grandpa told him the reason was "She (Maggie) doesn't nurse them." Which translates she can have kids sooner. –Kelly Boyers.

******

Dad had two women pregnant at the same time. He chose my mother to marry. Grandpa Boyers paid the court $600 and my dad had to pay him back. The girl's father used the $600 to buy a 40-acre farm. Fifty years later (1974) my dad bought the farm back for $250 an acre or $10,000, and gave it to the illegitimate son. Recently, 2009, that same farm sold for $100,000. My mom didn't resent my Dad's other son. He showed her a lot of respect. –Kelly Boyers.

******

One time Grandpa, Ira, and Byrd delivered a young team of mules to a buyer, and met him at a farm business at Pine and Broadway (where presently Myrtle's Café is). He had quoted the man $400 for the pair. While the man looked at the mules, Uncle Byrd overheard him say under his breath, "$450 is a lot of money for a young team of mules." Uncle Byrd slips around and tells Grandpa the man thinks the deal is for $450. Grandpa let him shell out the money. When the man left with them, he was riding one and leading one heading east on Pine Street. With the extra $50 Grandpa bought Ira a new saddle, and Byrd new harness. –Ira Boyers as recalled by Kelly Boyers.

******

Great-grandpa Granville Boyers and his two boys, Robert, and his older brother, John A., moved from Tennessee to Missouri in the mid-1870s and they camped at Cane Creek, where he died. John A. was born in 1861 and Grandpa was born in 1864. The boys were adopted out by neighbors. Supposedly the reason they moved was John A. was involved with the Jesse James' gang in Tennessee. I asked my dad, Ira, about this one time and he told me, "The old folks wouldn't talk about it."–Kelly Boyers.

******

The family and neighbor kids would get together at Grandpa's on Sunday evenings. He would let us ride calves in the long hallway of the big barn (at Hvam). I remember being under 5 years old and I was on the fence of the old jack's stall, putting my leg over him but a little uneasy about getting on, and Grandpa says to me in a quiet tone of voice, "Go ahead and get on. He won't buck." –Kelly Boyers.

******

When he died, I was 10. We called him "Pa." I remember being with him one time when he lanced a goat's shoulder that had swelled up. When we went to town the kids always rode in the back of the wagon. It seemed like it would take forever to get there. We would take cream and chickens to town. Momma (Maggie) canned and always had a big garden. She would help with the milking. She would fix dinner for him and all the hired hands. There was a bunkhouse off of the back porch where some hired hands would stay. He had cows every place. My older sister (Roberta) always rode in front of him on his horse ole "Tim" when he went to see about his cattle on open range. He called her "Tommy." They would be gone a half a day or longer. The day he died us kids were at school. He was sick and had walked outside to go to the outside john. On the way back he hollered for her and fell in the yard. A man helped her get him back in the house.–Bobbie Joe Boyers Waddell.

*According to Butler County records, R. J. Boyers and Maggie Nichols'
Application for License to Marry lists him as 60 when they were married in
May 1934. Handwritten across the top of the license is "Do not publish." According to Bobby Joe, her mother was born Dec. 12, 1899, and died Dec. 31,
1981. Her mother married William Sims probably in the early 1950s. Bobby
Joe was born in December 1935, and her older sister, Roberta, was born in December 1934. Roberta Conner was contacted and said, "I always went with
him. I was a tomboy. I used to ride goats." She didn't recall any details about
the open-range rides (author).*

He Would Trade a Pair of Mules for Forty Acres
Uncle Bobby Part II
as told by Ed Nichols

Robert (Uncle Bobby) Boyers had four sons, Chester, Hannibal,
Byrd and Ira. Chester had a son named Robert, Byrd had sons named
Ben and Meredith, and a daughter named Betty, and Ira had sons
named R.J. and Kelly.

My mom, Maggie, married Robert Boyers in 1934 when I was 9.
He must have been in his 60s. He had two farms, one in the bottoms
in the Hvam area and one in the hills. We lived in the bottom. All he
wanted to do was work. Mom wouldn't let him work on Sundays.
When I was 9, he made me a board that fit on a harrow for me to sit
on. He taught me how to guide mules.

He started me out with an old and gentle mule team, Blue and Jet.
They must have been 20 years old. I think they more or less followed
other mules. There must have been 10 mule teams working in the
fields. There were mules everywhere you looked.

I worked Blue and Jet three summers. Uncle Bobby said they be-
longed to me. The mules knew more than I knowed. We'd start out
early in the morning. Blue and Jet would start braying at 11. Uncle
Bobby told me to keep on driving them, that Blue would bray again.
At 11:30 she would start braying again, and pretty soon I would hear
Mom ringing the bell.

Uncle Bobby kept some mules so old they would die. He would drag them to the woods and bury them. Back then mules were really something. He would trade a pair of mules for 40 acres. He did that several times.

At Hvam there was free range. Uncle Bobby would breed 15 to 20 mares to the two jacks we had, and then he would turn the mares loose in them free-range woods. To catch the mares in the spring, he would ride out with a bag of salt on the saddle horn and call them. It wasn't long before they would start coming. When the mares came in, they would all have mule colts.

Some of the colts would be 3 or 4 and had never had a hand on them. They were so wild; it would take two or three hired hands to round up the older colts. They had to choke them down to harness them. They would try to eat you up. He would put a wild mule between two gentle mules, tie them to each mule. Sometimes he would have them wear harness for two or three days. That would gentle them down. That's the way he broke those mules.

Our hired hands were Bill Brown (main one), Jim Sims, brothers Otis and Herbert Lake and Charlie Franklin. Uncle Bobby owned 400 acres. I would see 10 teams working. They would be in different fields plowing, disking or harrowing.

I worked the gentle mules. Each hired hand had their own mule team to work. Bill had a certain pair of mules he would drive to town on Saturdays on dirt roads. Bill worked a pair of mules called Buck and Jet, a big red mule and a black mule. The big mule had knots on his knees. He was buck-kneed. Bill was the only one who worked those mules. He would work them all day, and think he had them worked down. He would unhook them in the field and walk them to the barn holding the lines behind them. When they reached the pasture gate that led to the barn, located about a quarter of a mile from the barn, they would take off running, dragging Bill until he would finally let go.

He was called "Uncle Bobby" because he was well liked by his neighbors. If they would lose a mule or a team, he would tell them to come over and they would get a pair of mules to work. In the spring people would come and say, "Uncle Bobby, I have a mare or two in heat, what you going to charge me?" He would say $5 or $10. He would breed their mares to one of our jacks, and they would say they couldn't pay until the colt was born. He would never see any money. He never would mention it to them.

Uncle Bobby had a favorite pair of mules, Buck and Jet, a bay and a black. He put nice harness on them. They were so fat you could roll eggs down their backs. They were good looking mules, and everybody in the county liked them. He sure knew how to drive a team, but he didn't know how to drive anything else.

We always had a smokehouse full of hog meat. We ate hog meat, beans and potatoes. We always had plenty to eat, but there wasn't no difference to it. We lived in a house that had no insulation. We had two wood stoves. I slept in a feather bed. We would get up early in the morning and feed the mules and horses. By the time we had all that done, Mom would have breakfast ready. Uncle Bobby wouldn't eat beef. He said beef cattle were meant to be sold.

We'd feed cattle all winter. We had lots of hay and corn. That's all we ever raised. The Black River would flood. One time after the water had gone down, Uncle Bobby and I rode back in there to look for cattle. We found several cattle, and several drowned ones too. Uncle Bobby always said, "If you got them, you're bound to lose some. If you don't have them, ain't going to lose them."

Uncle Bobby built a horse-and-mule barn on the Miller (hill) farm. It's still standing. He always got up at 3 or 4 a.m. One morning he didn't get up. Someone stopped by and said some cattle were loose on the Miller farm. He wasn't feeling well, and asked me and another boy, who was staying there, to take a horse or two and do the best we could. By the time we got back, he had died. Mom had a big sale after he died. Bobby didn't know how to drive a pickup truck. Mules were all he ever knowed.

Ed Nichols was born on Sept. 9, 1924, to Albert and Maggie Nichols. He never knew his father. He had two younger brothers (now deceased) and two younger half-sisters. He attended Pleasant Ridge School in southern Butler County through the sixth grade. He was self-employed for 28 years in the trash and truck-

ing business, retiring in the mid-1990s. He and his wife, Mildred, had been married many years when she died in the late 1990s. In a January 2007 interview, Nichols said, "I liked living back then. He had me plowing with a double shovel when I got older. I've been fooling with mules and horses all my life, sold an old jenny yesterday." In a follow-up telephone call in March 2008, Nichols, 83, still owned a mare. "I mostly look at her. I'll keep her around," he said.

We Farmed 150 Acres With Seven Mule Teams
as told by R.J. Boyers

We had mules because we could work them from early dawn to late in the evening. They didn't get tired and didn't eat nearly as much as a horse. A lot of people didn't have mules and I don't know why.

We only had mares to raise mules, and we kept a jack. My dad, Ira, always said a horse could step on a corn stalk and injure themselves, and they could do a lot of damage when turning equipment at the end of a row. Horses will get hot, mules don't. A horse will get hot and can't work anymore. A mule can go all day. Horses have big feet and are clumsy. Mules can get around better.

We got used to the mules. Sometimes we would work the mares, but they would give out and we'd have to go get the mules to replace them. We always used mules even when we went to town in a wagon. We teamed up young mules by which two got along the best. We used Jim and Zin when going to town, which was about 10 miles from our farm and took about three hours one way.

When I was 10, we farmed with seven teams of mules. I would cook dinner. Mom was in Mount Vernon sanitarium with TB. The only cure for TB was rest and she couldn't get that at home. She was at Mount Vernon twice, once in the 1940s and again in the 1950s. I had four sisters and four brothers. My older sisters had already left home by the time I was 10. Dad said, "Jay, you're the cook." I would pick blackberries and make cobblers, go down the creek and fish, cooked biscuits and gravy with meat. I taught myself to cook. I would cook in the morning, do dishes in the afternoon, then I would go to the field and work a team of mules to harrow. At first I had a certain team, Mary and Kit. They were a young team we had raised. All of us kids started working when we were little, and worked until we left home at 17 or 18.

We didn't have watches. Before dinner was ready, I would walk out in the yard and wave a white towel. The men would see me and come to lunch. They would bring their teams up, take off their harness and put them in a lot and throw out ears of corn and let them rest an hour. The harness was lined up in a row next to the fence. One time a mule got to chasing another mule and got into the harness. That was a mess. We like to never got it straightened out.

I plowed, harrowed, and cultivated with mules. I was harrowing one morning and didn't know what time it was. I had planned to get to the house early in time to fix dinner. When we got to the end of the row nearest the house, the mules headed for the house. I couldn't hold them, so I knew it was getting close to dinnertime. That's a mule for you. They were hungry and wanted to come to the house and eat, and they just brought me with them.

We had a team named Jim and Zin. Zin was broke to ride, Jim wasn't. One morning before he left, Dad told me to get on Zin at lunchtime, and bring him his lunch. Mom put his lunch in a metal bucket. I got on the mule and she handed me the bucket. A neighbor boy, John Faughn, wanted to go with me. When John got on behind me, she throwed both of us on the gravel road and ran off. She had never bucked before.

We lived at Hvam and the farm was a half mile south of where we lived. Dad would send me down to feed cattle on a mule. I would ride along the fence. I kept telling Dad I couldn't keep Zin away from the fence. Finally she got next to the fence, and I ended up with wire cuts on both legs, one going down, the other coming back. That's a mule for you.

At Hvam we would ride to town (Poplar Bluff) with mules pulling a wagon. It was four or five hours one way. We went to town about twice a year. We would take wheat and corn in to the mill, and have it ground to flour and corn meal. The only thing Mom would buy was sugar, baking soda, baking powder, and salt. We'd grow or raise everything else. I would say we didn't spend $10 a year on groceries. We grew up during the Depression. It was rough.

At Hvam, I would ride a mule to school about a half mile. It was four miles on to the store. Sometimes three or four of us kids would ride on a mule to the store to get something for Mom. Dad would send my brother to the store on the Fourth of July to buy 50 pounds of ice. He would haul it back in a gunnysack. We had a gallon bucket for the ice cream and we put it in a five-gallon bucket and would fill ice around the gallon bucket. We would move the gallon bucket handle back and forth to keep the cream stirred.

When Dad would break mules, we would catch them and harness them and hook two of them to a wagon. He'd get us eight kids in a wagon and turn those young mules loose and around and around in a circle we'd go. We'd hoop and holler and carry on. No wonder they would run. They would run until they gave out, sometimes close to an hour. That's the way we broke them at Hvam. He done that to break them and to have fun. One time the wagon almost tipped over and Mom said, "You're going to kill those kids." After the wagon episode, he would take the mules one at a time and put them with an older mule to finish breaking them.

We farmed 150 acres with seven mule teams. Dad, me, Auburn, John, a black guy named Bill Jordan, Charlie Franklin, and Arthur Tibbs. We had seven plows and seven disks and one planter. Dad drove the planter. Men were paid $1 a day. If they had a team they made $2 a day. At Hvam we raised corn, hay, cattle, sheep, goats, and mules.

One time when I was 12 Dad said, "Jay, go down to the corn crib and get some corn." At the time we had about 25 mules in a large barn pen, and you had to walk through the pen to get to the crib. I managed to make it through the mules, and when I made a 90-degree turn down to the door to the corn crib an old mule, Jim, was blocking the door. I reached over to move him away, and he kicked me with both hind feet, striking my legs and liked to have killed me. It knocked me down. I ran crying to Dad and he said, "Jay, guess I should have told you, a mule will live to be a 100 years old to get to kick you one time." I couldn't walk for two or three days.

 **R.J. Boyers was born Aug. 13, 1931, to Ira and Clelah Boyers. He had two older brothers and Kelly was seven years younger, and four sisters. His father farmed 150 acres 10 miles south of Poplar Bluff. In 1940, when R.J. was nine, the family moved to a 100-acre farm near Poplar Bluff. R.J. attended a one-room school at Hvam for three years and Cravens School in Poplar Bluff through the eighth grade. He never attended high school.** "Dad wouldn't let us kids go to high school. There was too much to do on the farm," he said.

R.J. was drafted into the Army in 1950 and was trained as a paratrooper. As a paratrooper he marched in the 1952 inauguration parade for President Eisenhower and jumped at separate demonstrations at Fort Bragg for President Truman and General McArthur. R.J. worked in factories in St. Louis for several years, then worked in oil fields in California through most of the 1960s and moved back to Poplar Bluff in 1971. He became a boilermaker, retiring in 1994. Since 1973, he has owned a cattle farm that was purchased by his grandparents, Robert and Cassie Boyers, in 1895. In 2008, R.J. and his wife, Donna, celebrated 41 years of marriage.

They Pulled the Tractor Out of the Creek
Pete and Jude
as told by Robert Boyers*

I started working mules when I was 8. They knew more than I did when I was a kid. Dad was crippled, had muscular dystrophy and could hardly walk. He tried to work, but he depended on me to get it done. He nearly worked me to death.

Dad farmed 216 acres on the west side of Cane Creek, 10 miles west of Poplar Bluff in Butler County. We broke and cultivated 100 acres of corn a year. We generally had three mule teams. You could always get help for a dollar a day.

We had a lot of groundhogs that would make holes on the edges of the fields. If a mule sees fresh dirt where a hole might be, they'd walk around it. They'd figure out they might get hurt, whereas a horse will plunge right on into it.

We started breaking ground in March. Dad would say, "Robert, we need to get our breaking done before it gets hot." We tried to start planting on the 10th of May and would try to be done plowing (cultivating) corn by the Fourth of July. By that time it would be tasseled out.

That was the only way we farmed back then. It was my Great-grandfather Ezekiel Miller's old farm. After a frost or two, we would gather the corn by hand in November. There would be three of us and we would gather five rows of corn as we drove a team of mules hooked to a wagon down the field. One would work the middle row the team knocked down with the wagon. Sometimes my mom would help us.

The last pair of mules I owned was named Pete and Jude. They were black with white noses. Pete was a horse mule and Jude was a mare mule. They were both good natured. They weighed around 1,400 pounds. He was a little bigger than she was. I raised them and broke them to work.

Photo taken in 1935 by a Poplar Bluff High School student. Pete on left, Jude on right. "A mare mule's a little finer than a male mule," Robert Boyers said.

I bought them at the Poplar Bluff Sale Barn in 1935. I was 14. A man brought in a pair of Percheron mares with six-month old mule colts. Somebody bought the mares and I bought the mule colts. I think I gave $125 for the pair.

My uncle, H.H. Boyers, was at the sale and he said, "Bob, would you like to have those mule colts?" I said, "Yeah, but I don't have that much money." He said to go ahead and bid on them, and that he would loan me the money.

I hauled them home in the back of a Ford pickup. I didn't go to the sale to buy them. I was just there and seen them and liked them. Their mothers were big mares. I knew they would make good mules. I run them in the pasture with cows until they got 2 year olds and started breaking them. I broke them to harness as coming 3 year olds.

I worked Pete with an older mule, tied his harness to the other's harness. That's the way you break a mule is to put them with an older mule already broke. He might try but he can't go anywhere. They soon catch on to what they're suppose to do. I broke Jude the same way.

You hook them to a plow. The older mule knew exactly where to go when you hooked them up. Mules are awful smart. They are smarter than a horse. I would take Pete and plow a little while with an older mule, then let him rest and plow with Jude. A young mule makes lunges. They don't know what's going on. They learn to follow the other mule. After a few days, I took the young mules and put them together to make a team.

We broke ground with a 12-inch breaking plow. If it wasn't too hot, I could plow two acres a day with Pete and Jude. I plowed all day and would bring them in at noon and feed them. Each one knew where their stall was. You'd take their bridle off and leave the harness on.

I'd go back at 1 p.m. and plow until about sundown. If they got too hot I would stop and let them blow a little for a while. When I brought them in in the evening, I would take their harness off and let them roll. There was a place in the back of the barn that they kept dirt loose. They would roll plumb over and back, get up and shake themselves off, then come to their stall to be fed. I gave them eight ears of corn and a full manger of hay.

I wouldn't let them out in the pasture in the summer. I kept them in a lot and fed them hay and corn. If they got a belly full of grass they would sweat a lot, get hot quicker. On corn and dry hay they could stand the hot weather better.

Jude was a little bit smarter and was dominant. He was a little bit slower. After the plowing was done, I would hook them to a double A harrow. I would harrow the field one-way, then go back and harrow crossways. They would get to be tough as nails. In July and August they would get sunburnt.

When corn got up to 2 to 3 inches, I had a walking cultivator that had two handles that you guided over a cornrow. You held the handles as close to the corn as you could in order to get the weeds and grass. We plowed it four different times.

One day I was plowing corn in a 40-acre field. Dad was in an adjoining field plowing with a used Ford Ferguson tractor. The rows ran out near the creek bank. There was a good pool of water in the creek. Dad pulled the plow up to the bank and stopped. He thought he had it in reverse, but instead had it in second. He went over the bank into the creek. Water was clear up to the bottom of the tractor seat. He walked over to where I was and said, "I'm into it." I said, "What did you do?" He said, "I'm in the creek."

I unhooked Pete and Jude and drove them across the creek, and drove them down to where the tractor was. But when they saw the tractor in the water, they were afraid and wouldn't go on. I finally drove them behind the tractor, and got them to back up enough to where I could hook a chain to the tractor. I was holding the mules in water belly deep. They got a little scared. My dad was guiding the tractor, which was flooded. When I hooked on, I'm telling you they took the tractor out of the creek; then panicked when the tractor started moving, and ran them and me up the bank into a barbed wire fence. It cut both my knees 4 inches long. I wouldn't have thought they would have pulled that tractor up that bank and over that fence, but they were scared.

After being drafted into the Army at age 18, Boyers sold Pete and Jude to a man in Williamsville who used them to skid logs.

When I got out of the Army, me, and my wife, went to look at them. I had raised them from 6 months old. We became pretty close after working them every day. I think they recognized me. The log cutters would take them to the logwoods, separate them, hook each mule to a log and turn them loose. They would go back to the sawmill by themselves and stop. Somebody would lead them back to the woods and they would repeat the process.

*Bob Boyers was interviewed by the author in 1998 and several times in 2008. Parts of the above story were previously published in the *Daily American Republic*, a newspaper in Poplar Bluff, MO.

 Robert Boyers was born April 26, 1921, to Chester and Grace Boyers. He had one brother eight years younger and eight sisters. After being discharged from the Army, Boyers farmed with his dad another five years, then worked in construction, mostly as a welder for about 40 years, until he suffered a heart problem in 1982 and was unable to go back to work. He and his wife, Mary, were married 49 years. She died in 2002. Boyers has lived in rural Poplar Bluff for over 50 years. Robert Boyers shares the same name of his grandfather. After he returned from the Army in 1943, his dad purchased a new Ford tractor with three pieces of equipment for $1,700. "Riding that tractor was like going to heaven. I could plow an acre an hour," he said.

Neighbors Would Call Us to Pull Them Out
Pat and Jet
as told by Ben Boyers*

Pat and Jet were brother and sister. They were out of the same mare, Maud, a big bay mare, nervous type. They were out of the same jack. Pat was a bay horse mule. He could jump anything he could see over. She (Jet) was a big black mule with a white nose with a big belly. She always looked like she was in foal. Jet was gentle and tame.

We had them 20 years, and I never seen them hooked to anything they couldn't pull out or break.

Ole Pat he was a good working mule, but he kicked my dad, Byrd, a couple of times, nearly killed him. Dad had to harness him over Jet, and unhitch him that way. When Dad reached over Jet's back to reach Pat, Pat would turn around and kick up with both feet.

We farmed 80 acres, corn and cotton, and hay. We worked them to the disk and harrow. I started working them when I was 11. We worked before daylight until after dark.

Dad, or a hired hand, would help me harness, and hook up. At dinnertime, I was expected to unhook them. I got so tired. I would stop and let the team rest. I would be so tired I would lie down. One time I went to sleep, and Dad found me at noontime. I didn't get a whipping, but he let me know it wasn't to happen again.

They were known as one of the best pulling teams in that part of the county. Jet was bigger, but you couldn't tell it when they were pullin'. We had a lot of big cypress trees and stumps to remove from the fields. We would get Jet and Pat to straddle a big stump and hook them up.

They didn't shoot craps. They just sat down and pulled. I've seen them break harness loose, and we would have to fix it. We carried spare parts on their collars.

If one of our neighbors got hung up with a team from pulling a wagon loaded with wood or hay, they would call us to pull them out. Dad would have them unhook their team, and we would hook Pat and Jet to the load. They would pull it out.

They were my dad's favorite team. He said they were the best team he ever owned. We had sharecroppers and tenants and kept about four teams. In the fall, Dad would turn them all out onto open range, with the exception of Pat and Jet. He kept them around to haul wood and to go to town. The other teams would get hand me downs. Pat and Jet always got new stuff.

Uncle George Pratt Sr. was a teamster, a good mule handler. He was farming for us. He was the only other person we let handle that team. Uncle Pratt had Pat one summer and had him where he could hook him to a single plow in his garden. We never could do that. He never whipped him. I never did figure out how he worked that old mule.

We had 80 acres where we lived. We had a few sharecroppers. Dad furnished everything. They provided labor. We would furnish mules, feed, and equipment. They lived on the place. They would farm for part of the crop. Dad would advance them some money to pay off summer loans. Some of them took the money, and the next week they would be moved out of the house. We would have to work double hard. Some stayed two or three years. We had three houses built for sharecroppers. The houses were named after the first occupant.

I went to horses when I was 18. They are prettier than mules. Mules were hard headed, but tough as a pine knot.

We always ate good, never went to bed hungry or cold. Our mules and horses helped us make it. That was the only power people had. A lot of times we would hook three or four head to a piece of equipment.

Pat was 16 or 17 which was pretty good for a work animal. One day Pat laid down in the dust to roll, went to sleep, and died. A hired hand buried him under a walnut tree.

*Ben Boyers was interviewed by the author in 1998 and again in 2008. Parts of this story were previously published in the *Daily American Republic*, a newspaper in Poplar Bluff, MO.

Ben Boyers was born Sept. 8, 1923, to Byrd and Hettie Boyers. His dad farmed in the Hvan area, north of Coon Island in Butler County, about 10 miles south of Poplar Bluff. He had five sisters and one brother, Meridith, who was five years younger. He attended three different one-room schools in Butler County through the eighth grade. "When I was eight, a cousin was cutting corn with a corn knife. Dad had planted some peas in with the corn. My cousin was cutting stalks, and missed cutting a vine. I said I would break it at the same time he said he would cut it, and he cut off part of my left thumb. When picking cotton, cotton would punch it and make it sore. I could pick good with my right hand. We picked our own cotton, and if other people had cotton to pick we rode a cotton truck. I think the first day I picked cotton I made 80 cents. I picked off and on from age 12 to 16," he said.

Boyers served in the U.S. Army during WWII and was stationed in the South Pacific. He was hit by shrapnel and later in life was awarded disability for his injuries. He and his wife, Mary, were married 42 years, until her death in 1988. For 25 years, he trained horses, mostly quarter horses, and for years was sought after by local veterinarians and others to round up wild stock that had gotten loose whose owners couldn't retrieve them.

He Liked to Have Scared Me to Death
Pat and Jet Part II
as told by Betty Boyers Webb

Betty is seven years younger than her brother, Ben Boyers, who talked about Pat and Jet in Part I

I was born and raised on a farm in the Hvam area. When I was 5, we moved north to a 90-acre farm that was about 10 miles south of Poplar Bluff. We still kept the Hvam farm, where we had sharecroppers.

We moved to the new farm in a team and wagon. When we got to the Aggerman Ditch, there was a log that people could cross on, but the team had to cross it. Pat and Jet pulled the load across; then Pat decided not to pull. Daddy jumped on Jet, and started yelling, and they pulled that wagon right up the bank of that ditch. That was the only time I have ever seen Pat balk.

I can close my eyes and still see that happening. I was 5 the other kids were at school.

If you're raised on a farm you learn to ride horses and drive a team at a young age. I was driving a mule team through gates to pick up pumpkins and corn when I was 10.

Back before we moved, there would be a bunch of us kids in the wagon, and Pat would look around and see us in the wagon, and want to runaway. That's when Dad put blinders on him.

Pat and Jet were skittish. None of us kids could harness them. We would stay our distance from them. You could never tell about ole Pat. I only took the harness off of Pat and Jet one time. Dad was gone; I kept my distance; I was afraid of them.

I've seen him kick my dad several times. He liked to have scared me to death. When I was 12, one winter day I was helping my dad cut trees, and drag logs out of the woods. Dad bent over to hook up the chain to the log. He was talking to Pat. When he got close, Pat kicked him in the chest. It knocked him to the ground, and knocked the wind out of him. I remember running to Dad thinking Pat had killed him.

Before I got to him, Dad rose up and told me to stay back. He got up and went on working. Pat kicked at him two or three more times that day. He had mean spells, I guess. Dad wasn't one to beat animals. One time, I saw a guy beat a horse until the horse fell down.

I started plowing with mules with a walking cultivator when I was 13. I remember it was the Fourth of July, because everyone else was picnicking. I took over when Ben left for the service. My younger brother, Meredith, was too little. I was Dad's right hand man for three summers. I worked from when school was out in the spring, until school started back in the fall.

I farmed with Toby and Nig, two gentle mules. Toby was a small buckskin mule with black mane and tail. Nig was a gentle ole mule; you could depend on him. He was brownish black, bigger than Toby.

You could ride Toby sometimes. We could be riding along pretty good and "Wham!" You'd find yourself on the ground. He bucked me, and my sister off when I was 5 years old. Dad was driving some cattle across a ditch, and my sister and I decided we wanted to go. I imagine the flies may have been a factor.

When I went to the field Mom made me wear bib overalls, a long-sleeve shirt, and a bonnet to protect me from the sun. Mom was very particular. I wore whatever shoes I had; sometimes I didn't have shoes to wear. I would get blisters on my feet, try to put something on them, and keep going.

I was usually in one field working Toby and Nig, while Dad was in a nearby field. I would have to disk and harrow, and he'd be in another field planting with Pat and Jet. I used the plow lines and commands gee and haw and getup and go. Dad usually kept a jug of water at the end of the field underneath a shade tree.

I stayed in school and worked Saturdays during the school year. We would get up at 5 a.m., do milking and chores, and then harness the mules, and go to the field. I usually milked five or six cows, morning and evening.

Dad didn't get a little Ford tractor until I was in high school in 1947. We didn't get electricity out where we lived until 1949, after I had graduated from high school.

The only time we got paid at home was from picking cotton. That's how I got money for my school clothes. I started picking cotton when I was 5, using a 24-pound flour sack, later I used a tow sack, then 9-foot sack when I was older. I got to where I could pick 200 pounds a day. When I started we got paid 75 cents per 100 pounds, by the time I quit when I was 17, we were making $2.50 a 100 pounds. I would get up in time to catch the truck at 4:30 that took us to the Clarkton area (Dunklin County). In a good day I could clear $5, after paying 50 cents for the ride. I thought I was doing pretty good. I couldn't go everyday because I was needed at the farm.

We picked cotton during cotton vacation at school, which usually lasted four weeks in late September, October.

We had goats, mules, horses, cows, pigs, chickens, ducks, and geese. At times, all seven of us kids were at home. We learned not to get attached to the animals, especially the goats. That might be our meal in the spring. We raised garden stuff and canned it. We raised our own peanuts and popcorn; otherwise we didn't have it. We had a sorghum grinder and made our own sorghum. We only had bare necessities. We didn't get anything from the government, such as the Civilian Conservation Camps. What we raised was what we ate.

I would rather work in the field than in the house anytime. I don't regret learning everything I learned. I liked Toby over the other mules because I thought he was pretty. I always wondered why we never had a white mule.

Betty Boyers Webb was born Sept. 11, 1930, to Byrd and Hettie Boyers and was raised in Butler County. She had four sisters and two brothers and was the second youngest child. She attended Carter School, a one-room school, for three years, then attended Black River School, a two-room school, for five years. She attended one year at Big Island High School and the last three years at Broseley High School, where she was graduated in 1949. She was the only one of her siblings to graduate from high school.

On June 5, 1949, she married John Webb, Jr., of Qulin; and in 1951 the young couple moved to Illinois where he worked for Caterpillar Tractor for 31 years. After he retired in 1982, they moved to rural Ellsinore in Carter County. Betty raised four boys and a daughter. John Webb died in 2005, and Betty lost

her daughter in 2006. She said her father was about 5'6" tall and weighed about 150 pounds when she was growing up, and she weighed 90 to 100 pounds. "I helped Dad disking and harrowing, putting up loose hay on a wagon, the part I didn't like because it fell down my back and neck. I sawed wood and made posts. I was a right-hand man for Daddy and pulled a crosscut saw with him. I guess that's what made me tough," she said.

His Ears Would Keep Pace With His Gait
Toby
as told by brothers R.J. and Kelly Boyers

R.J. Boyers:

Dad bought Toby in the 1930s. Us kids liked him because he was little and we could get on him easily. We rode mules with a sack on them. We didn't have saddles. Toby was my riding mule. I cleaned and took care of him. He was a gaited mule. My older brother Auburn had a nice mare. He and his friends rode horses. When we would all go riding they would run off, and leave Toby and me, and hide.

Dad sold Toby four times and each time the people couldn't finish paying for him, so Dad would take him back. One day, Dad rode Toby and when he got off said, "I won't ever sell him again," and Toby had a home.

When I was 6, and we were living in the Hvam area, the Black River got out and I got stranded out on a knoll way out in the field. Dad seen me, and got on ole Toby to come and get me. He got off and we both pulled our boots off and when we got on him, he throwed us both in the water and ran off. I don't know why he did that. We had to wade the water and swim back.

One day Toby got out in a neighbor's garden and the man gut shot him. Dad was so angry; he went over there and whipped him for doing it.

Kelly Boyers:

When I was growing up we had a pacing mule, not much larger than a Shetland pony, we called "Toby." My four brothers and older sisters and I all rode him. He would throw you, kick you, but he was a nice-riding little mule, fast paced, comfortable gait.

His ears would keep time with his gait. One of his ears would move forward the same time one of his feet would move forward, like he was keeping time with his feet.

Dad purchased him as a team. He got rid of his mate, but never got him back. He sold Toby a few times and would always get him back. Denver Timmons told me before he died, that he remembered trading a sow to my dad for ole Toby and they weighed about the same weight. I think he said 600 pounds. Toby kicked Denver's brother, Sylvester, and broke his jaw, and they brought him back to my dad.

He was a treacherous little rascal. You had to watch him. I remember one time I was suppose to take this set of scales somewhere and they were trying to hand them to me while I was on Toby. They were rattling and it was all I could do to stay on him. I can remember my older brother, John (now deceased), telling me he rode Toby one Saturday night 11 miles to Neelyville as a teenager, partying. On the

Shirley Berry, a great-granddaughter of Robert and Cassie Boyers on "Toby" mule. Auburn Boyers, son of Ira on "Tony."

way home he pulled up and rolled a cigarette in the dark. When he struck that kitchen match on the steel saddle horn, Toby threw him and he could hear him standing nearby snorting at him, and he just stood there and let him catch him.

Someone had shot at him on open range and he was gun shy. My older brother, R.J., and I were riding him double bareback in a lot when a neighbor boy, who was sitting on the fence, pointed a stick at him. He started bucking and threw us both off with R.J. landing on top of me. I was hurting. R.J. got up and took after the neighbor kid, who knew Toby was gun shy.

We rented pastures all over the place, all over the country, and drove livestock down the roads. Dad would try to rent cornfields (after harvest) for the cattle. We'd ride Toby to go check on them. Toby was kept in a lot to be used. My dad would say get on Toby and do this and do that. You'd just hop on him, mostly bareback. We'd run errands on him, drove stock with him.

I remember only one time that my dad worked him. It was in the late '50s. Toby was probably 25. My dad one spring got caught without a team. I guess he had sold them, swapped them, or something. We always planted 100 acres of corn. And he always wanted to plant corn with a team; so he'd get a good stand. So his team that spring was ole Toby, which I guess had been broke to work years before, and a spotted stud horse that had always run loose with the mares. It was an odd looking team, a little mule and a big spotted stud horse, hooked to a planter. My dad was quite a teamster. He evidently could handle stock. That's all he ever done. No one else would have attempted that.

He was gun shy. That's the way he died. He got in a neighbor's garden and the ole boy shot him. That was in the late '50s. He was old by then.

He'd Tell People, "Gin Broke Another Singletree"
as told by Kelly Boyers

When I was 5 (1943), my dad, Ira, had a team of big sorrel mules named Kit and Kate. One of them tried to jump a bull rake, and stuck a rake tooth in her belly. Dad tried to doctor her up. He thought she was coming along. One evening he saw her walking to get water and said, "I think she's a little better." That mule fell over dead.

Later I saw Dad sitting on the front porch crying. It was crop time, and it was terrible for him. An ole mule had a lot to do with people making a living.

When I was 7, Dad and some others had killed some hogs to butcher, and loaded them on a sled to skid to the kettle. A mule was hooked to the sled. When that mule smelled those hogs, she ran off and scattered dead hogs all over the hillside. She got into a grove of saplings and tore up the sled and harness.

I came along when mule teams had begun to be phased out. Tractors took over after World War II. I was the last of four brothers and four sisters.

I started plowing with mules in 1949 when I was 11. If you got the plow hung up on a stump, it was hell to get it off. I've worked mules on a riding disk. R.J. and I would turn the earth over and disk it. Dad did all the planting. We would have three mule teams in the field. I have worked three mules to a three-abreast harrow. We farmed in what would be called today, patches, 10 acres here, 20 acres there. We planted mostly corn.

Breaking plows came in different sizes, 8-inch, 10-inch, 12-inch, etc. My dad bought a new walking plow for $3 back in 1918. He told my mother the reason he bought a walking cultivator, instead of a riding plow, was because it wouldn't be so hard on the team.

My dad stood a draft horse stallion and a jack up into the mid-1950s at Poplar Bluff. He traded mules at the local Poplar Bluff Sale Barn. We raised mules, broke mules, and traded mules. A lot of my dad's customers were from the black population who lived in the Bacon Pasture area down Highway 142 south, and the Morocco and Province areas east of Poplar Bluff off of Highway 60.

I remember one time a black man brought a mule back and Dad told him to lead him in a lot and take his bridle off, which he did. After he walked off my dad said, "That's the sixth time I've owned that mule." They would buy in the spring and sell in the fall. Dad would get a substantial down payment in the spring knowing they would bring them back in the fall. Sometimes they would just buy one to match with another.

Mules were big, medium, and small. Each had their own place in the world, like different size tractors do today. Some mules you had to watch or they'd kick you. A lot of them were touchy around the ears when you went to bridle them. I worked a big team of mules that were gentle and good natured named Jim and Gin that were over 16 hands. Dad used to brag how strong Gin was. He'd tell people, "Gin broke another singletree."

We had a smaller team named Ben and Coalie, which were bad about getting scared and running off. In the mid-1950s we purchased our first hay baler that had a Wisconsin engine on it, that you had to crank to start. Ben and Coalie were tied up in the yard. When that engine started up, they spooked, broke their reins, and ran through Mom's clotheslines.

One time Dad sent me to pull a bull rake with Ben and Coalie, and before I worked them he told me if they started running, not to fall forward into the rake, but to fall backwards over the seat. How in the hell would I know which way I was going to fall off? I would rake the mowed hay until the rake filled up, then I would trip it, which caused the rake to rise and dump the hay, When the hay would load up and get under the team's rear, especially Coalie's, he would start twitching his tail, and I knew then I had better dump.

One time Dad was skidding logs on the other side of Highway 67 and he asked me to catch a gray mare mule, harness her, and bring her to him. I was riding her with the harness on and when we got to Highway 67, she lit into bucking. She threw me, the harness, and the bridle, everything except the collar. She let me catch her, and I bridled and harnessed her and went on.

We gathered corn with a mule team in the fall. We called it "snapping corn." You would snap an ear off and throw it in the wagon. Since I was the smallest, I always got the down row. A team had to straddle a row pulling a wagon, which would knock the row down. That was the hardest job because you had to bend over more. One person would work two rows on one side, and another two rows on the other side. When picking corn with a team we only used voice commands. We'd pick until we got even with the front of the wagon and one of us would clutch our tongue or say "getty-up." When we got to the back of the wagon picking we would say, "whoa." The lines were always tied up. Our voice commands came from our ancestors. Although the universal language for turning teams was gee for turning right, and haw for turning left, we said "Yah, come ere" for left and "Yah to the right" for turning right.

Dad bought a new 8N Ford tractor and equipment in 1952. I lived on that tractor as a 14-year-old boy. With the tractor we row cropped 120 acres, mostly corn, and we put up hay. Dad still did all the planting with a mule team because he was particular. He wanted to see every kernel of corn drop out of that planter box.

 **Kelly Boyers was born March 7, 1938, to Ira and Clelah Boyers. In the 1940s his father farmed 100 acres, which is today part of Poplar Bluff Industrial Park. He had three brothers and four sisters and was the youngest child. His brother, R.J., is seven years older. Boyers attended Cravens School in Poplar Bluff through the eighth grade, and was graduated from Poplar Bluff High School in 1957. When he was 13, he talked his dad into buying him an American Saddlebred yearling chestnut colt that he named Master. Young Boyers earned several hundred dollars a year in stud fees, using Master to breed up to 40 mares a year at $20 to $40 a mare. "I hauled him in the back of a pickup that had a stock rack. When I'd start it up, he'd come running," Boyers said. Master died on the farm in 1968 from liver complications. He is buried in their backyard.**

Boyers worked as an electrical lineman for 30 years, retiring in 1994. In 2008, he and his wife, Judy, celebrated their 46th wedding anniversary. Since 1994, Boyers has raised American Saddlebreds and sells colts at weaning time. Some of his mares trace back to Master. In 2002, he held back a colt named Durange that went on to win the Four Year Old Stallion class at the 2006 Missouri State Fair. Durange later sold for $25,000.

He Would Start a Split Second Sooner.
They Knew to Pull Together
Pete and Dave
as told by Robert Boyers

In the mid-1940s, Dad had a pair of mules called Pete and Dave. Dave was a bay mule and weighed around 1,100 pounds. Pete was a dark-brown mule and weighed 1,200 pounds. The guy he bought them from had trained them to work in the logwoods. He would cut 3,000 feet of big logs off that farm and use Pete and Dave to skid them out and load on the truck.

Buck Hayes, a one-armed man, and Charlie Ward, worked Pete and Dave in the logwoods. Dad furnished the team and harness. They would hook the logs to a skid and skid them to the truck and load them. They tried to load four or five loads a day. The soft wood was taken to Harviell to a stave mill where they made barrel staves; the hardwood, red oak, and white oak, was taken to Poplar Bluff.

Back then we only used crosscut saws and axes. Sometimes you would drive a wedge in where you had sawed to make the tree fall. They used a cross haul to load the truck. The mules would line up in front of the truck; and chains and the cross haul were used to hook a chain to the mules' doubletree, and they would pull the logs up on skids that had been placed on the back of the truck. Some of the logs would be 16 feet long.

One time they had Pete and Dave hooked to some large logs, and the chains were up high and pulled the mules rear ends up where they couldn't get enough traction. Two big lumbermen, Dan Kirk and Red Niederstadt both weighed over 200 pounds; they each sat on the backend of one of the mules where the mules could get enough traction to pull the logs up on the truck. They got down and pulled that log up on the truck with the men on them. I've never seen anything like it. Everybody there had a fit.

You could hook them to a big log and you'd swear they'd never pull it. They would get down on their bellies to pull it. They were the best pulling pair of mules I've ever seen to be as light as they were.

Dave was a little lighter and quicker. He knew he had to get a head start to keep up with Pete. He would start a split second sooner. They knew to pull together. Pete had to do some scratching to level the doubletree. When pulling a stump, they would just dig, wouldn't give up until you told them to whoa.

Dad later purchased a bigger pair of blue mules that weighed 1,400 to 1,500 pounds. He was going to use them in the logwoods. But they never came up to what Pete and Dave could do. One would try to pull, then the other, what we called "shoot craps." Dad didn't log with them very long. He used them for plowing.

Pete and Dave were also good mules for farming when we didn't use them in the logwoods. They were two of the best.

Jack Would Buck a Circle Around the Barn Lot
Jack
as told by Alvin "Bob" Hager by letter and phone conversation

I grew up on a farm, working mules until I was 18. I started working mules when I was 8 or 9. I didn't start out using a breaking plow. I started by using a riding disk and riding harrow. We had three teams, a mule team, horse team, and a mule and a horse team. My dad and brother would each work a team; I would work the mule team.

Mules were a premium back then. We used them for farming, logging. These mules were trained and smart.

We had one mule which was very smart. Jack was his name. He was brownish and weighed about 1,200 pounds. My dad bought Jack when he was about 3 or a 4 year old from a man by the name of Lodgee for $100. He was a good taught mule to work. Jack did his part.

Jack would buck while putting harness on him. His mate's name was George, a black mule with a white nose. When you opened the barn door, George would go out first. He knew what Jack was going to do. Jack would run out and buck a circle around the barn lot, then he would go up to the side of his mate, stop at his side, to be hitched together. He done that for years, about every time you'd hook him up. He was kind of a spoilt mule.

After they were hooked together, and you opened the barnyard gate, they would walk out and straddle the wagon tongue, ready to be hooked up to go. All the mules we had were very smart. They could always tell when they were going to have a hard pull. They would pick up speed to go over it.

I worked Jack and George for 10 years. They were a tough team of mules, very alert. They noticed anything around them. They made a good team. I used voice commands. You never had to whip them.

We used to have a rodeo on Sundays at home. We had a few boys in the community who wanted to ride. One of these boys, Bill Burke, wanted to ride Jack. Well Jack was never rode. He would buck until he got them off. You could try to ride him every day, and he would still get you off.

To really tell a good mule, you judge them by their physical shape. You looked for one who has ears erect when moving, ears that were up and not flopping. The ones with floppy ears and head not erect were not as good a mule.

In training and breaking them, the right mule was the off mule; the left was head mule. They learned in turning, right was gee, left was haw. They knew and learned this. A mule with a Roman nose was a good animal, one with a dish face was not as good.

Jack died on the farm when he was about 20 years old.

Alvin Lloyd Hager, Sr., was born Sept. 21, 1921, to Jake and Agnes Boyers Hager. He was the oldest of eight siblings, two brothers and five sisters. His father farmed 130 acres, mostly corn, soybeans, oats, and hay seven miles south of Poplar Bluff in Butler County. Hager attended Pike Slough School, a two-room country school, through the eighth grade.
He served in the Army Air Corps during World War II (1942-1946) as a mechanic and flight engineer on the B-25 bomber. He worked in aircraft maintenance for TWA 23 years, retiring in 1984. He lost his wife, Maurine, in 2008. They were married 61 years. "My mother was Agnes Boyers. Her father,

Robert Boyers, raised mules. He kept a black-and-white-nosed jack and raised black-and-white-nosed mules. He had a gray-colored jack and raised all other colors of mules. Mules have been around for many years, back in 1800 or before," he said.

V. Mules That Worked by Voice Commands/ Without Lines

I'd Hunt Awhile and Come Back, and There Was My Bridle
Gin
as told by Ralph Higgerson

My grandfather had an ole gentle mule. Her name was Gin. She was real smart and she could jump a fence and not even touch it, like a deer. She'd jump a 4- or 5-foot fence like a deer does. They just stand and leap over it.

She was a good riding mule. Gin had a good, soft trot. Most farmers had a special mule for riding. And I'd ride her hunting or visiting, to hunt ducks or squirrels, whatever was available. I'd lead her to a stump or anything I could get off the ground with, and jump on her and take off. I might be gone half a day.

And she'd slip a bridle. I'd ride her three or four miles back in the woods hunting. And I'd tie her to a tree while I went hunting. I'd hunt awhile and come back, and there was my bridle. So I got smart. I took a rope and tied it around her neck. She'd slip the bridle but couldn't get away.

Gin was just as gentle as a dog. But she was smart. Grandfather worked her in the garden. She was his favorite mule for that. He could drive her without any lines. He'd holler "gee" and "haw" and all of that. She could plow a row of potatoes without any lines. He'd have harness and bridle on her.

Ole Kit was her mate. When you work them as a team, they get to be real close. She liked to stay with her mate. I worked ole Kit and Gin several years. Gin was easy to catch and to harness and to put a bridle on. She knew more about what she was doing than some of the farmhands did. She was just a gentle mule.

Ole Gin had a breathing problem. Some mules breathe loud, kind of like people with asthma. When she was young she was that away. They called it wind broke or something. Sometimes she'd wear an apparatus around her nose. She finally got over that.

She must have lived over 20 years. That's unusual for a work animal. Back then when they got old, they just retired them. An old mule will stand in the lot and eat or be on pasture. She died when anthrax hit the livestock.

Higgerson also has a story in the Farming With Mules chapter.

People Can't Imagine How Smart Mules Were Back Then
Jim and Bill
as told by Lloyd Massey

We had a young team, a small team of mules; we called them Jim and Bill. They were as small a mule as there were back in those days. Bill was brown, and Jim was black. I had a half brother, Paul, that always taught animals, dogs, mules, etc. And he had these two mules where you could just walk out in the lot with a bridle, and they would come to him, and put their head in that bridle. They were just like a human being. They had more sense than you gave them credit for.

He'd take both bridles to the lot. He'd lay one of them down, and hold the other one up, and holler for whichever mule he wanted, Bill or Jim, and they'd come, and put their head down in there. It's just unbelievable. Then he would lead them into the barn hallway and put their harness on. And then we'd be ready for the day.

I was 10 (1931) when I first worked with them. Being that small I was nervous when I started out. They learned to accept me as commander. In other words, I'd tell them what to do and they'd do it. I'd just call them by name, "Jim, do this, and do that." They were wonderful little mules. I plowed with them, planted, even used one of them a lot with a one-row planter, planting one row at a time, which nowadays don't seem possible with all these 40-and-50-foot planters they have.

One time my older brother, H.L., and I were hauling manure on a sled out of a muddy lot. We got the sled loaded and told them to "Get up. Get up Jim. Get up Bill." They begin to seesaw back and forth, wouldn't pull together. So my brother hit Bill over the head with a two-by-four. Bill reared up and fell back on the sled. He lay there a little bit. We thought he had killed him. We begin to kind of pet him and directly he jumped up. His harness was messed up. We had to straighten it out.

We got him back in place with the other mule. We hollered, "Get up. Get up Jim, Bill," and they took off as if they weren't pulling anything. They were that smart. That lick over that mule's head put them together to where they would pull together.

One day a friend, Woodrow "Woody" Duffy, and I were going to gather corn. We hooked Bill and Jim to a wagon and headed for the cornfield. We had to go through a gate. Woody jumped out and opened the gate. I drove the team through and stopped on the field turning road. Woody closed the gate and started getting back in the wagon; just as he was ready to step over the wagon tailgate, those mules went crazy.

They jumped against their trace chains and took off running. It was so quick! It threw Woody off the wagon. I was afraid the mules might not act right in the cornfield, so I began to lay leather to their butts. We went almost a quarter of a mile and I turned them around and went back for Woody.

Those mules acted perfect the rest of the day. I'd holler "get up" and they would go forward until we hollered "whoa."

Bill was so smart. To give you an idea, a friend of mine and I were riding him one time down a turning row. Back then we didn't have tiles. We had wooden bridges out in the fields. We were loping along on that mule, and he comes to this bridge, and instead of going on over it; he puts his front feet out in front of him and stops, and throws his head down. And both of us went off over his head onto that bridge. That mule stood there as if he was laughing at us. He didn't turn or run off or nothing. He just stood there. We got up, got back on him, and went across the bridge and went on our way.

Jim, we used him to pull hay up in the big barn with a loft hayrack and fork. Jim was smart enough that we would put him on this rope way down in the bottom of the barn. We'd take this hayfork and put on a load of hay, and we'd holler all the way from the loft, "Get up Jim!" And he'd pull that load of hay up in the barn, until that fork tripped, and immediately when that fork tripped, he'd stop. He'd turn around and come back and get in place ready for another load without anyone around him. It's just unbelievable. I mean people can't imagine how smart mules were back then.

This is the second of four stories Massey has in this book. See chapters Mule Teams and Runaways and the story, "And Guess What? That Tractor Didn't Stop."

He Didn't Have No Lines on That Ole Mule
Gin and Bill
as told by Naman Caldwell

We used to plant a lot of cotton back then (1930s). When I was 9 years old Dad planted cotton with a one-row planter with one ole mule. He didn't have no lines on that ole mule. We planted cotton on ridges back then. Dad would holler, "get-up" when he wanted him to go, and "whoa" when he wanted him to stop.

That ole Bill mule would go down that ridge, get to the other end and Dad would holler "gee" or "haw" whichever way he wanted him to go. The ole mule would come right back on the next row. All he had on him was harness and a bridle.

I'd take the other ole mule, Gin, and I'd knock them ridges down pulling a section harrow. That was the first job I had with a mule. I'd work Bill and Gin together whenever we needed two to pull something. They were both black with blazed faces, and weighed around 1,100 pounds. Dad raised Gin. She was born the same year I was. I'm not sure where he got Bill, but he was already trained to work when he got him. Bill was stubborn. You had to show him ever little bit who was boss.

They were kinda tough-mouthed. I can recollect one time, me, and, my older brother, were breaking ground and weeds were probably 3-foot high. My brother had to wrap the lines around his waist (to hold them), and they hit a stump. When they hit that stump they broke the middle clevis; them lines pulled him over the plow handles and knocked the breath out of him. The mules went a little ways and stopped. It was hot weather. He was laying out in that sun, and I didn't know what to do of course. He wasn't injured.

We used to work taxes out on the road. I remember Dad taking them ole mules out there with a scraper, and pulling dirt out of the ditches and putting it on the road. There wasn't many gravel roads back then. It was all dirt. That's the way he worked his poll tax out.

I worked with mules 10 or 12 years. Dad grew corn, cotton, and cane for the sorghum mill. Kids picked cotton to raise money to buy school clothes.

Dad always said he could hold them mules if they ever took a notion to run. We were farming down there by Dudley one year, and he was going to go down there and get his welder back. He had a rubber-tired wagon. Going down there one of those tires blowed out on that old wagon, scared them mules. They runaway with him. He fell off, drug him a little ways.

He came back and I said, "Dad, I thought you said you could hold them ole mules." He said, "Yeah, but I didn't have no chance then."

 **Naman Caldwell was born Nov. 7, 1919, to Ova and Orfa Caldwell. He had two older brothers and two younger sisters. His father farmed on 40 acres of rented land six miles south of Puxico in Stoddard County. Naman attended Edmondson School through the fourth grade, then attended Rock Hill School through the eighth grade, both rural schools. He farmed with his**

dad for four years after the eighth grade, then farmed on his own for 12 years. He worked on the railroad for three years and drove a school bus for 33 years, retiring in 1985. Rita, his wife of 67 years, died in 2006.

If a Storm Came, I'd Tie Them to a Fencerow and Get Under Their Bellies
Jude and Jean
as told by John Hammon

My dad could take any mule, put it in the logwoods, and it wasn't long until he could just hang the lines on their hames. He could load logs without them (lines). He'd say, "Just give me a little bit," and they would antsy along just a little bit at a time.

Dad wouldn't have anything but a mule. He said a horse didn't have any sense. They'd founder themselves. My dad had no use for a horse at all. He said a horse would kill you and kill itself, that you won't ever get a mule to run through a fence.

We had a mule team named Jude and Jean. Mules got about four different personalities. One's called a good mule, then you got what's called a mischievous mule, you got a mean mule, then you got a mule that never forgets. That Jude mule was one of them that never forgot. And she'd lay down on you ever once in a while, and wouldn't work.

My dad, he was about 6 feet 6 inches tall and weighed about 260. He'd take a chain and put on her hame. He'd flip it around and bring it under her ribs and take the hide, hair, all off of her. Then us boys when we'd work them, if she wanted to lay down. We'd rattle the chain, and she'd get with it.

They (Jude and Jean) were around 15 hands. They were big Missouri mules. Jude was reddish brown. Jean was a black with a white nose. Jean was the best mule we had. We used her to plow the garden with a double shovel. She wouldn't step on nothing. You could talk to her like a person. (Her) lines were on the hames. She'd turn around and go right back down the other row. She was 13 or 14 years old, an old steady mule.

Saulus Whitener, a neighbor, was plowing corn with her (Jude) and my dad was hunting up the creek. He told Dad he would take a hundred dollars for that mule. Dad said, "I'll just buy her." The first thing he done was take her to the logwoods with that ole Jean mule, and when he got done with her, that mule was just as good of mule as you could find.

Dad always told us, "Boys, don't never open the (stall) door and go in and try to put a bridle on them. Make them stick their nose around to you." By the time we were 7 or 8 years old we could put the bridle on them, and harness them, and work them. We'd stand on a box to put harness on. When he first got that ole Jude mule, she wouldn't turn around (in the stall). Dad took a pitchfork to her hind end. She learned that when you opened that stable door and say, "come here" she'd turn around and stick her nose in that bridle.

Dad had four different teams. Us boys all had a team we'd work ourselves. I worked Jude and Jean six or seven years, cultivating, logging, harrowing, just anything. I planted corn with them. At first we had a one-row (planter), and finally we got a two-row. Dad fed them corn. You couldn't work a mule without feeding them corn or oats.

Us boys started plowing when we were 7 or 8 years old. Because the mules would turn the plow, we'd just follow them ole mules all day long. They could tell time better than a human being. When it got noon at the end (of the row) closest to the house, they'd stop. They didn't want to go any further. They wanted to go to the stable. You couldn't hardly get them to move around. All you had to do was unhook them. That's the way us boys could tell when it was time to go in for dinner. We'd get our butts whipped if we rode them mules. My dad said them mules worked to. We walked them to the house.

Jude and Jean worked good together. That Jude mule wouldn't work with any other mule. With Jean she couldn't get away with anything. Jean wouldn't run with her. She wouldn't let her go off to the side. Jean was a big ole Missouri mule. She was a heavy blocked-up mule.

We (boys) all worked one field. We would follow each other. All four of us could break 20 acres in a day. Dad would be working nearby clearing new ground. But he was never very far from us. He kept an eye on us and made sure we done stuff right. If we didn't do it right, he would take a brush to our hind end. He told you how to do it, and that's the way you better do it. Back in them days you didn't disobey your parents.

You walk 14 hours a day with a breaking plow. Your legs get tired. My mom used to come in my bedroom and rub down my legs with alcohol. Back then we were in the Depression. We didn't have a choice. You either worked, or you didn't eat.

Only one of us would harrow (a field). Sometimes we'd have to put weights on the harrow. Sometimes you even rode it. There were three sections to a harrow. We'd put three big rocks on it and sit in the middle. Those ole mules were steady. There was no reason for you to get injured. Dad always wired a board to it, and with that rock, you'd sit there with your feet on the board. We were told to sit there, just drive the mules and that's the way we done it.

If a rainstorm came I'd tie Jude and Jean to a fencerow, and get under their bellies. They'd hold their heads down. They wouldn't flinch or move. They'd just stand right there.

I never did like to farm. You had to get up at 4 o'clock every morning. You worked from when you couldn't see, to when you couldn't see, and you never got done with your work. Didn't make any difference if you were sick; there wasn't no doctors. Our mom and dad doctored us. They done the best they could.

When I was 15, I put my clothes in an old sack and went south to Kennett. My mother said, "Where are you going?" I said, "I'm going to pick cotton and make some money and go to St. Louis and get a job." That's how I got out of there.

 John Thomas Hammon, Jr., was born July 7, 1928, to John T. Hammon, Sr. and Clara Ette Hammon. He had two older and two younger brothers and four sisters. His father farmed 80 acres about 18 miles northeast of Wappapello Lake in Wayne County. They farmed mostly corn and oats, some wheat, no cotton. He attended McGee School, a two-room rural school, through the eighth grade. When he left home at age 15, he worked at Meyer Brother Drug Company in St. Louis.

Hammon was drafted into the Army at age 17 (he had lied about his age) and spent four years overseas in France helping to build bridges, airport runways, and Quonset huts as part of the 69th Engineering Battalion.

After being discharged from the service, he worked at Fisher Body for five years in St. Louis, then worked at Balls Brothers Glass Company in Hillsboro, Illinois as a glass blower for 39 years, retiring in 1990. He and his wife, Barbara, were married 54 years. She died in December 2006.

"We didn't sell corn; fed it to the hogs. Back then was open range. We ran 300 head in the Mingo swamps. It was eight or 10 miles to the swamp. They'd fatten up on acorns, then we'd go down and catch them in the wintertime," Hammon said. "We'd take two or three wagons with the mules. We didn't catch all of them. We had an ole bulldog named Jack. He'd go catch them. We'd wire their feet and load eight or 10 in a wagon, bring them home, feed them corn, and ship them to St. Louis. That's how we paid for our groceries. My mom and dad were very religious. They depended on the Lord. They attended Shady Dale Church on McGee Creek all day Sunday. I don't know what denomination it was."

Henry, I've Skidded Ties With Him Without Using Lines
Henry and Joe
as told by Mitch Threlkeld

They were big black mules. Henry weighed 1,400 pounds and Joe weighed 1,300. They were over 15 hands. Henry may have been a half a hand taller. We bought them up on (Highway) 160 about a mile from where we lived for $200. They were 2 when we got them.

They were able to pull more than the little team (we'd had before). We had used a 12-inch plow with the little team, but these mules could pull a 14-inch plow, that's 2 inches deeper. We cultivated with them and disked some of the small patches. If we had a big patch, we'd hire a tractor to do the disking.

Dad and I farmed together. We had a team of horses besides the mules. I'd usually work the mules. We rented river bottomland to raise corn in. The owner of the land would get every third load. We lived in the hills. There was a steep hill just before we got home.

Those mules could pull 30 bushel of corn up that hill. We'd put the brakes on to slide one of the wheels going down so the wagon wouldn't run over them.

One time I was plowing and had a half a quarter of a row to go; it came a hard rain. When that rain hit them in the face they turned around facing me, so the rain would hit their butts. I had to undo the lines and get them straightened out. I got pretty wet.

This Henry was a real good mule. He'd come to you when you wanted to catch him, and the other one would follow him in. But you'd have to point his ears forward and gently work the bridle over them, or you wouldn't get the bridle on him if you didn't, because he was so tall. He injured his back leg when he was a colt running out of the barn. He caught it between the sills. The leg didn't seem to bother him. He'd raise it up funny sometimes. But he could pull with it and everything. Sometimes when it swelled too much, we'd put horse liniment on it.

Henry, I've skidded (railroad) ties with him without using lines. My brother and I worked timber in the summers after we got the crops laid by. We'd hook Henry up (to a tie) and say "get up" and he'd take off for the wagon and I'd follow. I just tied his lines up on the hames. I would follow him back to the woods. My brother and I used to experiment with them, and after we'd had them awhile we just tried it

Threlkeld on Joe, Henry on right. Note Henry's big ankle.

one day. We'd had Henry a couple of years and knew he was real gentle. The other one (Joe) probably would have taken off to the barn if we had tried that with him. We'd haul the ties to Naylor to sell.

I knew the mother of Joe and that was a bronc mare. He was a little mean I guess because of that. Sometimes he wouldn't want to pull and we'd wrap (hit) him with a chain and he would.

When we went on the highway a little ways to bottom ground that we rented, if a big truck would come by with a tarp flopping, he'd (Joe) jump back and if we didn't rattle that chain, he's liable to have pulled the wagon in front of that truck. He worked on the left so he was out there close to the trucks.

I have a sister five years younger than me, and one time she was down there in the lot when we took the harness off of Joe. He just felt good and was glad to get that harness off, and he started jumping and running over to her. We thought he was going to run over her. But he just ran up to her and stopped. He just playing.

We'd use the big one to plow a garden. If we used Joe and there was a plant growing, he would step on it. He was just a little mean. But he wouldn't do that cultivating, just in the garden.

Neither one of them was very good to ride. But my brother and I would lead them to a stump and get on. Sometimes Dad would oversee us (in the field) and one of us worked the horses, and the other one worked the mules. When we took off for lunch, we'd help each other up or we'd find a bank or a stump to get on. We'd ride them to the barn and eat our lunch and ride them back to the field. We always fed them corn and hay (at lunch time.)

We'd start at 7 a.m. and work them until about 4 o'clock. An old train would go by at 11:30. They got used to that train and when they got to the end of the row, they wouldn't want to make another round. You could make them go back, but they didn't like it. They wanted to head for the barn.

We kept them shod. A neighbor would shoe them. Sometimes they'd get tired of holding a leg up, and you'd have to hit them in the side to straighten them up.

I guess we got those mules in 1940 when I was 16 and had them until 1944 when we sold out and quit farming. In 1944 Dad went back on the railroad and I was drafted. We sold everything, sold the farm. They were always good mules. I was never afraid to work them to anything.

 **Mitchel Elijah Threlkeld was born July 29, 1923, to George Carlos and Eula Bell Threlkeld. He had four sisters, one younger and three older, and one brother three years older. He was raised in Ripley County about four miles north of Naylor, a mile and half southeast of Fairdealing. While their father worked on the railroad, Mitch and his older brother, Champ, farmed 24 acres of corn and cotton and 12 acres of hay.** Champ left the farm at age 17 to work at a Civilian Conservation Camp, leaving most of the farming to Mitch, who was 14. Mitch attended Burham, a one-room school through the eighth grade and was graduated from Doniphan High School in 1942. He farmed for a year with Joe and Henry and was drafted into the U.S. Army in 1944. He served one year overseas in France as a medic at the same time that his brother, Champ, served on the front lines. "He would come back to see me," Mitch said. "Champ was awarded two Purple Hearts. One time he was hit in the chest. A bullet hit his New Testament."

After being discharged Mitch worked for Montgomery Ward and the Missouri Pacific Railroad. He retired in 1984 after working 26 years for the Missouri State Highway Patrol as a driver's license examiner. He married Betty Davis on Dec. 30, 1947, and the couple celebrated their 62nd anniversary in 2009. After retiring, Mitch bought an old pickup and worked flea markets for 12 years. Mitch said after he was drafted in 1944 his father sold the farm and Joe and Henry at auction and that he never saw the mules again. "I drove a tractor four days for a cousin when I was a teenager, an old steel-wheeled Farmall, and I was so sore I couldn't hardly walk. But I liked working the mules," he said.

They Pulled Better If They Knew He Was Over a Wheel
Pete and Nig
as told by Paul Jenkins

These mules would pull. We had to have them to pull the baler, see. And they would pull. There were not many teams back then in the farming that pulled. You know, really get down and pull.

Pete and Nig, one was a red mule; the other was a black mare mule. They were between 700 and 800 pounds. They wouldn't weigh a thousand. We bought them together from an individual when they were 3 or 4. We used them for general farming, plowing, and with the cultivator, and the baler. We used them for transportation a lot then, to go to town. We had them close to 20 years.

My older brother, Harold, claimed them, but they were still on our farm. He mainly worked them, but I worked them some.

We went from the bottoms here at Harviell to Stringtown in 1929, and we stayed up there about three years and we logged. We had a couple of big teams of horses and the team of mules. And we hauled ties with these little mules from Stringtown to Grandin, which was 15 miles. We might have had eight ties per load. It would take eight to nine hours to go over there and back. You'd try to make it over there by noon. Then you fed the mules and had something yourself, then you would head back.

There would be three wagons together, different people going with ties about every day. There were mud holes and bad places. They (Pete and Nig) were kind of a team of wrecker mules. We would have to take them out to pull the big wagons through. We'd go through first, unhook the mules, and go back and help the others. We would hook on to the front of them, to the tongue. That would give you two horses and two mules. If the wagon was stuck, they'd swing and they'd swing to see if the front wheel was loose. If it was, they would go with it. They knowed when to pull.

They pulled better if they knew my brother was over a wheel. He'd get hold of a back wheel. He had their lines on the hames. He'd talk to them. They'd swing one-way, then the other. Them little mules would get down to where you could hardly see under their bellies. They'd pull really good.

We lived on a road that ran in front of the house. He could sit on the porch, have the mules out in the road hooked to a wagon, and he could make them turn around. He'd say, "haw" or "gee", or "Get up Nig, Pete" and they'd turn around. They done that without any lines.

They were good mules. They were just little. He would do that just to show people how well they could do that. He used them really too hard, because they would do the job. If they'd been heavier, they would have been really good.

It was very seldom that they had teams that would really pull. There were a few horses that would pull. We never did have any that would. Our horses never would really get down and pull. They would pull a pretty good load, but if they got stuck, they didn't like that. They would seesaw.

I worked the mules to a cultivator that had six plows, three on each wing. We straddled the row and maneuvered blades however you wanted them. There was a Frisco that went down the Frisco track through Taft, down through Naylor and into Arkansas. That train came through at 11:30. When that train came through, it blew its whistle. Then we knowed it was about dinnertime. There was open range then and there was a jack or two that ran loose, and they would fight our mules, and we had to keep them run off.

And them little mules also pulled a big separator (thresher). A tractor (steam engine) couldn't pull it. They would blow the whistle to the steam engine of the morning if they were going to work. My brother hauled water to the steam engine. If they were going to work, my brother would take the team of mules, go get a load of water, and take it to the steam engine. That was two of the main duties with a thresher, the water wagon, and pulling it over hills. They'd swing back and forth (to get the thresher moving).

We raised watermelon at that time and we shipped them from Taft. We'd load that freight car, hauling loads with them mules. It'd take 1,200 to 1,500 watermelon to make a carload. One year we shipped 15 cars of watermelons. That's a lot of watermelons. We had them in different patches, probably had 20 acres. We also bought watermelons from neighbors. They would see we were making a little bit of money, and they'd say,"I can make some money, too." They didn't know how to sell them, so we would buy them.

My brother got married and took the mules with him. And when he sold out, he had a farm sale. He sold the mules at the sale. It would have been about 1938 or 1940. They would have been 20 or 22 years old. I never did see them after that.

Paul R. Jenkins was born Sept. 29, 1923, to Roy and Minnie Jenkins. His dad farmed between Neelyville and Harviell in Butler County. Jenkins had a twin sister, three other sisters, and three brothers. He attended three one-room schools: Oak Dale, Pine View, and was graduated from the eighth grade at McIntosh School. "There were six of us kids, and we would ride horses to school. We had two horses; and six of us could ride the two horses. Pine View was two and a half miles from home. We went there two years and moved back to the sand country," he said. Jenkins married Wilma Adams, a classmate, in 1941. She passed away in 2005. Jenkins worked for Porter DeWitt Construction Company in Poplar Bluff for 43 years, mainly as a truck driver, retiring in 1985. From 1985 to 1995 he made 400 doghouses and sold them, all of them by word of mouth. He constructed a farm home in 1977 and in 2009 was living in the basement after selling the home to his son, Earl.

VI. Plantation Farming/Sharecropping

The Little River Drainage District of Southeast Missouri

Prior to the 20th century, parts of seven southeast Missouri counties were covered in swampland, and the land was considered useless for farming or logging. These counties were Bollinger, Cape Girardeau, Dunklin, New Madrid, Pemiscot, Scott, and Stoddard.

The swamp consisted of 500,000 acres in an area 90 miles long and 10 to 20 miles wide. The swamp was a mass of trees, bogs, and standing water, with only a few roads and railroad crossings. French explorers in the 1800s called the swamp area, "The Little River" to distinguish it from the Mississippi River, located a few miles to the east.

In 1907, The Little River Drainage District was formed to drain the swamp in order to produce sellable and productive land. Bonds were issued and landowners in the district were taxed to raise money to construct the drainage system. Engineers devised a system of levees and gravity-flow ditches.

The drainage was accomplished from 1914 to 1928, through construction of 957.8 miles of ditches and 304.43 miles of levees. This is the same facilities the district now operates and maintains. Since 1931, they have been assisted by the U.S. Army Corps of Engineers. The original ditches were built with floating dredge boats. Mule teams were used in the project.

Two separate drainage systems were built, the Northern District, and the Southern District. The Northern District consists of a diversion channel that diverts the flows of the Castor River and four creeks east into the Mississippi River, just below Cape Girardeau. The channel extends about 45 miles, from near Greenbriar in Bollinger County to the Mississippi River. The Northern District has over 50 miles of channels and nearly 45 miles of levees.

The Southern District is much larger. Ditch Number 1 extends 100 miles from the diversion channel levee, located between the two districts, south to the Arkansas line. The Southern District has nearly 850 miles of ditches or canals, and nearly 250 miles of levees.

The 15-year project drained 1.2 million acres of land—an area approximate to the size of Delaware. When it was finished, more than one million cubic yards of earth had been displaced (a greater amount than was moved during construction of the Panama Canal.) The Little River Drainage District is the largest drainage district in the United States.

Many of the men featured in this book knew of the drainage district, and some farmed near some of its ditches and levees. Plantation owners David Barton and Charles B. Baker, who are both mentioned in some of the Plantation/Sharecropping stories, served on the drainage district's board of supervisors. Baker served from 1942 to 1957. Barton served from 1952 to 1987 and served as board president from 1964 to 1987.

Former swampland now yields cotton, soybeans, corn, wheat, barley, rice, vegetable crops, melons, and nuts. Today, one third of Missouri's agriculture income is produced in the seven counties in the

Bootheel area, which were transformed by the drainage project. There are 114 Missouri counties.

Information used for this story came from booklets authorized by The Little River Drainage District's board of supervisors.

Forty Acres and a Mule–
The David Barton Plantation at Catron

The David Barton Plantation at Catron in New Madrid County, has been in existence since 1935, when David's father, P.M. Barton, moved to the area from Marie, Arkansas, and formed the P.M. Barton and Son Plantation. P.M. Barton accumulated acreage by buying up farmland, some of which was not cleared or drained. At one time in the mid-1940s, the plantation consisted of 10,000 acres, located in Stoddard and New Madrid counties.

Opal Bondurant went to work for David Barton as a bookkeeper in 1943, and at age 88, in 2008, she was still working at the plantation two half days a week.

"It was row to row cotton in the 1940s," Bondurant said. "There were 200 sharecroppers, and over 200 three-room houses. They called them shotgun houses because they were lined up in a row. There was no running water. All of them had wells. Most of them didn't have electricity."

Bondurant said almost all of the 200 sharecroppers were black. "All of the sharecroppers had their own mules, and the mules were kept in a large lot on the farm," she said. "The mules were cared for by a hostler. There was a blacksmith there, too. Both of them were black. Sharecroppers came in each morning to pick up their mules."

She said there were about 300 mules on the

Barton plantation house at Catron.
2009 Photo.

plantation and that those who share-cropped 40 acres had one mule; those who sharecropped 80 acres had two mules. "Each family had about half an acre they could grow a garden in. Some of them kept chickens. The men worked the mules, and the women and children chopped cotton. All of them picked cotton," Bondurant said.

"We had one overseer, Charlie Jacks. He rode a saddlebred horse. He made sure they were working (the cotton) and keeping it clean. The sharecroppers were not mistreated. He would be out before daylight, and he would work after dark. He was a real good one.

Opal Bondurant at David Barton headquarters in Catron. June 2008.

"Some of them (sharecroppers) stayed here 10 or 20 years. They would stay through the winter. We rarely had a turnover. They had a school for blacks on the plantation that bordered the town (Catron)." Bondurant said the school could house 40 to 50 students and that many of the black children didn't go to school.

Sharecroppers received half of the crop money. "When we made a sale, we figured out what each one got. We took out our farm part, and gave them the rest," she said. "In good years," she added, "A sharecropper might make a bale and a half an acre, and some years cotton sold for $200 a bale." Bondurant stated that David Barton owned one of the four cotton gins in Catron.

"Sharecroppers would pick cotton all day. They would weigh it in the field. They would eat, and then haul it to the gin," Bondurant explained. "We could hear the wagons coming. We would weigh all evening, from 20 to 40 wagons. The gin could bale four to five bales an hour. Most of the fall we ginned 24 hours a day. It was a busy place around here."

DAVID M. BARTON

According to Bondurant, the first 20 or so loaded wagons got their cotton ginned that evening, while they waited. The rest stored their cotton in stalls inside one of two cotton houses that Barton owned. "We made a list from the cotton houses, so we would know the order in which they came in."

Bondurant stated that during the picking season she would often get to work at 4:30 a.m. and go home at 10 p.m. "David Barton used to call me a workaholic," she said. "Cotton picking would run from mid-August to February depending on the weather."

"In 1947 we had a flood, and the levee on the big drainage ditch broke, and water covered up half of the plantation," Bondurant said. "A lot of the sharecroppers didn't make anything. They didn't leave. They didn't have anywhere to go."

Bondurant remembered that in the 1940s, there were two grocery stores, two service stations, and a restaurant in Catron. "There was a honky-tonk west of town on the north side of the road. Dad Foster managed it all.

"In 1947, Barton started buying John Deere and International tractors, and sharecropping was phased out. Some of the families stayed in the houses until the men could find work elsewhere."

After the sharecroppers left, day laborers were hired to pick cotton. "Our last ginning year was 1982. We didn't grow cotton after that," she said.

David Barton owned and managed the plantation from 1940 until his death in 1987. In 1940, David Barton started construction on a southern-style plantation house just west of Catron and he and his first wife, Marion, moved into the house in 1943.

In 1957, David Barton rented the plantation out to a man and his sons.

Since 1987, June Barton (David's second wife) has managed the plantation. In 2007, she rented out land to five area farmers, and they planted 2,050 acres of cotton, 3,290 acres of soybeans, 827 acres of corn, and 509 acres of rice, for a total of 6,676 acres planted.

Mechanical pickers started ginning cotton in the early 1990s, and in 2002, the plantation started growing some cotton again.

Bondurant stated there were two other plantations in the Catron area in the 1940s, the Baker Plantation, and the Carouthers Plantation, which is still in existence.

I Can Still See Those Knees Coming At Me
Plantation Mules
as told by Bob Alsup

When I was 12, I was feeding up to 100 mules at wintertime at a plantation at Catron (New Madrid County). There wasn't always that many. Mules were coming and going all the time. They were always buying and selling. There might be 60 there one week and 100 the next.

There were two plantations west of Catron. The P.M. Barton Plantation was on the north side of the road that ran west of Catron. Charlie Baker, who lived in Kennett, owned the plantation on the south side of the road. It was a mile wide and two miles deep. This is where my Dad worked.

We lived in a house on the Baker Plantation; that was just across from the floodway ditch. That's what it was known as at that time. It was the main ditch. Just across the water was a black honky-tonk. It was a four-room house someone turned into a honky-tonk. They played continuous blues. The music was wonderful. I was captivated by that. They played music continuously (jukebox). Most of it was instrumental, piano, saxophone, and trumpets. They played blues well into the night. I knew most of the people who went to that place, because I worked with them during the day.

Connie Thompson was the headman of the plantation Baker owned. Thompson was a

CHARLES B. BAKER

mule trader. He bought mules during the winter, mostly unbroken two year olds. He would haul them in to the plantation by the truckload. There was a huge barn and a huge lot at the plantation where the mules were kept. I would spend most of my day shucking corn in the corncrib, and putting out hay, which was stored in the barn loft.

I worked for Thompson but didn't get paid for it. It was part of the arrangement he had with my dad (day laborer). I quit school at age 11. I quit on my own. We moved around so much, and I would stay in the cotton fields until December before I could start going to school. Sometimes I would go to school for a week or two, after getting cotton out of the fields. Dad would move to another place and I would have to start at another school.

In the barn lot, mud would be knee deep if you walked through it. There were so many mules I don't hardly remember a dry spot. I drove an old Farmal "M" tractor hooked to a wagon with feed and corn on it. I would put the corn in feed troughs, and the hay in outside hay mangers. Thompson had hand-operated water pumps side by side. I would work two pumps at one time that fed water into a big water trough. If I ever had any spare time, I would be at the blacksmith shop helping a giant of a black man called "Saul." I would help him temper plow points he had forged for cultivators and plows.

Thompson would take unbroken mules, and drive them in a chute, and harness them. Some were really wild. Before they could pen one of them, he turned around and came running down the barn aisle at full speed. I was standing at the entrance. At first I attempted to stop him. About the time I moved to get out of his way, he turned the same way and tried to jump over me. The last thing I remember was his knees hitting me in the head. I was knocked out for a couple of minutes. I can still see those knees coming at me.

In the spring before they would start making crops, Thompson would start choosing mule teams from over 100 unbroke mules. He would start with the biggest and best that looked alike. He had one pair that weighed 1,800 pounds each.

They would catch them in the chute and pair them up, harness them, and hook them to a wagon. Wagons never had brakes in the flat country, because you didn't need them. But the one they used to break mules had brakes. Two of the black day laborers would sit in the wagon. The driver would get on the left side, and the one with the whip would sit to his right. They would head the unbroken team down a straight two-mile road that ran between sections of land.

The driver would turn the team loose and they would start running down the road. He could keep them in the road with the reins. They would go as hard as they could go until they would start to slow down. At this time, the driver would put on the brakes, and the other man would start laying the whip to them. They would again go as hard as they could go, then they would stop. The driver would then turn them around and drive them back to the barn, and that team of mules would be broke. They would break them in 15 to 20 minutes. I doubt if that story has ever been told.

They would then choose two more that looked alike and weighed about the same. They would pair them, and break them all the way down to the last pair, and Thompson would sell them as broke to work. In those days a team of mules was the most expensive thing you could buy. You could buy a car for $200, a team of mules would fetch up to $500.

During the spring there would be 40 day laborers going to the fields each with a mule and a double shovel. Thompson had two or three American Saddlebreds men would ride to oversee the workers.

When the day laborers would come in from the fields with the mules and take their harnesses off, I had a fly spray can filled with a blue medicine to treat sores created by the collars put on the mules. The spray can took both hands to use, one to hold it, the other to operate the plunger. When they took the collars off, sometimes there would be sores twice as big as a silver dollar, where the collar had rubbed.

I could tell a mean mule by looking at them. There was a small black mule that after I had sprayed her, she wheeled and kicked. One of her feet hit flat on my right buttock. I went rolling approximately 20 feet. At the moment she wheeled around, I knew what was going to happen, and had started to turn away from her. I'm sure that helped in how far I rolled. I got right up and don't remember being sore. A mule knows where that foot is going to land when they kick.

On a rainy day the workers would come in from the field. Their favorite activity was to shoot craps. They would clear out a corner of a corncrib. I would join them. They mostly bet 15 cents. Blacks outnumbered whites nine to one around Catron. There wasn't any trouble between blacks and whites.

In the fall when the day laborers were picking cotton in the fields, I would drive the M Farmall from the fields to the gin at Parma, about four miles away. I would pull four loaded cotton wagons at a time. It looked like a train.

I was around 7 when I started picking cotton. I picked cotton for 10 years up until I was married. We'd pick from before sunup to sundown five and a half days a week, from August to into December. I probably picked 20 to 30 pounds a day starting out. The last two years I picked I was picking over 400 pounds a day. I would usually get up to 410 to 415 pounds. A lot of times we would get our own cotton out, and go and pick for somebody else. All of our family were big-cotton pickers.

We would start out when the cotton was heavy with dew. Walking to the end of the row, you would hold your sack in front of you so you wouldn't get wet. A lot of pickers crawled on their knees a lot. They would wear kneepads. Cotton would stand 2 to 3 feet high. They didn't fertilize in those days, so we seldom saw cotton 4-feet high. I didn't crawl that much. I would work all week and might get a dime, or if we had a good week, a quarter. Dad would hook up the team and we would go to town. It might be a five- or six-mile ride to town.

On the Fourth of July the workers would gather enough 30-foot poles to stack 4 feet high and 5 feet deep. They would dig a pit 3 feet wide and 3 feet deep. They would set the poles in the pit and set them afire the morning before. The next day they would place three or four hogs and three or four goats over the pit. Thompson would furnish the hogs and goats. All of the workers and their families would be invited.

 Bob Alsup was born Dec. 2, 1925, to Charlie and Vilena Alsup in a log cabin on a sharecropper's farm in Dunklin County. He had a brother four years older and two sisters. From the time he was born until he married Margery in 1943, Alsup estimated his father moved more than 20 times throughout the Bootheel area. Two of these years, when Bob was 12 to 14 years old, his father worked as a "Riding Boss" for a plantation near Catron in New Madrid County. His father rode an American Saddlebred to oversee about 50 black day laborers who worked approximately two sections of land, or 1,240 acres. While living on the plantation, Bob was in charge of feeding, haying, and watering mules during winter months. Bob attended several schools through the fifth grade. He was drafted into the U.S. Army in 1944 and served in Europe as World War II was coming to an end. Alsup worked as a bricklayer for 24 years, retiring in 1974. He moved from Kennett to Greenville in 1974 and worked small jobs for Carlos Hicks Construction in Poplar Bluff into the 1990s. For the past 25 years he has bought and sold musical instruments at flea markets. "I buy old ones and fix them up," he said. In 2008, Bob and Margery celebrated their 65th wedding anniversary. Alsup said the barn lot at the plantation was about three acres and the barn was 80 foot by 100 foot. The laborers lived in houses near the barn along a line that bordered the road. The west side of the plantation bordered the main floodway drainage ditch. See photo on page 286.

Jack Would Nose the Chain Off of a Gate, and Let the Cattle Drink
as told by Bob Lincoln

My dad worked by the day, then got into sharecropping, then renting. He would work by the day and get paid by the day. The largest he ever farmed was 50 to 60 acres. I was born in a farmhouse near White Oak, south of Holcomb in Dunklin County.

I was 10 when he (Dad) got into sharecropping. The person who owned the land would furnish the mules and equipment; you'd do the work and get half of the crop. I helped my dad from the time I was 9. Sometimes I would ride the cultivator. Dad would keep his hands on the cultivator's handles, and I would sit in front of him and watch the mules. I enjoyed it.

Mules come from breeding a mare to a jack. When stallions are bred to jennies, they never turn out to be as good of workers. My dad sharecropped for Charles Davis, Lon Lutes and Sam Hassler. They would furnish the mules. The mules were named human names like Charlie, Tom, Jack, and one we called "Hoss." My father was fairly harsh. I've seen him beat mules quite a bit.

Dad and I broke a few mule teams for landowners. We would harness them up, take them to a field and hook them to a log. They would be ready to go, they would run, jump, thrash around, and after a while the logs would pull them down. After they did that for a while they were not ready to run anymore.

Many times I would feed livestock for owners and pump water. I did a lot of that pumping. When you've got cattle and mules coming to drink, you can't keep it pumped fast enough. Sometimes the cattle would come up all at once. I'd have the trough full, but I would have to keep pumping.

On a typical day I would get up around 5 o'clock. While Mom was fixing breakfast, Dad and I would go out and feed the mules corn and hay and water them. During working season we would try to feed them quite a bit of corn. We'd brush them down. We'd go in and eat and when we came back we would harness them and go to the field, usually we'd go to the farm implement where we had stopped the day before and start right there. When I was young I would carry a lunch to Dad in the field. When I was older we would unhook the mules and bring them in at lunch and water them, but we didn't feed them. We would tie them up with the harness on. We would only take 15 or 20 minutes for lunch, and then we would head back to the field. When we came in in the evening; after we would get them free of the harness, they liked to roll on the ground.

Mules are temperamental and will run. One time we were pulling fence poles out of the ground; I was in the wagon driving the mules. Dad picked up a piece of barbed wire with a pole and it hit the tail of one of the mules. They sprinted forward. I knew I wouldn't be able to hold them so I grabbed one of the lines, and threw the other one out of the wagon. I pulled the one line and made them go in a circle, and when they came back around to where Dad was he grabbed the line and made them stop.

We plowed with a breaking plow, which throws dirt one way, and also plowed with a lister plow, which throws dirt two ways. We used the lister plow for planting potatoes and watermelons. Since you couldn't turn the lister to the side we put a tin can on the point. Dad was plowing one day and hit a snag causing the plow to come out of the ground and hit one of the mules in the rear end. The mules bolted. We thought they would tear the plow loose, but they ran with it all the way to the gate of the lot and stopped, which was a quarter of a mile away. When we got up to them we could see they were okay.

When I was 15, Dad got to the point where he could afford a team of mules. We bought a pair of brown mules from a local farmer for around $160. They were named Blue and Red. I don't know if they were related. When I was 16, Dad bought a tractor. He'd work the tractor and I'd work the mules. I think we were farming 60 acres of rented land then. When we sharecropped we usually raised 40 acres of cotton.

If we hadn't had the mules we would have been in trouble. There were tractors, but it was like someone who owns a fancy car today. Very few had one, most had a team of mules. I've worked both mules and horses. I liked mules better. Horses will work until they drop and hurt themselves. Mules work only so long and they'll stop. We worked some mare teams. Mares have a good temperament and are easier to handle. The last team we had was a team of mares (in 1951).

One time we worked a pair of black mules owned by Charles Davis. They each weighed around 1,200 pounds and were good workers. We lived in a tenant house on one of his farms. He kept a few head of mixed breed cattle on the farm. They pastured in a field along with the mules. We watered them a couple of times a day, and kept the gate to the barn lot locked. Davis didn't want cattle standing around a water tank. He wanted them out in the field so they would graze.

One of the black mules was named Jack. If the cattle went to the barn lot to drink and the gate was closed, Jack would nose the chain off the gate, and let the cattle drink. After they drank he would move them out of the barn lot, and would push that gate closed.

Sometimes when they were in the barn lot I would get a handful of grain and the mules would come up and eat out of my hand. If I went out there and didn't have grain and they were in the lot, they would come up and push their noses against my hand.

We usually fed the mules at a certain time each day, around 5:30 p.m. Jack got accustomed to that. If we were just a few minutes late, Jack would walk to the door that led to the corncrib, take his right foot and paw at that part of the barn as a reminder for us to come out and feed.

We were very, very poor. In 1944, we lost all of the crop, it rained so much. We all three, Mom, Dad and I, worked the fields for others picking cotton. The grocery owner let us buy groceries on credit. Mom did house cleaning and washing for others. We worked all year and lacked $25 of paying the grocer. I drove a team of mules to haul cotton trailers to the cotton gin. I'd wait there until they blew the cotton into the bin area. When we had corn, we used the mule team pulling a wagon to gather corn, but we'd make sure we had tame mules that would stop and stand on command. We used sickle mowers to mow hay and a frame put on a wagon to pick up and pile up hay and we would throw it in the wagon, and take the wagon to the barn and throw it up in the barn. One time we raised soybeans in a swamp area. We couldn't get the picker in so we harnessed the mules to a sled, and pulled the soybeans up by hand and beat them on the side of the sled to save the soybean crop.

Cotton was the best money crop in the Bootheel. You could do good with soybeans and corn, but you had to have quite a bit of land. We worked hard but we didn't think of it that way. When picking cotton we would have enough money to go to the movies on Saturday nights. I would walk to Holcomb to go to the movies. When I was working quite a bit, Dad would give me a dollar for Saturday night. Sometimes I would ride into town with an owner in a pickup to get groceries. Back then they would deliver groceries if we wanted to stay later. I liked the westerns, Gene Autry, Charles Starrett who played the Durango Kid, William Elliot who did the Hickok type of movies.

In a good year, we would clear $1,000. That was unusual. We considered ourselves fortunate if we had enough to buy my school clothes. Mother was very good at sewing and made my sister's clothes out of feed sacks with printed cloth. I worked in cotton fields from the time I was 4. I would walk the rows and put cotton in Mom's sack. By the time I was 6, I was given a sack of my own and given a row by myself and I kept it up. I picked cotton up until I was 18. They used to have a cotton-picking contest in Arkansas where the winner got $1,000. I got good enough to enter, but we could never afford the entry fee or the time off. The most I ever picked in one day was 542 or 547 pounds. That was considered very exceptional. Usually good pickers picked 300 to 350 a day.

The day I picked over 500 pounds, I started at 6:45 a.m. and worked until dark. The only breaks I got was when I would carry loaded cotton sacks to the trailer and unload, which never took longer than 15 minutes. I carried a sack lunch and would eat at the trailer. The more weight I got in the sack the better I could pick. When I would lean forward it would help support me, I could really work then. With the weight on I could carry 130 pounds with a strap around my neck to keep the sack straight. Often the amount of dew in the morning determined how long we would pick. Owners didn't want to pay for cotton that was wet because water dries out.

 **Bob Lincoln was born in 1932 to Elmer and Grace Lincoln. He had one sibling, a younger sister. He was graduated from Holcomb High School in 1950 and worked as a clerk in a general store before joining the U.S. Navy in 1951. He was a turret gunner and a co-pilot for P2-V patrol planes during the Korean Conflict. He and his wife, Mary Lou, were married in 1959 and have resided in Columbia, Missouri ever since. Bob taught at elementary and high schools before becoming a principal and retired in 1989. "When I was a junior in high school I made A's in English. One time the English teacher was going to be gone two weeks, and she went to the superintend-**

ent and asked that I substitute while she was gone. I taught all of her English classes including senior classes, plus I had to keep up my own homework. The district paid me," he said. "If I could grow up again, I would be tickled to grow up the same way. I found out we were poverty stricken when I joined the Navy. I never knew that before. We always had food to eat, a place to live, and clothes to wear. That was fine. One time I complained to Dad that I wasn't getting paid enough ,and he had me keep expenses for food, clothing, etc. and at the end of the year he owed me $25. Dad never owned a car. He bought a Ford-Ferguson tractor when I left home." Lincoln was interviewed in December 2007. He died July 21, 2010.

Here He'd Come With Another Blame Mule
as told by Ervin Cates

There were different sizes of mule, and the little mules were for cultivators, and the big mules were used for heavier plowing and pulling, and rolling logs and things like that. They had to be broke. Odie Reeves owned 140 acres in town (Charleston) and had different farms in the country. Dad sharecropped 40 acres from him, and he furnished the mules and equipment. It was all mules, very seldom seen horses.

He'd (Reeves) buy mules from Jock Ward's mule farm. Jock would buy anything they brought in. He could tell by looking at them if they were a cultivator team or could pull a road grader. At that time they used a lot of slip shovels behind a team. These levees were built years ago by teams pulling those slip shovels. When Odie bought mules, he didn't know anything about them, which side he'd work on or nothing. There was always someone ready to buy a team of mules that was broke. And Odie was steady buying those blime (blame) mules.

So Odie would bring a mule out there while I was plowing with a team of mules. And he'd want to take one mule loose, and doggone I had to break these mules in. If you get a mule used to working on the right, and you put him on the left, he'll act crazy for several days, walking sideways and acting up. That's what I had to put up with. He traded me two different times in one day. About the time I'd get a team broke, here he'd come with another blime (blame) mule. That went on for two years.

I was 15 when we moved up here. (We) moved up from the Ozarks. Daddy was a timber cutter. Back during the Depression time, anytime he got a job cutting timber, I had to come out of school to help him. I didn't get an education. We had mules back there, family mules, and I got to learning about mules. (I) didn't work with them then. Dad had them.

I went to (grade) school when I could, but there was a teacher (Hytator) that told me, "Ervin, you just need to go to school long enough to learn the basics, then you can exercise your education by reading and all of that." I can read. Of the mornings when I'd get up I'd say, "I'll study my twos, threes or fours all day long. Two times two is four, two times three is six." I'd repeat that (out loud) all day long while I was plowing. I've looked at the south end of a north-bound mule for years studying multiplication tables. I got to where I knew all of the multiplications and adding and dividing. He was right. You learn the basics on that and if you learn to read a little you can exercise that. I ordered books, history books and enjoyed that.

Down here (Charleston) we had this broke up ground and when we found a blame mule that wouldn't ride, we'd ride these doggone mules. The way you break a mule to ride is after you have worked him. He's tired. Take a sack and put two spades of dirt in it and tie it. Divide it and throw it on his back. If he's all right with that sack, he'll ride. Boy! I've seen them jump, run, do everything. But you know then you're not going to belly up on that son of a gun.

We'd get in this plowed ground. I'd have a rope around his neck and a bridle (on him) too. My two brothers are the ones who'd do the riding, because I was bigger and I would hold the mule. If they carried the sack a little bit, they'd jump up on him. One would get the other by the foot and throw him on him. But they didn't mind getting throwed because of the soft dirt, and I had this rope. We broke them to work. We broke them to ride, no telling how many, probably 20 or 30. Somewhere (in the county) there was a man that all he done was break mules and he (Reeves) was getting all of this done for nothing. But us boys were getting a kick out of breaking them to ride out in that plowed ground.

Sometimes they'd get scared, rear up and jerk me down and drag me around. My brothers would laugh. But if they got throwed, I'd laugh. They'd throw them easy. They were just sitting bareback. They didn't have nothing to hold on to. If they broke loose from me, they'd head to the barn, because that's where the feed was. They'd go right in the stall. The feed was there.

That's the way you break a mule. You just don't jump on a mule, not knowing he's broke to ride. Because those buggers will kick. And I was always scared of them, because when I was a boy, there was a man who got kicked right in the face. His whole face was caved in.

Back in '37, we had a flood. Reeves bought mules in from his country farms. We had 21 mules in the lot all winter. Those mules would want out so bad. Those mules would come up to the gate wanting you to put a bridle on them. There would be three of us, on a mule apiece. After we'd turn one loose, we'd grab another one. We were steady riding them things. We had friends in town that would come up and help us ride them.

I worked about 30 different mules in the field. I used double shovels, a one-row cultivator and breaking plows. I worked a one-row planter with one mule tied to it that I walked behind. Small mules were the best at cultivating because in turning they wouldn't tear up as much. And you didn't need the strength of that big mule to put up with. A good team of cultivating mules, it was kind of fun to plow with them because they were good stepping. You wanted a team that would really step out, not poke along. Most of the time, one of us (brothers, Dad and I) would work the team, and the others would be hoeing and things like that. We traded off. I've done all of it. However it worked out.

I weighed 149 pounds when I was 17. I wore overalls and we went barefoot in the summer time in that sand. Most of the cultivator men went barefooted. In the sand it was fun. This was cotton country. That's the reason we came up here. I did a lot of plowing cotton.

I never had a team to get scared and run in the field. My dad was plowing with a cultivator and a piece of paper came blowing across there, and off they went as hard as they could run, jerked my dad down, the cultivator plows were just missing him. He'd had the lines around his back and they were dragging him, had him scared to death. It's a wonder those plows didn't get him.

The only mules that ever run away from me, I had taken a load of cotton to the gin and I got back to the farm. I was in an empty wagon and was going down a sandy road and something happened and off they went. I just let them run. I was going around the farm. When they got to slowing down, I took the lines and really put it to them. When they did stop, they were ready. They were broke to work.

Some mules were just a hunting trouble. Some mules, buggers they called them. They were always hunting something to get scared of.

Henry Ervin Cates was born March 12, 1921, to Henry and Mae Cates. He had three younger brothers and one sister. He was raised in Ripley County, 16 miles southwest of Doniphan, and attended Bellview School for a while but didn't make it past the third grade. His father moved the family to sharecrop in Charleston when Ervin was 15. He failed a physical at Fort Leonard Wood for the draft due to a back injury he sustained at age 17 from jumping a levee fence and landing/slipping on a soda bottle that threw him abruptly backwards. After attending a welding class at Charleston High School he worked as a shop man for Clay County Cotton Company in Charleston for 40 years, retiring in 1986. He lost his wife, Violet, in April 2007 after 65 years of marriage.

Red Would Catch Them by the Neck
and Set Them Over the Fence
Red
as told by Wilma Cavness

The one mule I remember in particular was ole Red. He was a big mule because I was a little-bitty-scrawny kid. But ole Red, he knew everything. I guess he was old.

I worked Red by himself, "get up Red" and "whoa." He just knew when to stop. Dad had to harness him. I was 9 or 10, might have been 4-foot tall, real-scrawny kid. I guess Dad told me to do it, because we didn't have no boys. Momma was busy with twin girls four years younger.

I was so little there was a lot of things I couldn't do on the farm. I had an older sister, Lillie. She was larger and four-years older than I was and she worked with Poppa about every day. We always had two teams of mules.

Poppa knew Red wouldn't hurt me or run away with me. I wasn't afraid because I had been around ole Red. We were always giving him (Red) apples and carrots. We'd sneak out of the house without Momma knowing it. He was a pet. We just put our arms around his neck and petted him. We wasn't afraid to walk around behind him because he wouldn't kick us or anything.

Poppa wouldn't let us girls ride him. He was too big. All I did (with Red) was plant cotton. It was a one-row planter, had handles on it. Dad was sitting up the rows and I'd follow along with the mule and try to stay on the top of the ridge that he made. I was planting and he was preparing the rows.

Papa said, "When you get to the end, don't worry about holding on to that planter, just turn it loose. Ole Red knows what to do." When I got to the end of the row, I'd let go and he'd just turn. I wasn't strong enough to hold it to turn it. But I could balance it (down the rows). My rows weren't straight. Dad would say, "Well, Hon, do the best you can." He was a good dad. I didn't mind working with him.

I just worked part of a day. I couldn't hold up all day. I'd work maybe a half a day and my sister would take over. She would work with Poppa when I worked Red. Then she would take over for me because I was wore out from the walking. We tried to find a bush to hide behind (if we needed to go to the bathroom). Poppa always took us in early if a storm was coming. I was terrified of storms.

That's when we lived south of Hayti about two or three miles. We could walk to town. Dad sharecropped probably 40 acres. Momma and Poppa didn't have no boys at that time. Poppa usually borrowed I think $100 to sharecrop. That had to buy feed, groceries, everything else that was needed. So it had to be spent wisely. We had our dress clothes, our dress shoes to go to church in, but we didn't wear them everyday. And when we weren't working in the field, we went bare-footed.

Poppa would let us wear overalls and a shirt, dressed like a boy. When we got through working, we had to take them off. He wouldn't let us wear them. We had to wear a dress or a skirt.

He (Red) belonged to Dad, because as a sharecropper you had to furnish your own mules. I could make two or three rounds without stopping. I was used to walking because we had no other way to go. We had to wear shoes and a bonnet to cover our face with. Momma made us wear long sleeves. Dad let us know he was proud of us. Me and Poppa was buddies. He'd say, "Come on Bill, let's go to town," to get feed or whatever we happened to need.

He called me "Bill." I was called Bill until I started to school. I guess because Poppa wanted a son so bad. I took the boy's place. We planted cotton. After it came up we had to chop it. We called it hoe-ing at that time.

That was a rough life for a child, but it was a good life. I loved it. I didn't know nothing else, but that.

Our pigs, hogs, and horses were all in the same lot. Ole Red would take the baby pigs, catch them by the back of the neck, and set them over the fence.

Another thing he would do, Poppa had buttons to fasten the barn doors with. Red learnt how to open those doors and get in there and get to the corn. He knew how to open it, but he didn't know how to shut it, so he would let all the rest of the animals in the corn. Dad had to go to wiring the doors shut.

He was a smart mule. I don't know what ever become of him, because when he quit farming, Poppa sold him. And to tell you the truth it was like selling one of his kids.

Wilma Cavness was born March 22, 1919, to Vander and Emma Mabry. In addition to Lillie, she had twin sisters four years younger and a younger brother and sister. She attended schools in Hayti, to the 10th grade. "I had to help Poppa pick cotton and gather corn. I got disgusted and quit school. I couldn't keep up with both," she said. She married O'Dell "Jack" Cavness on Jan. 22, 1939, and the couple moved to Poplar Bluff in 1947. They raised three boys and one daughter. "Lillie (McIntosh) was my sister and my best friend. My husband and her both expired on the same night. My husband died at 8:30 and she died at 9:30. That was on March 17, 1995. "Wilma has worked various jobs and in 2009 she was volunteering three days a week at Northside Nutrition Center in Poplar Bluff.

"We canned everything we could. We didn't have no deep freeze, had to can it. When the blackberries were ripe, Poppa would take me and my older sister and a washtub in the back of a wagon, and he knew where the berries were at. We picked that washtub full of berries. I picked and chopped cotton. I got to where I could pick 300 pounds a day, if I didn't have to carry the sacks. Momma would make me a sack to put around my shoulder when I was young. When I have an extra dollar now, I appreciate it; because I know what it is when we didn't have it. We never did go hungry. We always had plenty to eat. The last bale of cotton that we picked Poppa would take the money and buy it up in groceries. He'd buy 50 pounds of flour, a big bag of sugar, rolled oats, and he always had fruit on the table. He'd say, 'Kids got to have fruit.' We canned apples, peaches, berries, and plums. He always had a great big bottle of cod liver oil sitting on the table. And we had to take a teaspoon of that before we ate, every day. I don't use cod liver oil today," she said.

You Don't Bother Them. They Just Know What to Do
Working as a Plow Hand on a Plantation
as told by Alfonse Webb

You either plowed or chopped cotton, and I'd rather plow mules any day than chop cotton. Once you get used to mules, they pretty well do what you ask them. When you get to the end, and you get ready to turn around, after you do it so long, they know what to do. You don't bother them. They just know what to do.

I worked on the AB Rushing Plantation near Cooter from about 1946 to 1949. Quite a few around 40 or 50 people were working there. Some would work with tractors, H Farmalls or F-20s, and some would work with mules. My dad sharecropped about 40 acres. They would furnish everything and Dad would get half the crop. We lived on the plantation.

I was the plow hand. I would either break ground or cultivate. My dad told me when I wasn't plowing at home, I could plow and make some money, and that's what I'd do. They wasn't paying much of nothing, about three and a half (dollars) a day, and that was from can to can't. From when you can see in the morning to when you can't see at night. We didn't hardly take no breaks, unless it was real hot. Sometimes it would be me and another guy with a team working the same field.

On a good day I could cultivate seven or eight acres. I liked it at the time. I farmed with Bell and Roadie. They were big mules, nice, mainly brown. They weighed about 1,000 pounds. They knowed what they was. Guess someone else had trained them. You could put one line on the right hand mule and plow them with one line with a cultivator and tell them "whoa." When you'd get to the end, they would come right on around. You have one pair of mules and you teach them that and they know what to do. But it would take a little while and can't everybody do that. I would sharecrop with them, or plow by the day for AB. I helped Dad when he needed help, and when I worked out by the day the other guy would pay me. If you were working away from home, you'd carry your lunch with you.

They had a straw boss. He never did bother me. He'd tell me what he wanted done and I'd go and do it. He didn't worry about me, or nothing. He knowed I could do it, and would do it.

I'd work with those mules five or six months a year. We'd start in March and sometimes would work into September.

Webb talks about his favorite mule in a story in the Nubbins chapter.

Alfonse Webb was born Jan. 29, 1929, to John and Mattie Mae Webb near Dundee, Mississippi. He attended school through the sixth grade. He had six brothers and six sisters. The family moved to Pemiscot County in 1946, where his dad sharecropped for several years. Alfonse worked on Extra Gang No. 9 for the Cotton Bell Railroad in 1951-1952 and was drafted into the U.S. Army on Oct. 9, 1952, and spent 13 months in Korea, mostly in the infantry. He was in Korea when the armistice was signed in July 1953. He was discharged on Oct. 9, 1954 and farmed with his dad awhile before moving to Butler County in 1957, where he started farming on his own. He farmed up into the late 1990s until failing health forced him to turn the farming over to his sons, Ronnie and Bruce. Alfonse and his wife, June Marie, celebrated their 57th anniversary in 2009.

Unhook Those Horses and Get Out of the Way
Sharecropping in Butler County
as told by Paul Woods

Out east of town (Poplar Bluff), before you get to the levee on the old highway, Dad helped clear that ground. He put the first crop in out there. He farmed with two black mules, Andy and Queen. Andy was the small one. Queen was a big mule. When he'd run into a root or something the plow wouldn't cut, he'd just back the mules up, raise the plow up and go over it. When he plowed I picked up worms and sold them to a bait shop for a dollar a gallon.

Those mules fed us. But I remember he was afraid of them. Dad sharecropped for five years in the late '40s. He farmed mainly corn and peas that was used for hay.

When I was with the mules I was with Dad and he knew how to handle them. He wouldn't let me work them. But I helped with gathering corn. Because I was the smallest, I would pick the down row. All you had to do to move them forward was to plop a line down on their backs and they'd go. I remember one day we were picking corn with Andy and Queen and my brother, Walter, jumped a rabbit. He had an ear of corn in his hand and threw it at the rabbit and missed it. The rabbit hopped about 10 feet forward. He picked up the ear of corn, yanked a shuck off and creeped up on it and wham! He hit him. We had rabbit for supper.

I remember one year it was wet and we didn't get the corn out. When the ground froze we took the team, hooked them to a mud boat (and pulled it out in the field). The boat was about 4 foot wide. Dad picked one side and I picked the other. We would fill the mud boat up and take it out. We'd scoop the corn into a wagon, then go get another load.

Andy and Queen were the hardest working things. In the spring he used them to plow the garden. He would plow other gardens for a fee.

We lived on the (Black) river. When they built the levee (est. 1948) it went right through the house. Dad took the money we got for

Andy and Queen with Woods' uncle and dad.

the house and went to the bank and borrowed $300 and bought the house across the street and it's still there. One time we had bought a load of hay and it started raining; I don't know why I wasn't in school. He laid into the mules and ran them as hard as he could to try to keep the hay from getting wet. He only used his whip to get them to go faster. He never mistreated them. We pulled into the yard and we were both soaking wet. He said, "Go into the house to the refrigerator and get a bottle of beer, tip it up and take a drink. It will warm you. Then bring the rest to me." That was almost 70 years ago and I can still taste that stuff. That was my only taste of liquor, Hyde Park Beer.

Dad used the mules for logging, skidding logs, and he hauled ties from the mill out to the tie yard and stacked them all by himself, no help. He used Andy and Queen to help clean out all the timber in Neelyville and in the Coon Island area. He would skid three logs out with the mules to two for the horses. Lots of times someone would get stuck in a mud hole and you couldn't go around them and Dad would say, "Unhook those horses and get out of the way!" He'd hook his mules to it and pull it out. While others would stop and fix their harness, Dad never did. He'd come in Friday night and on Saturday morning he got his harness out and checked it and if there was anything weak, he'd fix it.

One year (1920s), his brother-in-law, Levi McCoy, came down with TB. The doctor told Dad if you can get him to Colorado in the mountain air, he might be okay. Dad took him out there in the wagon with the mules. McCoy died in Kansas on the way out there and Dad buried him on the side of the road, turned around and came back home.

The biggest work project Dad had with the mules was he used them to scoop out the ground in layers, that was used to make the seats for the (Poplar Bluff High School) football stadium. One year he had surgery at Jefferson Barracks Hospital (in St. Louis) and was there for almost a month and I helped take care of feeding and watering the mules. I would toss them a couple ears of corn and a flake of hay a piece.

Andy slipped one time and banged up a knee and it swelled up. But he always pulled his weight, even with the bad knee. There was a circus in town and Dad took Andy down to the auction. He said he hated to sell him because he knew he went to animal food. Andy was getting old and he figured he would drop dead on him. He bought a big mule named John to work with Queen. He was as big as Queen. She was really a big one. I don't remember what happened to her. Those mules were our transportation. When we went someplace, we'd all go in the wagon.

 **Paul E. Woods was born Dec. 6, 1933 to Charles and Hazel Woods. He had four brothers and five sisters and was the youngest boy. Paul attended J. Minnie Smith grade school and was graduated from Poplar Bluff High School in 1951. He graduated on Thursday, and started working in the composing room for *The Daily American Republic* newspaper on Monday and retired in 1999. In 2010 at the time he was interviewed, Woods still wrote a weekly column for the newspaper, *The Ridge Runner,* which he has written for 30 years. He married Elaine York in 1954. The couple celebrated their 55th anniversary in 2009. "Dad was the best shot in his company in World War I," Woods said. "They nicknamed him Trigger Foot, because he could shoot with his foot and beat anybody else. His commanding officer entered him in a lot of marksmanship competitions. Dad said he (C.O.) always shared his winnings with him. One time the drummer from Winchester Arms came to Poplar Bluff and he took on all challengers who were crack shots. Dad beat him. Throw a cork up in the air and he would bust it with a .22. They tried to hire him. If they would have, I wouldn't be here. Right now the way he disciplined us, he would be thrown in jail. But it didn't kill us. The last whipping I got; he had a mule whip made out of an automobile fan belt, and I got it. Me, and my sister didn't know that that oatmeal box would burn. We built a stove out of it and filled it up with hay where our hay was stored. When it took off, they called the fire department and they put the fire out. Dad took an ax and chopped the burned ends off of the bales. But I can remember that whipping. When Dad got old my oldest brother cussed the old man because he didn't provide very good. I told him, "Bill, Dad did the best he could. We never went hungry. We always had a roof over our heads. So don't blast the old man." I was his last boy and we were buddies. The night he died (Dec. 4, 1960), we had planned to go coon hunting the next night. He died in his sleep, 68 years of age. He worked himself to death."**

Anytime They Walk Behind Them Mules, You Didn't Take No Break
Working Mules on a Mississippi Plantation
as told by Tim Whitney, Sr.

Dad sharecropped at the CP Owens Plantation (late 1930s into 1940s) that was located south of Robinsonville, Mississippi. He moved from one farm to the next. It was a big plantation that had a big bell. You couldn't quit until you heard that big bell. We'd start at just about daylight and work from 6 to 6, 12 hours a day. We would work five days a week and half-day Saturday. We were paid $12.50 a week. A man in a pickup truck would go around to your house picking your dinner up and would bring it to us when working at the back of the farm. Sometimes we would eat at home.

We mostly farmed cotton. The man (CP Owens) had his own gin, (and a) great big ole store. Had everything you wanted in that store, (He'd) kill hogs, (and we'd) have meat.

I worked there four years starting at age 18, when I was single. There is no way in the world I would have been married, (I) would have cut out. (I) lived in home with my parents on the plantation. There were three boys, two worked on farm. Only one of us boys worked at a time.

You walkin' 12 hours behind a darn mule, plowing. If that didn't give you exercise you won't ever have none. Lemont and Alex, (were the) two brown horse mules I worked with. My brother worked with Rock Island and Frisco. They were iron gray. They was good. We had them trained. We broke them. While harnessing them, put the bridle on first. Then after you put harness on, carry them on to the field.

We broke them with a gang plow (one-row-walk-behind cultivator) in rough ground. We'd have an old one and young one together. That's the way to break them. We got them broke. Got bit by one.

The boss man came out there and told me, "You're tearing up his mouth with those bits. You put those big bits in there." He come out there, man that mule came up and came down. I said "Boss man you better get back, he don't know you, he'll paw you." By the time he left, I put them others back in his mouth. You can't break no mule with those big bits. If he sets his teeth down on those big bits, you can't handle him. You got to have a twist on their lips to put the bridle on and all that. You'd carry your bridle home with you, make sure nobody would get it.

We took breaks. Straw bosses don't want you to break, see. Anytime they walk behind them mules, you didn't take no break. We wore shoes, overalls, gum boots when muddy. You might take a break, but the straw boss is out there to keep you going. We kept them three straw bosses in the middle of the field and 25 or 30 men out there plowing. You had to walk behind them mules that long and not take a break. Work the shit out of us.

When you were done working them, all of them went to that big barn. A hostler took care of them. They were fed hay and oats.

(You'd) start work in spring maybe April to August. There was nothing to do in the wintertime. (In the fall we'd) work at that gin, me, and my brother. In the spring we'd clean that barn out, take all that mule stuff out and spread it out in the field. We tore up a lot of things, though. Mules were scared of those trains, had coal burners at that time. We tore up wagons, plows. Mules pull those wagons half in too. Many a mule came out of their harness.

He raised mules. Had a big ole jack out there. He'd bring them mares to that jack, well that mare wasn't ready; that jack fell down in that hole. They had a board in front of her. When that jack hit her, she broke that board. That jack disappeared. Nobody know'd where that jack went. He bought another young one.

Day work (also included) hauling hay, running a combine, checking sacks in combine. Trucks come along and pick it up. Now, you got one man doing all of it. To put out fertilize, come out with two mules and a man spread with a buster, two mules to it. What you call hipping the ground. I'd fill those planters up. Put fertilize with that. Planter had a little bucket in front of the seed bucket for fertilize.

In cotton-picking time, we'd pick cotton. All of us together could pick a bale and a half a day. I was picking about 200 or 300 (pounds) myself. We made more picking cotton than working on that farm. We could make more in two days than a whole week. Boss would say, "What you boys going to do with all that money?" $12.50 ain't nothing. We couldn't save nothing. We didn't need nothing; cause everything we needed was on the farm at the store there.

When you get older the legs are the first thing to break down on you. I can't hardly walk now, see. I did landscape when I got up here, until age 65.

 Tim Whitney, Sr., was born Aug. 21, 1921, in Coahoma County, Mississippi to Walter and Susie Whitney. He was the oldest of five brothers and had five sisters. He attended schools through the seventh grade, and farmed most of his life. He followed his dad to Missouri in December 1946. He married Elsie Clemon on Dec. 15, 1948. She died in 1993, after the couple had been married 44 years. Whitney also worked for a Chicago box car manufacturer, and in landscaping. He resided in Charleston, Missouri in 2008 at the time he was interviewed.

Come Up Dan, "Whoa." We'd Work Until We Got Through, the Whole Day
Dan
as told by Flora Currie

When I started farming with the mules I was about 12 or 13. Have to get out there early and catch them, shear'em and brush them up, put the gathering thing on, and hook them up to the plow, and go to the field.

That was a double shovel; sometimes he would let us use the turning plow, that was too heavy for us, harrowing, run the middles out in the field, all of that. Sometimes I'd have one mule. I had two mules with the cultivator, but the double shovel it was just one mule.

There was ole Dan, and the other mule. The horse was named Daisy. Dan was brown and wasn't too big. He'd pull that double shovel. I'd walk behind the plow. Sometimes I'd have the lines around my waist, and then again had them in my hands. "Come up

Dan, whoa." We'd work until we got through, the whole day.

I was older than my brothers, and the other girls were gone. My dad made us get out there and work. We'd go home at lunch. They say when you can step on your shadow it's 12 o'clock. We'd take the gear off of ole Dan. We'd go out and cut Johnson grass and go feed ole Dan. Give ole Dan some water. And we'd stay there till 1 o'clock. After 1 o'clock, we'd go back to the field.

I worked with my younger brother, Henry. Sometimes my brother would be driving the mule, and I'd be holding the plow. We'd walk side by side. He had the mule with the lines, and I had the cultivator with the handles. Dad would be somewhere else, maybe cutting wood or something.

It got so hot, you could see little things jumping up. We always called them little mawkees (monkeys). It was hot. Back then we'd wear dresses or shorts and a straw hat. It was hot. Sometimes, a big shade tree, we'd carry ole Dan beneath that shade tree and rest awhile. I just didn't like going to the field. They didn't bring me up like they do today. Children have their way. My parents made me. If I didn't want to do it, I went anyhow.

We didn't have feed to feed them. We had to carry him out to graze on grass, Johnson grass. We'd set out there in the shade. They (mules and horse) had a halter and rope. As long as he can sit out there and eat, we'd stay out there. But when he started to walk, we had to bring him back. Sometimes it would be early in the morning with the dew on, sometimes it was late in the evening when it's kind of cool.

Me, and him would get out there and throw that harness on there. Get the collar on, me, and Son, that's what I called Henry. He was a little boy. Dan stayed gentle all the time. Sometimes you'd have to pull him back on the row, but most of the time, he'd just go straight down that row.

I still had a hold of the plow when he'd go around. I had my plow and he had the lines. At that time it was fun. We just probably didn't know no better. Mosquitoes, flies, and gnats, horse flies, they will bite you while we were plowing. We wore long sleeves. If we were in soft ground, we didn't wear shoes. If we were in rough ground, we wore shoes, what we had.

When it was hot, sometimes he would stop on his own. Sometimes we'd stop him. We'd get out there about 7 o'clock in the morning, and maybe stay out there until 11 or 11:30. Then we'd take him out and come to the house and bring him water and get him some feed. About 1:30 or a little bit later, we'd hook him up, get out again, me, and Son go back to the field.

Sometimes we'd take water; sometimes we'd holler at the house for someone to bring us some water. We lived close to where the farm is, in a four-room house. Well I tell you, I'd rather plow than to chop cotton. You know, chopping cotton all day long.

I worked ole Dan about two years. I didn't like when he'd heist his tail up and put out all that drop, drop, drop. We had to go right behind him. I didn't like that so well.

When he got away from the house, he just wouldn't make it, but when he got his head going to the house, you had to run to keep up with him. Get him going back towards the house, ole Dan would fly. We'd try to hold him back, he'd walk so fast. Going away from the house, we didn't care if he didn't. But we didn't want to go no how.

We used to ride him to the field; just jump up on him. Sometimes I'd be in front and Son would be behind me. If we wanted to ride him, we'd put the saddle on him, put our feet up in the stirrups. To keep from walking to the field, we'd just ride ole Dan to the field. Never did fall off of him. He wasn't all that tall.

Dad would make us get out there and keep the mules looking good, shear them, curry comb, get the cockleburs out. We kept them mules looking good. Can't think of that other mule's name. We hardly ever fooled with him.

Daisy was a gray horse. We were scared of Daisy. She'd snort at you. Dad just wouldn't let us be with her. Sometimes he'd ride her to town, about four miles. Sometimes he'd hook the wagon with ole Dan and that other mule to go to town. At one time we had a surrey. We had chickens, hogs, and milk cows. That's how we lived, with those chickens and hogs. I had to milk; my older sister, Colee, had to

milk. Sometimes we'd milk three cows. We chop cotton. Sometimes
be so much grass, couldn't see the cotton. Highest I ever picked was
500. That's picking. Pulling, I pulled 700 one day. I had to pick. That
was in Mississippi. They like to worked us to death. My main job
was going to the field and chopping cotton. I used to pick cotton, but
not in Mississippi. After I left Mississippi, we come to Arkansas. I
was about 14.

 **Flora Mae Currie was born June 6, 1916, to Colie and Careda
Doss near Houston, in north-central Mississippi. She had four
brothers and six sisters. Her dad sharecropped 20 acres in Mississippi, and the family moved to Clarksdale, Arkansas in about
1930 and to Butler County, Missouri in 1938. "Whenever the
weather was bad, we went to school; but when the sun was out,
we worked. My dad didn't believe in sending us to school, so I
never got an education," she said. Flora married Cleveland Palmer in 1932
and left him four years later. She married William Currie in 1936, and this
union lasted 10 years. "I raised nine of my own, and four of my grandchildren," she said. Flora worked as a maid in Poplar Bluff for over 30 years,
mostly for doctors, until she was 92. She has outlived all of her brothers and
sisters. She purchased 23 acres southeast of Poplar Bluff in the 1980s and for
years raised cotton. She hired out the plowing and planting, and she and her
children chopped and picked it.**

VII. RUNAWAYS

I Crawled on My Knees Until I Got Ahold of the Lines
as told by James King

When I was a young boy we had a team of gray mules. Sam and
Joe was their names. They were a big team, 8 or 10 years old. They
were a good team to work with. I pretty well started out with them. It
was before I graduated from the eighth grade, so I was probably 12
years old (1933).

The first day I worked them was with a breaking plow. My dad and older brother, Harold, were also working teams. We had three teams plowing together. The lead team made their furrow, the other teams walked in the furrow and plowed behind them.

You'd follow the team ahead about 10 to 15 feet. I got behind them, maybe 300 yards. I tried to catch up, so I made them (Sam and Joe) run with the plow, and the plow fell over dragging me and the plow too until we caught up with the others. Then I got them stopped, and set the plow back up. My dad asked if I was hurt. I wasn't. We then went back to plowing. My lines were around my waist. I've seen people put them around their shoulder, but we always put them around our waist when plowing or cultivating.

We didn't have any riding cultivators, all walking cultivators. That first day or two (cultivating), it was pretty rough, but you got toughened to it. I worked mostly with Harold, who was about two years older.

We used to gather corn, me, and my brothers, with wagons. We had three teams all the time, mules and horses. We each had a team and wagon. If one runaway started, they all three went. And we were knocking corn every way. We were young and quick enough we'd grab the side of a wagon and swing ourselves until we got up in the wagon, and got a hold of the lines and stopped them. Something in the corn would scare them. We had many a runaway, right in that field of corn, especially if the team behind were the first to get scared. They scared the others. They'd be running one team behind the other.

You never let the rear wheel get past you. That way, you'd be ready, because you knew they would do it. So you'd be ready to run up beside that wagon, and swing yourself in it. They'd run about once a week, until we got all the corn out. If you didn't catch them, they'd run all the way to the barn.

One day I had that same team of mules, Joe and Sam. We were breaking ground with a plow. We didn't get to go out very much of a night, but we (Harold and I) had went out and had to be back in by 10 o'clock. Some reason we were a little tired, and Harold had to use the bathroom. Then, you just went to the woods. So he had a team of horses in front of me, and I had the team of mules behind. I just sat down in the furrow with the lines in my hands.

He made a little sound out there when he got up, and when he done that, they just, zoom! Them horses jumped, the mules jumped! They were right on those horses before they hardly got started. Before I could get up, they took the lines right out of my hands. Joe and Sam jumped this plow the horses were pulling. They went out on the highway, and went up that highway and went all the way to the house, and went around and around that house pulling the plows, which had fallen over on their sides. I knew in my mind they'd have a leg cut off when I got down there. They didn't. They were all in pretty good shape, pretty well run down.

While they were running the mules spread out wide enough the plow didn't get them. Their check lines let them spread out pretty wide. They couldn't pull around the horses, the check lines caught the backend of the horses. His horses had blinds on where they couldn't see behind. When they heard that noise, zoom!

Joe was a little more active than Sam, little more skittish. He backed me all the way to the corner of the barn one day kicking at me, but he never did hit me. I had walked behind him, wasn't paying any attention, didn't think he'd do it. He kind of squealed, made a funny noise with his mouth. He was kicking with both (hind) feet. I was lucky enough I was between the legs when he kicked out, and I got all the way back in the corner, and he kicked three or four times and quit. I was about 15. He'd never kicked that way before, but he was eating his corn. You fed them corn. He was eating. I don't know if I surprised him, or what.

I worked Joe and Sam to a threshing machine. Back then we didn't have combines. We cut wheat and oats with a binder, and put them in bundles. The thresher machine sat stationary, and you drove your team up with a wagon with a hay frame, on each side of that thresher. These mules were skittish. The side I got that day was where the sackers caught the wheat in a sack. I had to head the mules straight in to them. I didn't have a hold of the lines. They were tied up to the hay frame. The sackers made some noise, and those mules wheeled real quick, and went out of there really fast. I was down on my knees almost in the back of the wagon. By luck, they were going straight enough they didn't turn it over. I crawled on my knees until I got ahold of the lines, and the minute I got a hold of the lines, I stopped them. They had run about a quarter of a mile, down a hill, this way and that. The bed of the frame had little cracks in it. When crawling, I'd take hold of the cracks and hold on.

We would be in the field by 7 o'clock in the morning and stay until 6 o'clock in the evening. You got up, and while my mother was fixing breakfast, we'd go out, milk the cows, feed the horses and mules their corn to eat, feed the hogs, had the cream separator, where you separated your milk. About the time we were done with that, Mom would holler, "Breakfast!" and we'd go in and eat.

The dinner bell rang at 11 o'clock, and about 11:30, we'd take off for the house. Our neighbor just across the road from us, he had a team of mules and when they rang that bell; if they were halfway across the field, they'd turn right around and go to the house. He couldn't stop them. They didn't run. They just turned around walking. When that bell rang, they knew it was lunchtime. Ours wasn't like that.

We worked Joe and Sam seven or eight years. We were working them back in the river (St. Francis). They had a pretty good hill to go up with loads of corn on. Sam got to where we had to stop him several times to rest him. There was something wrong with him. (So) Dad swapped a team of horses for them at a sale barn in Campbell. You couldn't tell anything was wrong with him, unless you were working them real hard. He (Sam) couldn't take it.

It was hard to see them go. It was almost like one of the family moving away.

James R. King was born Sept. 12, 1921, to Walter and Alaska King. He had one older brother, two younger brothers, and four sisters. At the time of this story his father farmed 80 acres four miles west of Campbell in Dunklin County. King attended a one-room rural school through the eighth grade, then worked on the

farm. He was drafted into the U.S. Army in 1942, and was assigned to an anti-aircraft battalion as a driver and mechanic. After being discharged, he worked for the Minton Brothers in Dexter, as a bulldozer operator for four years, clearing land for farming. He then worked a dragline for five years for a Bloomfield Ditch District, and from 1976 to 1980 worked as a mechanic at the Malden Air Base. He drove a school bus for Campbell R-II Schools for seven years, retiring in 1991. He then did farm work for Kenneth Fortner of Bernie until 2001, when he turned 80. King's left ankle was permanently injured in a roofing accident in 1955. He and his wife, Ruby, celebrated 62 years of marriage in 2008.

His Tail Went Round and Round.
He Let Out a Toot-Toot and Took Off
as told by Lloyd Massey

My mother sent my brother, H.L., and I to a woods farm a quarter of a mile from our home. She had made us waistband bags to gather blackberries in. We were to fill those bags and come back home as quick as we could. So we did as Mother commanded.

I was in the timber some 30 to 45 minutes. I got my bag full and started home. Just as I was ready to leave the woods, I walked to the edge of the timber and saw a team of mules hooked to a walking cultivator some 50 to 60 feet out in a field of cotton.

Kid's thinking; I took my slingshot out of a pocket, put a rock in it and shot one of those mules. His tail went round and round. He let out a toot-toot and took off with his mate in a hard run. The cultivator was bouncing like a rubber ball. Their driver, a black man, was down at a field water pump getting a drink. He saw them running and took off after them.

I'm back in the woods so no one knew where I was. I stayed hid as much as possible.

Those mules ran all the way through the field, even went through a pasture fence at the end of the cotton rows, and wound up at a lot gate close to a barn.

I never told anyone what had happened. It went on that way for 30 to 40 years; until I went to Greenville, Mississippi and saw my brother-in-law, the owner of that team of mules. He was getting along in years. So I told him about that mishap. He remembered it well and said they always wondered what happened to those mules. What kids will do.

This is Massey's third of four stories. He also has stories in the Mule Teams and Mules That Worked Without Lines chapters and the story, "And Guess What. That Tractor Didn't Stop." He said this incident probably took place in 1934, when he was 13; and at the time his brother was still back in the woods picking berries and didn't see what happened.

I Can Still See Those Plow Points Going Up in the Air
as told by Lindell Hoggard

My father raised and broke mules for the Army. They were sold through the Pug Moore Mule Barn in Portageville and had to be saddle broke. I think he got $200 per mule. He kept a jack and we had four mares. We always had a different set of mules to work with. I don't remember their names. We had 40 acres of ground we farmed as tenants and another 40 Dad purchased. We used mules and horses for breaking of ground, bedding of ground with harrows, and planting. Dad never had a tractor.

I was about 12 when I started driving them (mules) to pick corn. My dad and a brother would pick the corn, while I drove the wagon. I graduated to breaking (ground), pulling a harrow. Dad wouldn't let me plant.

There was some new ground you'd go along with a plow and hit those roots. They'd spring back and hit you on the shin.

We'd sometimes have problems putting harness on new mules. First you have to move slowly so as not to frighten them. If necessary, there was a post at the barn to tie the mule to, before putting the harness on. To start them out, we'd hook them to a plow and sink it as deep in the ground as we could. Pretty soon it'd take the starch out of them.

One morning I was using a one-row cultivator and something spooked the mules. They ran a half-mile down the field. They ran until they came to a fence. They didn't follow a row. When they went, I got out from under the lines, which I had around my shoulders. The lines were positioned where I could get out quick. They didn't have any sense of direction and each time they changed direction, they uprooted more cotton plants.

Dad was chopping cotton nearby and came over and asked me if I was hurt. I didn't get scolded. I think he knew I could of gotten hurt. That run took a lot of starch out of those mules. Those ole mules were tired. I don't think they ever gave me any more trouble.

There were some people sharecropping with us that saw it from a different field. I can still see those plow points going up in the air and dropping down, scattering cotton plants.

Lindell Hoggard was born Jan. 28, 1929, to Albert and Alma Hoggard. His father farmed in New Madrid County, three miles north of Portageville. He had three brothers and four sisters and was the youngest boy. James, the next oldest, was five years older and was not at home when Lindell was helping his dad farm. He graduated from Portageville High School in 1947. He married Doris in 1948. He worked 40 years for Cypress Supply in Portageville. Hoggard was interviewed April 14, 2008. He died June 10, 2009.

I Sprinkled It On and Let It Run Down Their Necks
as told by Chalk Givens

Me, and a feller were trading together and we went up to the other side of Poplar Bluff, and bought these mules from a trader, fella name of Hilderbrand. They were mare mules and just as near alike as you could get two and stick them together. They were 4-year-old blue mules. I mean they were crackerjacks. They were 15 hands and weighed 1,200 or more. They weren't tall, but as broad as a bale of cotton.

I was planting corn with them, had a fertilizer attachment with the planter, and that made it heavy on their necks. Their necks begin to get lower. I told the old man on whose farm I was working on and he said, "What I usually do. I take dry dirt off the top of the ground and pour it down their necks."

I got me a handful of that real fine dirt, pulled their collars up, and sprinkled it on and let it run down their necks. When I was doing that, that scared that mule, running down her shoulders tickled her.

I had them to a new John Deere corn planter that had a pair of wooden doubletrees. I was standing between the planter, and the mules, when they started up. I hollered "whoa" but they were scared and they just took off. I just got behind the marker and let them go.

They ran off in the field a ways and made a circle and when they did they pulled one clip off of one end of the planter; and when that come off, they just run off a little piece and just stopped. I went to them and got them and come back to where I was started and went back to filling up everything. I looked around and I was lucky enough in that loose ground that I found that clip. I took it and hammered it back on there and went about my business.

In the fall, I had that same pair to a mowing machine. I was mowing a little ole pasture field, me, and a hired hand. He had a pair of horses mowing, and he was down ahead of me. And what happened to cause this runaway? The pitman connecting rod and all of them little rabbets that hold that pitman on there, they all came off at one time. You talk about making a racket. I lived down there by Delta close to a railroad track. That made more racket than the train would make when it went by, and it just scared them mules to death.

And when it did, it scared me too. And they both started to run. I seen it. You can't hold a pair of mules with them wanting to runaway. I was young too, kind of laid back in the seat. I tried to hold them a little bit, but I didn't want to get tangled up in that damn mower, and I just throwed the lines up and baled off of it. The mower blade was down on the ground bouncing around. They didn't knock the hair off of them on either one. I had been going down a fence line and they just ran over close to the fence, and the left wheel hit a fence post, and it broke the casting on the mower. And when it done that, they just come apart more or less. They ran down the field a piece, maybe a 100 yards. They run out there just like they did with that corn planter. They made a circle in that field. The other man that was mowing, he just went on. He didn't know what was going on. Hell, I fooled around a little bit walked out in the field, they just done the same thing, let me go up to them.

I grabbed the lines and drove them on out of the field and I said, "Well, you sons of bitches, you'll never run away with me again, cause I'll never put the harness on you again." I sold them to a man in Kennett, Ted Holloway. I had sold him a pair of horse mules and he was strictly a mare mule man. I called him that night and said, "You still interested in those mare mules?" He said, "Yeah, I am. Are they just like they was?" I said, "There ain't a hair off of them outside where the harness has knocked a few loose. They're just fat and ready to go." And I told him kind of what happened and said, "If you're still interested, send your truck man up here. And I'll load them up and send them to you." And he said, "I'll have to trade you them horse mules in on them." And I said, "That will be all right. I'll damn sure take them." Cause I'd rather had them because you could just sic the get out of them.

Givens also has a story in the Mule Teams chapter.

VIII. And Guess What. That Tractor Didn't Stop
as told by Lloyd Massey

Mostly, back in those days (1930s), people had bob trucks, which was a truck a little larger than a pickup that had a flat wooden bed. My dad had a 1928 Chevrolet bob truck that he drove all the time. And my dad drove that truck like a mule. He'd pull back on the steering wheel and say, "whoa now." Or turn it to the left and holler "haw."

In 1938, when I would have been 17, my dad and I decided to buy a tractor. We went to look at tractors. They had an H Farmall two row and an A Farmall one row. Now, I drove both of them.

Of course I wanted the large one. I wanted the H. Dad pointed his finger right in my face and said, "Now son, you think of it. There's no way a man can watch two rows at one time." So guess what. We bought the A Farmall.

One day I came in from school and I run through the house. Mother always kept us bacon and cornbread. I got my sandwich and I heard that little tractor running in the pasture behind the house.

I ran on through the house and out into the backyard a ways. This tractor was coming right towards me pulling a team wheat drill. There was nobody in the seat of the tractor. It was running by itself. It scared me. I thought Dad had fallen off and got run over or something.

I ran out to the fence and about the time I started to get over the fence, Dad came running up behind the wheat drill and ran up beside the tractor and instead of getting back on it, he started hollering, "Whoa, damn it, whoa! Whoa, damn it whoa!" Over and over, and guess what, that tractor didn't stop until it run up on a lumber pile at the fence, an old scrap lumber pile. It ran up on it and the wheels ran over the fence down on the oil pan and killed the motor.

Dad and I worked well after dark getting that tractor out.

This is Massey's fourth story. He also has stories in the Mule Teams, Mules That Worked Without Lines, and Runaways chapters.

IX. Elmer Mallett Understood Mules
as told by Leland Mallett

My dad farmed all of his life with mules. He quit farming in 1965 when he turned 65, and he died in 1992 at age 92.

We moved to a 160-acre farm east of Malden, from Conway, Arkansas in 1948, when I was 12.

I was small when we moved up. That spring he told me he was going to buy me some mules so I could help him. I think he bought them at the Poplar Bluff Sale Barn. I know at that time they had a lot of mules for sale over there.

We were the only ones that had teams when we moved up here. Everyone else had tractors. The guy across the road had a team, but he had tractors too, and he never used the team for anything except picking up hay. Dad never had a tractor. He always said, "Them mules were doing fine for him."

They were two gentle, brown-and-tan mare mules, Kate and Jude. They matched pretty well. They were big mules. I was raised with them.

At first I wasn't big enough to put their bridles on. They'd raise their heads up. He (Dad) helped me harness until I got big enough. He started out letting me harrow with them and different things. It wasn't long until I was using them to a breaking plow.

I remember that breaking plow would throw me down. I'd be between the handles trying to hold it, and if it hit anything; it would just throw me down. I'd just holler, "whoa" and they'd stop, and I'd straighten it up.

When Dad came by with his team, he'd straighten up my mistake, where it threw me down and I didn't plow. He had two teams. He had his team and I had mine.

Kate and Jude worked together really good. It was cultivating where I had the problem with her (Jude). When she'd get close to the end of a row, she'd want to run, maybe a 100 yards from the end. When she got to the end, she'd turn and go right with the other mule.

When she'd run, it pulled the one-row cultivator sideways, because the other mule wasn't running. It would be bumping Kate.
When she'd get to running, it would cause you to plow up some of
the crop. Dad didn't like that. He didn't want no skips, or plowing up
anything.

He was very particular with his mules (team). He wouldn't hardly
let me do anything with them. I guess they got used to him and
minded him good. He treated them different than I did. If they didn't
do what I said, I'd want to jerk the line and jerk them or something.
And he didn't do his that way. He wouldn't have to jerk them around.
He'd just talk to them. He claimed that's what ruined mine. So he
didn't want me using his.

Jude kept doing that and getting worse. Her bridle had bills over
the eyes. I cut out a piece of cotton sack and hung over that bill,
where she could only look down. It worked really well. Dad was
amazed by that.

*Elmer Mallett cultivating beans with Maude and Dixie in early 1950s.
Photo provided by family.*

He had his one-row cultivator and I had mine. He gave me the new cultivator when I got big enough to start plowing, and he kept the old one. We'd start plowing at daylight and be there till dark. When we got to the field, he'd skip ever other row. And I'd pick that one up.

They were quarter-mile-long rows. We could cultivate 10 acres a day. We'd walk all day. Dad never did complain. When I first started, my legs would get tired, being young. After I got to be a teenager, I'd walk behind them all day and go to town that night.

We'd cultivate all summer. If it rained, it would knock us out. We'd start in March and cultivate into part of July, six days a week. It took that for both of them teams to plow that 160 acres. One row at a time, you didn't get far. Before we got done, it was time to do it again. He had the rest of the family chopping cotton. We just raised cotton and beans and what corn we thought the mules would eat.

We'd take an hour off for noon; take their harness off. They'd go woller, get them a drink, and he fed them corn and hay. The heat never bothered me. Sometimes the mules would get a little hot, and we'd stop at the end of a row and sit on the cultivator for a while, 15 minutes at the most. If it was real hot, we might rest them three times. Most of the time we kept them going.

We always kept plenty of corn for them. Dad fed them in the mornings. My job was to water them, pump the water. At first, I'd have to lay on the pump handle to pull it down. Them mules can drink a lot of water. I got a whippin over that.

I had run them off with a stick because they were drinking it faster than I could pump it; he saw me, so I got a whipping. He got a peach tree limb by where we were at; I remember that. I didn't run those mules off anymore. They got water noon and night and in the morning before we started. I pumped water at noon and in the evening. We had a 50-gallon-barrel tank.

We never put shoes on them. Sometimes the mules would get sore at the collar. He had a salve he'd put on it. One time one of them had a pretty good size sore, and he cut a hole in the collar. We never quit using them.

Kate was just a gentle mule. I rode her a lot. I just rode her back in the fields when we weren't working. Dad wouldn't let me get near the highway. I never did ride Jude. I don't think I ever tried to ride her. She (Kate) wasn't hard to bridle. Sometimes I'd ride her back to our neighbor's, which was a mile back in the field. And I could just get off there, and she'd stand there until I got ready to go. She didn't ever run off and leave me. I'd leave the bridle on and just drop the reins down, and she'd stand right there.

One time I was riding her back to the neighbor, and I was running her. A mule isn't like a horse; they're kinda clumsy. She got to stumbling and fell and kind of throwed me away from her. I landed out in the field. She just got up and stood there. I got up and got a hold of a rein. I couldn't get back on her. She was too tall. I had to lead her to the house and get on a bucket, and I could jump up on her.

When I was in the 11th grade, I came in one day (from school) and Dad said he needed me to plow. I told him I was going to quit school. He didn't say nothing either way. I just started helping him plow.

I farmed with Kate and Jude the next year (1954), and he gave me nine acres to sharecrop. After I made that sharecrop, I got married. The next year I started farming 80 acres and got me an H Farmall. He went ahead and farmed with his team, Maud and Dixie.

For the next two years I went back and used a team planter, and planted with Kate and Jude. Then I got me a two-row planter for the tractor.

Dad kept Kate and Jude until one of them died in 1973. He just kept them in a 10-acre pasture with his mules. I asked him one time why he never got rid of them. He said they weren't doing nothing but eating grass, and he'd just keep them.

 **Leland Mallett was born July 2, 1936, to Elmer and Mildred Mallett. His father farmed five miles east of Malden in New Madrid County. Leland and his twin sister, Lillian, have three younger sisters and a brother, 12 years younger, who never worked on the farm. Leland attended Risco schools through the**

10th grade. He farmed until he was 62, and at one time farmed 1,200 acres, most of which was rented. In 2009, he and his wife, Shirley, celebrated their 52nd wedding anniversary. "Mother and the girls took care of two milk cows, and we had quite a few pigs at one time. We'd kill some for winter. I got out of chopping (cotton). I didn't like to chop. But I did a lot of picking. There wasn't nothing going on with the mules during picking time," he said.

X. His Work Led to the Mule Being Named Missouri's Official State Animal
Melvin Bradley

Melvin Bradley's work with mules helped lead, in 1995, to the mule being named Missouri's official state animal. Bradley, who worked mules as a boy in Missouri cornfields, once said, "I found that the mule has so much more personality than a horse. A mule is highly intelligent. He will outsmart you."

Bradley was born in 1922 and studied at the University of Missouri (MU) at Columbia and Oklahoma University, where he took a doctorate. He taught at MU in Columbia from 1948 to 1990, becoming professor of animal science. In 1982, he embarked on an oral history project to preserve Missouri's mule heritage, touring the state to record reminiscences about the breeding, rearing, training, showing, and selling of mules which led to his publishing a 540-page two-volume set entitled *The Missouri Mule: His Origins and Times.*

In Bradley's book, beginning on page 313, there is a chapter called "Mule Psychology." Below, I quote some of Bradley's comments in this chapter dealing with the intelligence and behavior of mules, and reference quotes from stories in this book that support Bradley's comments.

Bradley states on page 313, "Researchers in Texas and elsewhere have done a number of maze trials with horses to determine trainability, but none are known to have included mules. It is doubtful if maze trials, using food as the only motivator, would be satisfactory for a comparison of horse and mule behavior. Perhaps the gluttonous horse would place a higher value on food than would the fastidious mule." ("..horses would overeat and founder themselves, whereas a mule won't"[Jim Becker, from "If Hired Hands Were Working Them, Dad Preferred Mules"]. And "Every night we'd put more corn in it. There'd better be a little corn in there the next morning. If you did that with horses, there'd be some foundered horses" [Jay McCurry, from "You'd Soon Learn to Jump Working a Breaking Plow"]. Both stories are in Farming with Mules chapter.)

"The mule is a survivor. He will seldom get injured" (page 313). ("I knew in my mind they'd have a leg cut off when I got down there. They didn't" [James King, from "I Crawled on My Knees Until I Got A Hold of the Lines" in Runaways chapter].)

"Many mules will kick when surprised from behind"(page 315). ("My brother, Joe, got kicked by Toby one time. Joe was always trying to do something funny. He slipped around the barn, caught Toby when he wasn't looking [Francis Hulshof, from "I Heard Him Start to Chuckle, 'Hee, Hee, Hee,' All of a Sudden It Got Quiet" in Mule Teams chapter].)

"If rapidly approached from behind, with or without a loud noise, it (a mule) will likely panic into flight. If not restrained, it may stop after 100 yards and look back while it re-evaluates its' decision"(page 315). ("One time we had them tied up and someone shot off a firecracker and away they went. We thought the disk was going to tear them up, but it didn't. They stopped after about 100 yards" [Ancil Robertson from "I Didn't Care Much For It" in Farming With Mules chapter].)

"They (mules) know exactly what they want, and they are willing to pay a price to get it. Mules, like horses, prefer good food, shade, shelter, kind treatment, companionship, and peace of mind. Most of a mule's behavior is slanted toward these pleasures. When it perceives denial of one or more of them, it may scheme to restore its pastoral heritage." ("...and they got away from him and started to run down the road to our house" [Armon Keaster, from "I Can't Believe I'm Not Dead"]. And "After they were done for the day, the old man would unhook the mules and turn them loose, and they'd come to our house" [Ed Beasley from "Well, It Was Right Up One of Them's Butt"]. Both stories are in the Mule Teams chapter.)

"Mules will attack a fence, gate, barn, or other restraint with more vigor, and usually more success, than will their horse half-brothers." ("He was pawing the whole end off the barn. I could see the boards coming loose from the barn"[Wilma VanGennip, from "I'd Just Love to Hit

Him With This Stick"] and "If there was a gate he couldn't open, he would put his head over it, and break it down by pushing it with his front end"[Wyman Hampton, from "That Son of a Gun Had Sense"]. Both stories are in the Mules chapter.)

"If it (a mule) learns of its considerable talent to jump fences, it will be most difficult to contain behind a fence under six or seven feet" (page 315). **("Jake would jump a railroad fence six-foot high. He would back up 30 feet or so, ring his tail a couple of times, and run and jump the fence to get to some grass on the other side"[Floyd Howe, from "Jake Was the Meanest Mule Ever Born" in the Mules chapter] and "All He Wanted to Do Was Jump That Fence" [Rodney Eddleman's story in Nubbins chapter].)**

"Mules have very different personalities than horses and they differ from each other. They want to be friends with humans and with their companion." (page 316). **("She liked me and I liked her. She'd come to me, but she would run from those other guys. If they wanted to catch her, they'd say, 'Go get that damn mule'" [Paul Vance, from "Her Ole Ears Would Flop and She'd Just Pace Along" in Mules chapter] and "If I went out there and didn't have grain, and they were in the lot, they would come up and push their noses against my hand"[Bob Lincoln, from "Jack Would Nose the Chain off the Gate, and Let the Cattle Drink" in the Plantation Farming/Sharecroppers chapter].)**

"Clearly the mule's ability to tell time is remarkable. He can pinpoint break-time, noon-time, and quitting time within minutes when he is taken on a regular schedule. When it is his turn to rest or eat, he will bray loudly, try to stop, and look you in the eye while he sharply resists normal performance" (page 316). **("At quarter till 12, when we would get to the end of the row, he would stop and wait for you to unhook him...He seemed like he knew when it was a quarter till 12 better than we did looking at the clock" [Johnny Williams, from "He Would Get Down on His Knees for You to Ride Him to the Barn"] and "After a hard day of plowing, come around 5 o'clock, the horse mule would bray. He wouldn't miss it 10 minutes either way" [Ping Davis, from "I Don't Know What Kept Me From Killing That Mule"] and "He knew when it was 12 o'clock as well as I did" [James Patton, from "Neighbors Were Always Saying How Pretty He Was"]. All three stories are in the Mules chapter.)**

"As a youth, my privilege was to 'gentle' the new foals. We thought then that the ideal time to start was about the second or third day of life. The mule was caught by the neck and caressed throughout its body. This procedure dispelled its natural fear of people and taught

it to enjoy a good back-scratching session ....An advantage to im-
printing is that human dominance can be established with minimum
trauma to both person and animal..." (pages 317-318). **("We played
with Frank. My older brothers would wrestle with him when he was a colt, but
he would never hurt us" [Wyman Hampton, from "That Son of a Gun Had
Sense" in the Mules chapter].)**

"Soon the youngster learns that a raised voice registers an objec-
tion to the behavior in which it just engaged. When such mules are
'minimum-error' trained, they usually remain obedient and have good
work habits throughout life" (page 319). **("I'd want to jerk them around
or something. And he didn't do his that way. He wouldn't have to jerk them
around. He'd just talk to them"[Leland Mallett, from "Elmer Mallett Understood Mules" and "Dad always had more patience with an animal. He could
get them to do anything he wanted them to"[Lloyd Payne from "Jack and Jim
Were the Best Team He Ever Had,]" Both stories are in the Mule Teams chapter.)**

"Persons unfamiliar with mules often fear getting kicked by
them. They have read and heard that most mules are kickers. In real-
ity, only a few have ever kicked at a human. Only about half of the
life-long mule handlers interviewed admitted to having been kicked
by a mule. Those who had often explained why they, not the mule,
were at fault." **("It scared him and he kicked at me. His hoof missed me but
the top part of his ankle hit me on the side of my head. It knocked me to my
knees. I got up and got out of there. I didn't hit him. It was my fault for not
letting him know I was behind him"Jim Hillis, from "Kate Shoved Mike Off
the Bridge" in the Mule Teams chapter] and "He backed me all the way to the
corner of the barn one day kicking at me. I had walked behind him, wasn't
paying any attention" [James King, from "I Crawled on My Knees Until I Got
A Hold of the Lines" in the Runaways chapter].)**

"Some mules do kick! If allowed to continue to practice, they can
get quite good at it" (page 320). **("When dad reached over Jet's back to
reach Pat. Pat would turn around and kick up with both feet" [Ben Boyers,
from "Neighbors Would Call Us to Pull Them Out" Pat and Jet] and "I've
seen him kick my dad several times. He liked to have scared me to death"
[Betty Boyers Webb, from "He Like to Have Scared Me to Death" Pat and Jet
Part II], Both stories are in the Mule Farming with Robert "Uncle Bob" Boyers Family of Butler County chapter and "He went around the back of one
with some hay and it penned him against the wall and kicked him"[Curtis**

Ashby, from "My Older Sister, Loeta, and I Had to Put in the Crops" in the **Farming With Mules chapter].")**

"It is a paradox that young mules are so willing to run away when hitched, and so seldom attempt to run away under saddle. Unlike claims of never having been kicked, all of the persons interviewed had experienced runaways with mules." (**They were young at the time. I had just filled the planter up with seed, and my brother-in-law was driving them....They took off and he jumped off. They got astraddle a pasture fence and tore it up..."[Ed Beasley, from "Well, It Was Right Up One of Them's Butt" in the Mule Teams chapter].)**

"The young team was expected sooner or later to 'spook' at something and attempt to run, or just run because they felt good and wanted to express their feelings....Since mules seldom hurt themselves in runaways, some teamsters claimed they, 'could ride as fast as the team could run' and dismissed the event as 'growing up' for the young team." (**"I was in an empty wagon and was going down a sandy road and something happened and off they went. I just let them run. I was going around the farm. When they got to slowing down, I took the lines and really put it to them. When they did stop. They were ready. They were broke to work" [Ervin Cates from "Here He'd Come With Another Blame Mule" in the Plantation Farming/Sharecroppers chapter].)**

"No small number of the old-time owners hitched two unbroken mules together and let them run. They took them to a parked wagon in an open field and with sufficient help they were able to get them hitched. They were released and allowed to run. When tired, they began to respond to guidance." (**"They would go as hard as they could until they would start to slow down. At this time the driver would put on the brakes, and the other man would start laying the whip to them. They would again go as hard as they could go, then they would stop. The driver would turn them around and drive them back to the barn, and that team of mules would be broke"[Bob Alsup from "I Can Still See Those Knees Coming at Me" in the Plantation Farming/Sharecroppers chapter].)**

"Many well-trained mules, both in harness and under saddle, will do their best to please their handlers. They need no punishment, just clearly understood commands" (page 335). (**They learned to accept me as commander. In other words, I'd tell them what to do and they'd do it. I'd just call them by name, 'Jim, do this and do that'"[Lloyd Massey, from "I Mean People Can't Imagine How Smart Mules Were Back Then" in the Mules That Worked by Voice Commands/Without Lines chapter].)**

P.S. I met Bradley in the mid-1970s at Columbia while attending a one-day horseshoeing seminar taught by Bradley. Bradley died in 2003 (the author).

Restored Higgerson School sits in downtown New Madrid.
(See Bud Henry bio on page 32.)

XI. What Happened to All Those Mules?

As Wyman Hampton noted in his introduction, God didn't create mules, man did, and when they were no longer needed, mankind got rid of them.

In 1930, there were 26,700 mules in the three Bootheel counties of Pemsicot, New Madrid and Dunklin.*

By 1945. these numbers had dropped 36 percent to 16,886 mules, and by 1954 there were only 882 mules left in the three counties.

That's 16,004 mules that disappeared from the three counties in 10 years (1945-1954), or in other words, 95 percent of the mules in the Bootheel disappeared. The efficiency of ridding the Bootheel of mules was greater than that of people killed (roughly 78%) in the atomic bombing of Hiroshima, Japan on August 6, 1945.

If you lined up those 16,004 mules in a single line, it would stretch more than 25 miles (allowing 8-feet per mule).

What happened to all those mules? There is no exact information available. Many were sold or traded in, but the vast majority of them in all likelihood went to killer markets. Francis Hulshof talks about anthrax killing their mules in 1951. He grew up near Portageville in New Madrid County. But anthrax probably wasn't much of a factor because there were only 440 mules and horses killed by anthrax in 1951 according to state records.

Kelly Boyers, who has stories in the Boyers family chapter, recalls as a young boy going to the Poplar Bluff Sale Barn and there being a lot of mules and horses for sale. "They would have a sale every Friday. They would sell the horses and mules first. They would start out in the morning, then they would get to the hogs and cattle," Boyers said. "A lot of them (mules and horses) went to the killer market. A Mr. Hildebrand had a big two-ton truck. He would buy killer animals. The way he loaded them in the truck was to have one headed one way, another the other way. They would be crisscrossed."

From 1942 to 1946, R.J. Boyers (Kelly's brother) worked at the Poplar Bluff Sale Barn helping to run stock in the sale ring. R. J. said a guy would come down from St. Louis and buy mules and horses that were crippled or old for the killer market, which R.J. thought was in East St. Louis, which would be about a three-hour drive from Poplar Bluff. "He'd haul 10 to 15 of them in a bob truck. He'd tie them crossways. It seems like the price he paid was 5 cents a pound," R. J. said.

Steve Dees of Marquand, Missouri, said his dad, Silas Dees, was an auctioneer in the 1940s and 1950s and his dad told him there was a horse and mule slaughterhouse in Rockford, Illinois, owned by Quaker Oats, and they made pet food at the location. Rockford would have been a 10-hour drive from Poplar Bluff in the 1950s.**
Charles Mangels, 73, of Oak Ridge, Missouri, a lifelong farmer who grew up with mules, has helped organize the Horse and Mule Show at the Southeast Missouri District Fair in Cape Girardeau for more than 40 years. "I imagine most of the mules went to the killer market.

The young mules could have gone to Memphis. There were still some mules in that area," Mangels said. "We still had a lot of mules around here in the 1950s, 1955 was the last year we had horses and mules at the district fair. Oscar Hildebrand (mentioned above) was from Perryville. He was still coming around here in the 1960s. At that time he had a contract (to furnish meat) with the St. Louis Zoo. Mules were brought back to the fair in 1969 and flourished through the 1970s and 1980s."

Another contact, who did not want his named used, said his father worked the killer market. He said the largest killer market during the 1940s and 1950s was Hills Pet Foods in Topeka, Kansas.*** He said there were two horse and mule slaughterhouses in the St. Louis area in the 1950s, and the largest mule slaughterhouse in Arkansas was at Conway, which is just north of Little Rock. This plant would have been about 4 hours from the Bootheel area.

Mechanization, of course, led to killing off the mules and draft horses. When tractor numbers increased, mule numbers dropped. In 1930, there were 416 tractors in the three Bootheel counties while there were 26,700 mules. By 1940 there were 1,892 tractors and

Buildings are where Baker's plantation was located. Main drainage ditch in foreground. See story on page 239.

23,900 mules and by 1950 there were 8,425 tractors and 6,243 mules.

Over time mechanization also moved people off of farms. For example, in Pemiscot County there were 5,546 farms in 1930. That number has gradually fallen over the decades to where in 2007 there were only 258 farms.

As tractors and equipment have become more efficient and larger; farmers have had to buy more land to compete. In 1930, in Pemiscot County, the average farm size was 38 acres, in 2007 it was 1,203 acres.

Mule numbers in the United States peaked in 1920 at 2.7 million. There were 2.4 million in 1935 and 1.9 million in 1940.

In Missouri, there were 300,000 mules in 1930 and 209,000 in 1940. Missouri ranked first in the nation in mule colt production in 1920 with 68,457 mule colts. Missouri also ranked first in registration of jacks and jennies from 1891 to 1917.

In years providing the main power source for farms, as of this date (2010), mules and horses out number tractors more than 100 years. Mules and horses were used for farming roughly 165 years (1785-1950). Tractors have been the main farm power source for 60 years (1950 to 2010).

Most of these 90-plus mule stories come from eight Southeast Missouri counties**** which combined had 52,800 mules in 1930. The mule stones in this book represent about one-fifth of 1 percent of farm mules in use at that time. Which means there were more than 52,000 farm mule stories in the Bootheel area that are not covered in this book.

According to the 2007 Census of Agriculture, there were only 69 mules, burros and donkeys listed for the three Bootheel counties of Pemsicot, New Madrid and Dunklin.

*Most of the statistical information for this story was provided by Thomas Sallee, agricultural statistician, USDA, National Agricultural Statistics Service, Missouri Field Office, Columbia, Missouri.

In the book titled *BRAND, TRADEMARKS AND GOOD WILL* (The Story of The Quaker Oats Company) published in 1967 on page 176 in the chapter titled "The Pet Foods" reads in part, "Soon Chappel and his brother had a profitable business in the export of pickled horsemeat. The American public had no tradition for this protein and apparently no desire to change its habits. Chappel begin to experiment with a canned dog food, an entirely new idea."

***An article in the July 16, 1939 issue of the *Topeka Daily Journal* reads in part, "The compact, three-acre Hill Packing Company plant sits on the edge of the Kansas River in Topeka and turns out millions of pounds of canned and fresh-frozen horse meat products annually for domestic consumption and export .... Last year, the company sold 15,800,000 pounds of frozen and 462,000 cases of canned horsemeat products."**

****The eight counties referred to are, Butler, Cape Girardeau, Dunklin, Mississippi, New Madrid, Pemiscot, Scott, and Stoddard.**

XII. Epilogue

Interviewing 78 people who farmed with mules back in the 1930s and 1940s provided me with information to compile data on (est.) 312 mules of that era, that is, allowing the average person interviewed worked with four mules.

Mule stories are more believable when similar incidents occur at another time and location. For example, Shipman and Massey talked about men throwing trimming shears at a fleeing mule and hitting the mule. And four people talked about working blind mules.

If only one person interviewed mentioned that a mule could tell when it was noontime, the reader would assume it was an unusual mule, but when nine people talk about this it becomes quite believable. As does mules that could unlock gates or doors, of which eight people talked about.

Nine people said they were either kicked at or kicked by a mule. Some of these incidents were brought on by the handlers, either by surprising a mule (see Joe Hillis story), kicking a mule (See Willcut story), or hitting a mule on the rump with a board (see Hulshof story).

Mules are such individuals there are many mule behaviors recorded in the book that are only mentioned once. Some of these could only have occurred with very smart mules, two of these mules were named Jack. Alfonse Webb, who spent several years working on plantations, talks about his favorite mule, Jack, in the Nubbins chapter. Jack would hit his head against the head of the slower mule he was working with to make the other mule mind. In his sharecropping adventures, Bob Lincoln talks about Jack, a mule that would not only open a gate, but would also close it.

In similar incidents mules don't always act alike. Six people mention falling off or being thrown by a mule, four of these six stated the mule didn't run off and they were able to get back on, but three people said the mule ran off. The Boyers' mule, Toby, did it both ways. But why are young mules inclined to run off while hitched? Eighteen of those interviewed talked about this. Perhaps the young mules just wanted to stretch their legs and did so with the slightest provocation. Melvin Bradley was aware of this. He states on page 321 of his book The Missouri Mule: His Origins and Times. "It is a paradox that young mules are so willing to runaway when hitched and so seldom attempt to runaway under saddle."

Abraham Maslow presented a hierarchy of needs for humans. First level or basic needs are physical such as for air, water, food and shelter. The second level care and safety needs and the third level belongingness. The fourth esteem and the fifth and final level is selfactualization.

Many mule behaviors appear to go beyond the first two levels. Two men, Alsup (in Nubbins chapter) and Caldwell, talk about incidents where their lives were in peril by farm equipment while working mules, and the mules stood without flinching for several minutes until help arrived. Hammon in his story talks about getting under his mule team when it was raining, which is a time you would expect mules to be antsy. Farmer, Henry, and Hager said their teams would line up to be hitched to equipment unassisted. Several talk about mules that would approach a bridle as if they were anxious to go to work.

Mules were good listeners and didn't need to be whipped to go all out for their owners. Several people talk about their dad's standing beside or on a mule and talking to them while they pulled a heavy load. See Webb's, Henry's and Jenkins' stories.

Several behaviors could be listed as tricky or teasing. The Van-Gennips talk about Jake who was quite adept at staying free. Hampton's Frank, Demerit's Tom and Kate, Floyd Howe's Jake, Fikuart's Harry and Williams' Rock, all couldn't resist checking out a field of corn or lush grass when they knew they weren't supposed to. Two men, Eddleman (in Nubbins chapter) and Davis, talk about mules who jumped a fence for the fun of it. Becker talks about a mule that would search out a handler's foot with his front foot and apply pressure. Ashby, Threlkeld and Massey talk about mule teams that appeared to be goofing off, yet, when disciplined, they easily pulled the load. Threlkeld also talks about Joe, after having his harness taken off, jumping and running up to his five year-old sister and abruptly stopping.

Did mules communicate with each other? They actually did this very well. How is it that when a young team bolted they did this in unison? How did they communicate this? There is no teamster that ever taught a mule team how to pull a heavy load. The mules figured this out themselves. Four men, Willcut, Hampton, Kesterson and Robert Boyers talk about how the weaker or younger mule would pull at a heavy load a split second ahead of the stronger mule that would jump up and grunt or stretch out, whatever it took to move it. Kesterson explained it this way, "The older one was better built. If they were hooked to a big load, the younger one would jump out, get the singletree set, and hold ground until the other one started pulling the load. Mules do have some sense." Neighbors knew who had the best pulling mules and often came over to watch the action (see Hampton's, Henry's and Ben Boyers' stories).

Two of the people interviewed talked about older brothers who were good at training mules. Massey's brother Paul could go out in a lot with two bridles and call for which mule he wanted to come out.

This team also pulled hay loads while yelled instructions from a barn loft. Paul Jenkins talks about his older brother, Harold, who had his team trained where he could give commands from the porch while the mules were hitched to a wagon in the road, and they would obey.

By allowing that 78 people I interviewed worked with 312 mules, I can estimate how many mules did certain things. For example, thirteen of the people interviewed talked about a mule that worked without using lines. If four percent of mules did this there would have been about 1,040 mules in just the three Bootheel counties of Dunklin, New Madrid and Pemiscot that worked without lines. Thirteen is 4% of 312. Four x 26,000, the approximate number of mules in the three counties in 1930, = 1040.

So will mules outsmart you as Melvin Bradley said? I think Van-Gennip's mules, Jake and Kate, outsmarted the neighbor that borrowed them. I think for a while Rock outsmarted Williams' dad and Kit did things that frustrated Ping Davis. I think mule teams that bolted were their way of telling their owners they had control too. There are many other instances mentioned in these stories.

XIII. Nubbins

A Mule Kicked Him as told by Joe Hillis (Hillis has a story is in the Mule Teams chapter.)

My dad's cousin, Calvin Robertson, was hooking mules up to a wagon in the 1920s. He reached down to loose a singletree and a mule kicked him, knocking his eye out. He was married with three kids.

He was called "Doc" as told by Judge Bill Batson (Batson has a story in the Mule Teams chapter.)

Dad knew some tricks on horse trading. He was called, "Doc." When we sold the mules in Arkansas they had begun to age and their hips were sunk in. Dad took a pocketknife and used it to jab a piece of leather for judging thickness. He kept the leather on the knife for judging depth. Then he would punch the mules' sunken hips several times. He would massage their skin causing it to swell. The punctures would hold up and hold the air in. It made them look like younger mules. It worked too. Their hips looked so much better.

Pete as told by Dr. Gene Leroux (Leroux has a story in the Mule Teams chapter.)

We had one ole mule called Pete, a red mule that was real high spirited. I went to a rodeo one Sunday at Glenn, a place a mile west of us in Ripley County. We took that mule over there. A cowboy from Oklahoma said he could ride anything. He was lean and as tough as nails. I can remember him wearing chaps and getting on that mule. There were 50 or 60 people there with several mules and horses to break. As I remember he would stay on Pete 10 or 15 seconds. That cowboy was bucked off two or three times. I can't remember if he rode him, but if he did, he didn't break him. None of the rest of us ever tried to ride that mule.

Mule Races as told by Ancil Robertson (Robertson has a story in Farming With Mules chapter.)

They had mule races at the Pemiscot fairgrounds in Caruthersville during the '30s and '40s. They really drew the crowds. Local farmers would race their mules. One guy tried to bring in a racing mule. He could outrun a race horse. They disqualified him. One mule would run from the track through a gap in the fence. They put blinders on him. He ran so close to the fence looking for that gap he hit the fence and fell down and fell on the rider.

Missed the Footrest as told by Bob Alsup (Alsup has story in the Plantation Mules/Sharecroppers chapter.)

I was about 10 years old and was working a three-mule disk early in the morning south of Canalou in New Madrid County. I had made several rounds and I missed the footrest and the disk caught the heel end of my shoe. It pulled my leg in under the disk almost to my knee. I pulled on the lines and hollered "whoa" and the mules stopped. I yelled "Help" to the top of my voice. I didn't have much confidence I would get anybody to hear me. The mules would get a little excited each time I hollered, so I would have to hold the lines. I was holding on to the lines all the time to keep them from going. I probably hollered between five and 10 minutes. A family lived about a half a quarter south of our house and close to a half of a mile from where I was at. They were sitting at the table eating breakfast. He heard me hollering and came straight out. The disk had two 3-foot sections. He lifted one section up where I could get my leg out. I was skinned on both sides of my leg.

Turn Around Jude as told by James R. King (King has a story in the Runaways chapter.)

My uncle lived near us below Campbell. He had a team of mules, Jude and Kate. He had to come up a levee with loads. He was pulling these mules so hard, trying to get loads of corn over that levee. They said that's what caused one of them to go blind. So they got rid of the other one and kept the ole blind mule. When we wanted to cultivate the garden with a double shovel, we went and got that ole blind mule. You didn't have to have lines or nothing on her. Just holler, "gee" or "haw" and when you got to the end you'd say, "turn around Jude." And she'd start turning. She'd get around, and you'd say "go." You never had to use a line with that mule, and she'd never run away.

I Didn't Like It. I Had To Do It as told by Julie Gilbreath Hillis (Julie's husband, Artie, is featured in Jim Becker's story in the Farming With Mules chapter.)

My dad would clean up new ground (Wayne county), but he wouldn't get all the stumps out. I started working a mule team when I was 9. One was black, and one was light brown. I don't remember their names. The black was a better worker. My dad had a mule team and a horse team. The mules were gentler. I worked them up until I was 17.

I worked mules to an A harrow, which consisted of two planks in an A shape. I would hit a stump, and I would try to throw one end over it. Sometimes it would jump, and bust my ankles. Once, I got my knees peeled up a little bit, causing them to bleed, and I would go ahead, and keep on working.

I didn't like it. I had to do it, because the boys weren't big enough, and too ornery to do it.

I walked three miles to Shook School, and I sometimes worked the mules after school. I also helped my dad milk (by hand) five cows, before and after school.

You'll Pull That Mule's Tail Off as told by Robert Boyers. Boyers has two stories in the Mule Farming With the Bob Boyers Family of Butler County chapter.*

When I was five we had a blue mare mule named Kate. One day Dad told me he was going to put a saddle on Kate, and that we were riding down to his dad's, and get a jenny. He put a saddle on her, got his rope, and I got on behind him. When we got about four miles down the road to the Miller bridge, Fred Chisler, the rural mail carrier, was driving a Model A Ford. There was no gravel, only mud. Wagon ruts were knee deep. He couldn't get his Model A up on the approach of the bridge. Once you got to the wooden bridge, it was flat. He tried two or three times and would get halfway up and get stuck, then he would back down and try it again. Dad said, "Fred drive up as far as you can and put your foot on the brakes and I'll pull you on up." Fred said, "How you going to pull me when you don't have any harness?" Dad said, "I got a rope." Dad took Kate in front of the Model A, put a slipknot on her tail as close to her butt as he could; and put a half hitch on the Model A and told Fred to start it up. He got in the saddle. I was sitting behind. Dad said, "Get up Kate!" Fred said, "You can't do that Chester, you'll pull her tail off." Dad said, "Naw, it won't hurt her." She just pulled that car upon the bridge.

For years after that ever time Dad saw Fred, Fred would say, "Chester, do you remember the time you pulled me up on Miller bridge with ole Kate?" And they would have a good laugh.

*This story was previously published in the *Daily American Republic*, a newspaper in Poplar Bluff, Missouri.

He Would Roll Over on His Back and Start Kicking at You as told by Johnny Williams (Williams has a story in the Mules chapter.)

When I was 8 or 9, Dad done some sharecropping for Frank Long near Braggadocio, eight or 10 miles southwest of Hayti in Pemiscot County. He farmed 20 acres for a third of the crop. Frank had several teams of mules. He furnished the mules and equipment.

The team Dad farmed with was a big mule named Red and a small brown mule named Toby. At age 22, Toby was as feisty as a 2 year old, and had never been ridden.

Toby was the unusual one. He would decide in the middle of the day he didn't want to work, and would lay down. Dad would take the whip to him, and he would roll over on his back and start kicking at you. No matter how much you'd whip him, he would kick at you until he decided to get up.

One time we were going to the cotton gin with a load of cotton, and we had to cross a slough that was a little bit muddy. There was no water in it. Toby took a notion that was as far as he was going to go. When we struck him with the whip to try to make him go, he dropped down, turned over, and was trying to kick back up in the trailer at us.

A lot of times he would do that for 20 to 30 minutes, then all of a sudden, he would get up on his own, and take the studs again.

That Scatterbrain Got Loose and Jumped Plumb Over It as told by Talmadge Gann (Gann has a story in the Mules chapter.)

A lot of times when you trimmed a mule's foot you've got to put a twister on his nose to hold him. We had a twister on Frank's nose one time. He was the nervous type. The gate in the stall was 6-foot high. That scatterbrain got loose and jumped plumb over it. We didn't know he could jump that high.

If the Other Mule Wouldn't Come Around, He'd Take His Head and Hit Him and Make Him Come Around as told by Alfonse Webb (Webb has a story in the Plantation Mules/Sharecroppers chapter.)

My favorite mule memory is when I was 10 to 12 years old on a plantation in Mississippi. Their names were Jack and Joe. They were two red mules. They was real good mules. The one they called Jack, worked him on the left, because he was the lead mule. He was the best mule I ever worked in my life. He was a smart mule. He was a tall mule, weighed about 1,200 pounds. He was a plantation mule.

You tell him what to do, and he'd do it. When you'd get to the end, tell him, "whoa" or "gee." If Joe wouldn't come around, Jack would take his head and hit him and knock him around. They'd come right on back around. You'd better have your plow ready, because he was coming around. He'd walk along as steady as you'd want any mule to be, but if you'd holler at him, he'd speed up all the time, get faster and faster.

Everybody else was using two lines, and I'd just plow with one line. Had the line to Jack, and the line to Joe, I'd just hang it on his hames. Jack would make him do anything I'd ask him to do.

He'd Find That Row And Then He Was Gone as told by Paul Jenkins (Jenkins has a story in the Mules That Worked Without Lines chapter.)

We had one mule, Mike, a big black mule that would work without lines. We mostly used him in the truck patches. The big mule was blind when we got him, might have been 10 or 12 years old. You'd just talk to him, "Get over Mike." He'd find that row and then he was gone. We used him with a double shovel and a lister (plow). We used the lister to make rows for turnips and potatoes. Instead of digging sweet potatoes with a hoe or shovel, we dug them with a lister. Take a lister down the ridge and it would throw them out each side. There's when we kids would come in, picking up potatoes.

Mike would get lost down in the pasture, then try to find the

fence. You'd holler at him and he'd raise his head, and he'd come towards you. He was a real good work mule. His mouth was cut way
back where they had cut it with bits. We figured he was a mean mule,
and they jerked and jerked, and they might have put his eyes out to
harness him. They done that back then some, especially with bulls, if
they were working close to a sawmill or something. They were scary.
It was a cruel thing, but that was done.

All He Wanted to Do Was Jump That Fence as told by Rodney
Eddleman. (Eddleman has a story in the Mule Teams chapter.)

Dad always told this story about his dad that farmed up by Long
Town. Grandpa had a mule. They turned him out of a stable in the
mornings when they wasn't working him. The mule would promptly
go down by the fence by the county road and jump the fence and pick
along the county road, till Grandpa wanted to try something. He put a
blindfold around the mule, led him out the gate to the county road
and took the blindfold off. The mule picked a couple of bites, then
jumped the fence back into the lot. All he wanted to do was jump the
fence.

He Took a Two-By-Four and Hit Him Right Between the Eyes
as told by Paul Woods. (Woods has a story in the Plantation Farm-
ing/Sharecropping" chapter.)

I had a mean uncle. He was heading home with his mules to a
wagon after working all day. One of the mules balked and he couldn't
get him to move at all. He just took a two-by-four and hit him right
between the eyes, and the mule fell to the ground. It killed him. He
took him out of the harness and left him there in the middle of the
road.

He Cut Himself Up Real Bad and Died That Night as told by
R.J. Boyers. (Boyers has two stories in the Boyers family chapter.)

When I was young (11-14) I worked at the (Poplar Bluff) sale
barn from 1942 to 1945 running stock through the sale ring. They'd
have from 10 to 25 head of mules each week. You'd buy a mule and

you had the option of hooking it up to Ole Ball, a big ole red gelding, a lead horse. They would hook them to a wagon and if the mule acted up, you didn't have to take him. One time a guy bought a mule that had never been caught. He gave me 5 dollars to ride him. Some men tied him to a post at the end of the sale barn. I got on him, someone turned him loose, and he took off a running and a bucking. He ran out of the barn, behind the office, and through a four-strand barbwire fence. I was still on him. He cut himself up real bad and died that night.

About the Author Lonny Thiele

Lonny, along with brother Gary (1942-2000) and sister Carolyn, were raised on a cattle and hog farm in Linn County, Missouri. After their dad was killed in a farm tractor accident in 1953, when Lonny was 8, the family moved to Rothville, Missouri where their mother, Emily, taught 5th and 6th grades at Rothville Elementary School for several years. Their mother married Quentin Smith, a college professor, in 1959.

Lonny attended high schools at Mendon, Kirksville and Kansas City, where he graduated from Paseo High School in 1962. He graduated with a B.A. degree from the University of Missouri at Columbia in 1966 with a major in English Literature. At graduation he was commissioned as a second lieutenant into the U.S. Army and spent 1968 serving at Nha Trang, South Vietnam.

He married Gail in 1973 and resided in Raymore. The marriage produced two daughters, Megan and Sheila. Lonny worked 15 years in finance at various employments in the Kansas City area, and in 1989 started a career in journalism, working at the *Linn County News* in Pleasanton, Kansas to 1994. He was divorced in 1994 and also worked at the *Holden-Image Progress* in Holden, Missouri, and from 1995 to 2004 worked as a general assignment/agriculture reporter at the *Daily American Republic* newspaper in Poplar Bluff, where he won several Missouri Press and Associated Press writing awards. During this time he also filled in for a few months as reporter at the *Prospect News* in Doniphan, Missouri.

His current hobbies include horseback riding, tennis, photography, making barn wood frames, and line dancing with his wife, Pauline, who is a medical transcriptionist in Poplar Bluff.

He researched on this book for more than three years starting in January 2007. In December 2008 he was diagnosed as a Type 2 diabetic.

He enjoys being with his wife and daughters, two step-daughters, two grandchildren and family and friends.